Michel Houellebecq

Modern **F**rench **I**dentities

Edited by Peter Collier

Volume 70

PETER LANG

Oxford· Bern· Berlin · Bruxelles · Frankfurt am Main · New York· Wien

John McCann

Michel Houellebecq

Author of our Times

PETER LANG

Oxford · Bern · Berlin · Bruxelles · Frankfurt am Main · New York · Wien

Bibliographic information published by Die Deutsche Nationalbibliothek
Die Deutsche Nationalbibliothek lists this publication in the Deutsche
Nationalbibliografie; detailed bibliographic data is available on the
Internet at http://dnb.d-nb.de.

A catalogue record for this book is available from the British Library and
from the Library of Congress.

ISSN 1422-9005
ISBN 978-3-03911-373-6

© Peter Lang AG, International Academic Publishers, Bern 2010
Hochfeldstrasse 32, CH-3012 Bern, Switzerland
info@peterlang.com, www.peterlang.com, www.peterlang.net

Printed in Germany

Contents

Acknowledgements   ix

INTRODUCTION
Michel Houellebecq: Author of our Times   1

CHAPTER 1
Extension du domaine de la lutte: Fighting to Survive?   5

CHAPTER 2
Les Particules élémentaires: A Tale of Two Humanities   51

CHAPTER 3
Lanzarote: A Detour?   101

CHAPTER 4
Plateforme: Writing about Sex-tourism   133

CHAPTER 5
La Possibilité d'une île: Life is Real   171

Select Bibliography   213

Index   217

Acknowledgements

I wish to thank the British Academy and the Humanities Research Institute at the University of Ulster for financial assistance to enable me to carry out this project. Thanks are also due to the staff of the Bibliothèque Nationale de France (Site Tolbiac) for their help and assistance.

Copyright on Michel Houellebecq's works is held as follows: Éditions Maurice Nadau for *Extension du domaine de la lutte*; Éditions Flammarion for *Les Particules élémentaires*, *Plateforme* and *Lanzarote*; and Librairie Arthème Fayard for *La possibilité d'une île*. Thanks are due to the copyright holders who kindly granted permission to quote from these works.

Colleagues in the School of Languages and Literature have been of invaluable help and support as have been colleagues in the wider academic community. They are too numerous to mention individually but I should particularly like to thank Larry Duffy who first introduced me to the work of Houellebecq as well as Philip Dine, Graham Gargett and the late Richard Bales, all of whom strongly supported this undertaking in its initial stages. David Barr, Loïc Guyon and Maeve Paris gave much needed help and support in the final stages.

Finally, I should like to thank Dr Graham Speake of Peter Lang AG and my series editor, Dr Peter Collier, for their encouragement, support and helpful suggestions throughout. I should also like to thank Peter Lang's Ireland representative, Joe Armstrong, for his initial interest in the project.

Michel Houellebecq: Author of our Times

Michel Houellebecq is a French author whose profile in the English speaking world is unusually high. His works receive prompt translation and publication in the UK. However, press reviews are frequently luke-warm, if not hostile, but this perhaps reflects a lack of proper appreciation of the artistic merit and incisiveness of an author who has put the humour back into the Absurd, without losing any of the awareness of the bleakness of the human condition. He is undoubtedly one of the most trenchant satirists of our time, deflating the projected utopias that we imagine to protect us from the ills that beset us. He faces the reader with the incipient totalitarianism that lies in our secular and religious faiths when they promise to secure the future in this world or the next – while at the same time showing the limits of our attempts to forge an all-encompassing view of the world. More than many other novelists, his work is a reflection of the social and economic reality of the contemporary life.

A close examination of Houellebecq's novels demonstrates how he creates a fictional world containing themes and characters that are recognizably contemporary. Houellebecq's world is post-industrial. Characters work in the tertiary sector, administrators and consumers rather than producers. They live in the knowledge economy. The latter does not just determine one's job but also penetrates all aspects of what it is to live today. His characters watch the same television shows as his readers and relate to them in similar ways. For example, a character can fix an event in time, not because he looked at his watch but because it coincided with the start of a favourite television show. His characters think about celebrities because they are part of the general culture – but these celebrities are not just French, they are global, as in the case of Jane Fonda, once married to Roger Vadim. He uses such references not in a superficial way but in order to investigate the workings of the human imagination in relation to the world. He shows how it is through the mind that we engage with the world (or even at times try to escape from it). Our mental experiences are not direct but rather are mediated through the knowledge and discourses that are already there. We are possessed by what obsesses us. Yet we are not totally victims. Just as we are subject to outside influences, we ourselves exert our influence on the world. Others can be controlled by us. The human subject is not autonomous but rather is like the nation-state which in the global economy finds that its boundaries are for good or ill more and more porous so that sovereignty is no longer clearly defined. This is the struggle that Houellebecq's characters face – a struggle that threatens to overwhelm them and from which they may seek relief in fantasy or, conversely, in dulling the mind through narcotics of various kinds. Indeed, in sado-masochism, fantasy and the narcotic are combined.

It is this which leads the reader to what many find problematic about Houellebecq. In dealing with the contemporary, he does not shy away from that which might be considered unmentionable and which yet obsesses us. He is pertinent and impertinent. The satirical narrators turn out to be satyrs as well. Houellebecq does not deal merely with subjects that are deemed permissible but also with those that are painful. Thus his novels will raise issues such as sex-tourism, paedophilia, globalization, the role of cults and religious fundamentalism. These are issues that we might not want to have to face and which we might want to wish away – if we had total control. But we do not. Knowledge, of various kinds, flows into and out of the human subject and we cannot isolate ourselves from them. Denial is futile.

Knowledge is pervasive. It is also value-free. It is not good in and of itself. Nor is it bad. Reason is dethroned. It is not a guide that leads to the truth. Its attempts to make sense of the world turn out to be no more than rationalization of the random flux of existence. The mind seeks to justify what is. Reason is in Houellebecq's fiction primarily an instrumental force, one that is in the service of the ideologies and other systems of belief, seeking to coerce by persuasion and seeking to provide justification for what suits the existing modes of thought. An important corollary of this is that reason will not be totally successful in predicting the outcomes of our actions since our plans will always be at the mercy of events not planned by us.

Houellebecq's world is bleak. An earlier generation of writers may have sought to change the world through embracing revolt against the absurdity and lack of meaning in the human condition. They advocate that we become self-aware and take responsibility for our actions, thereby gesturing towards a better world. Houellebecq denies the possibility of success to such a project in a world where the individual is no longer sovereign. Utopias are just what the name implies – they are nowhere to be found. We cannot take responsibility for our own actions if we are not the sole originator of those actions, nor are we able to use our reason to be sure that we choose only the good outcomes. If our actions are unpredictable in their effects, we may act from the best of intentions only to find that the consequences are not what we would have wished.

Consequently, Houellebecq's depiction of the controversial may be unflinching but, as a satirist, he does not take a stance. He may allow characters to voice opinions in favour of or against sex-tourism but he does not give either side a victory. Instead he manages to convey a debate that will never be resolved. The refusal to take a stance should not be taken as tantamount to approval. Some commentators seem to react to the subject rather than to the way Houellebecq deals with it. They condemn what they think he has written rather than what he did indeed write. They see what is in their own minds and lack the perspicacity to know so. In the knowledge-driven world we live in, there is always something that we do not know.

Houellebecq's fiction benefits from close scrutiny. Indeed, the presence of the detective in the opening pages of *Plateforme* and his discussion of Agatha Christie's *The Hollow* later in the novel would seem to justify a forensic investigation. Houellebecq's narrators are frequently cerebral investigators in perpetual conflict with the satyr who seeks to abnegate their mental capacities in sensual oblivion. It is by looking steadily at the novels instead of speculating on the basis of what we think is there or on what we would like to be there, that a better appreciation of the power of this major author can be appreciated.

CHAPTER 1

Extension du domaine de la lutte: Fighting to Survive?

Michel Houellebecq's writing revels in the derivative. Far from being a term of mere opprobrium, the derivative is to be seen as a way of understanding the world. It reminds us that what we encounter is not created out of nothing but always comes from somewhere. Origin becomes elusive – if not illusory. It is more like the point on a line of development. What passes for innovation is often derivation. Ideas, objects and people are not autonomous, self-sufficient or free-standing entities. They are derived from antecedents to which they remain attached. Derivation is a process of differentiation which never results in total separation. There always remains a connecting thread.

The world Houellebecq depicts is a web of proliferating connections. These connections reach back towards the past. The emphasis is on coming from somewhere rather than going towards a particular goal. The world tends towards no purpose. The universe has a dynamic but it is not goal-driven. It evolves not because it has a goal it seeks to attain or a purpose to fulfil, but rather because of the circumstances past and present which operate on it. Thus, though two of the novels describe a future, that future is always the outcome of trends already established. In *La Possibilité d'une île* the future is littered with the debris of its past – our present.

This is also true Houellebecq's characters who are the outcome of their past. They bear the scars. The past is a web that binds them. The narrator of *Extension du domaine de la lutte* undergoes an unsuccessful course of psychotherapy and Bruno in *Les Particules élémentaires* finishes his days in an asylum. Characters are not driven by a goal or by a mission to accomplish something. Ambitious characters, such as the head of administration in *Extension du domaine de la lutte*, seem to be bundles of pointless, poorly directed energy rather than pursuing ruthlessly a particular path. The character Michel in *Les Particules élémentaires* achieves what he does not by having a vision that he wants to realize but rather by taking into account what is already there by grasping the relevance of a different set of insights to a well-established discipline. He is concerned with how to develop knowledge. His insights comes from the past, not the future. It is not surprising in the context that his admiration for the *Book of Kells* should prove an important element in the way his thought evolves.

The novel also details the family circumstances of the two principal characters, Bruno and Michel – where they come from in terms of both place and ancestry. They are both men who have had to leave their birth places – for different reasons in each case. Michel is neglected by his mother and rescued by his father, who in turn leaves him in the care of his own mother. Bruno is, with his grandmother, pushed out of Algeria when the country gains independence. Like his brother, he has been left by his parents. It is as though he is of no importance. Being cared for by his grandmother seems to emphasize that, as in the case of Michel, his mother feels no sense of obligation.

Yet though he may have no impact on his mother, what she does is shape his personality. Not only does a strong bond of attachment develop but Bruno's upbringing, like Michel's, makes him the man he is. Bruno's son is of little importance to him – just as Bruno and Michel are of little importance to Jane. Children are often badly treated in Houellebecq's fiction – a contrast with the tenderness evinced towards the older generation. Indeed, the mistreatment of Bruno and Michel pales in comparison to the sexual abuse visited on children at various points in the novels. Children are not valued. They have little impact. At worst, they become the playthings of careless and cruel adults.

Affection and care tend to be directed towards the progenitors, even when not merited. Both Bruno and Michel are rightly very fond of their grandmothers. Michel's attendance at his grandmother's reburial is more than simply a fulfilment of bureaucratic requirements. However, both men rally to their mother's side at the moment of her death, showing a degree of filial obligation never reciprocated in the other direction. Similarly, Daniel1 in *La Possibilité d'une île* can barely remember his son – even though the latter committed suicide. Daniel24 in the same novel is derived from Daniel1 but his link to his replacement, Daniel25, is of almost no importance. We are who we are because of our derivation from our antecedents. Those who derive in turn from us do not have the same power to make us who we are.

This raises an intriguing question about our true natures. If the past has more influence on us than the future, if our characters are formed by circumstances, then the possibility arises that we are no more than the sum of our memories – whether those memories are the ones that we retain in our minds or the ones that are encoded in our DNA. Is our humanity only something that we have absorbed from our surroundings? If so, then it might be possible to envisage the personality as something that inhabits the body rather than being an integral part of who we are. Our personality is a visitor. Since visitors are mobile and can move (or be moved) from place to place, then can the memory or thoughts be transferred from body to body? This is an issue suggested by *Extension du domaine de la lutte*, where software programmes can be moved between one piece of computing hardware and another. It also informs *La Possibilité d'une île*. Indeed, the moving of our minds between different bodies would appear to find a parallel in the way the extraterrestrial intelligent beings are apparently able to move from planet to planet, staying for a while in each and passing on their knowledge. The extraterrestrials never stay. In other words, they do not cut themselves off from their home world in order to take up permanent abode on earth. Residence is temporary, as indicated by the fact that the cultists in *La Possibilité d'une île* are not building a permanent base for the returning visitors but an embassy. The separation of the extraterrestrials from their home worlds will not happen. Similarly, human intelligence or the personality cannot in the end be separated from the body from which it originates. It is only in the case of machines that software programmes (the means by which machines appear to think) can be transferred between physical incarnations. Breaking the link between us and the body in which (and with which) we were born means destroying the self.

But derivation is not a smooth process, a mere unfolding of what is implied. There is no underlying plan or purpose to evolution – or to our lives. There is no divine plan for individuals or humanity, despite attempts to find or manufacture one. Evolution itself is neither goal-directed nor a process of growth that realizes some potential essence. It proceeds by natural selection, the means by which the fittest survive. The struggle eliminates those who do not fit into the circumstances. We evolve as we live. The two are almost synonymous. Houellebecq's fiction takes place in a Darwinian world, as the title of his first novel presupposes. Remaining at a point of origin is stasis.

What is at one remove from the point of origin is already moving on a creative path. Again and again in the novels, it is the people who are one remove along from the innovators that bring to fruition the work of their predecessors. It is not some single, new idea that has the power to change – even supposing that a totally new idea, one not derived from any preceding ideas, were possible – but rather a process of development from previous thinking that transforms the world. A prime example is Hubczejak in *Les Particules élémentaires*. It is he, not Michel Djerzinski, who brings about change. The derivative is a point of departure for a series of novels that are rich expressions of the modern world and some of its preoccupations. Everything evolves and all life – and all matter – is derived from what preceded it.

But Houellebecq also warns us that there are perils, losses as well as benefits. A preoccupation with what one has derived from who or what has preceded us indicates a mind-set that is more focussed on receiving than on giving – hence Daniel1's lack of connection to his son. He is a man who has no interest in what he is passing on. Like so many of Houellebecq's characters he is a consumer not a producer. In *Plateforme*, Valérie's father starts out as a farmer. The farm does not pay and so it has to be sold to a leisure company which gives the ex-farmer enough money for him to spend the rest of his life as a consumer. The producer is transformed into the consumer. We are living in a world that is eating itself up – so that the ecological disasters of *La Possibilité d'une île* are all too credible. Lack of responsibility for future generations is a characteristic of Houellebecq's world. The neo-humans in *Les Particules élémentaires* feel a connection to the remnants of their predecessor race, a need to pay them homage. The humans display no such feelings towards the new beings they have created.

Less dramatically, the derivative can become the second-hand, the tired recycling to what has gone before. Fitness to survive can degenerate into comfort and conformity. An entity that fits its environment too comfortably will survive but will not have any reason to develop. It goes nowhere. Mere repetitiveness is deadly. It gives the lives of the clones in *La Possibilité d'une île* such dreariness. They are derivative in the worst sense. Unable to do anything more than read and re-read the lives of their progenitor – they cannot free themselves from their antecedents' life stories – they do not really lead lives of their own but consume a life already lived. Similarly, tourists who follow the itineraries of the guidebooks are having a derivative experience in the worst sense. It is those who dare to depart from what has been experienced and recorded that have a richer experience. Thus it is only when Daniel25 leaves the compound in which he re-lives Daniel1's life that the possibility of a future can be envisaged.

The departure from the established is an important theme in Houellebecq's novels – it constitutes a 'dérive' or a 'détournement'. It is thus not an undermining of the theme of the derivative. Rather, it is a development of it, a derivation. However, such departures are not always positive – as the expression 'détournement de mineurs' indicates. The corruption of innocence is a theme in both *Plateforme* and *Lanzarote*. Degeneration is a related theme, dealing with how things deteriorate over time. This is particularly striking in *Les Particules élémentaires*, where degenerative illnesses such as cancer are frequent. Indeed the very notion of the derivative seems to proliferate like cancerous cells, splitting and spreading out as they go. Furthermore, degeneration is also a retreat from what has been achieved. It is a defeat. Many, if not all, of Houellebecq's characters could be seen as moral degenerates. The sex-tourists in *Plateforme* are clear examples of this and the depiction of their activities aroused outrage when the novel was published. Their exploitation of others could be seen as inhuman.

Houellebecq seems in general to depict characters that depart from the norm. His characters are a mixture of degenerates and overachievers. Indeed, a character can be both at the same time. It is as though he is exploring not humanity but the extent to which we can fall short of the human – or go beyond it. He shows us what there is of the animal in us. He imagines post-humans. He explores our potential not to be human. Curiously, by showing what we lose in failing to realize or in going beyond the human, he helps us value our humanity. This is the paradox of his writing.

The epigraph to the first chapter of *Extension du domaine de la lutte* is a quotation from Paul's Epistle to the Romans:

> La nuit est avancée, le jour approche. Dépouillons-nous donc des œuvres des ténèbres, et revêtons les armes de la lumière.[1]

This is the first of the epistles to be written and is the earliest book of the New Testament. It is, therefore, a work that marks a new departure but it is launched not by Christ but by a follower, someone who came after him. Saint Paul stands in the same relation to Christ as Hubczejak to Michel Djerzinski.

The epigraph is not simply a reiteration of the original. Houellebecq is doing more than repeating from a venerable source in order to give his prose an air of decorative learning. The context reveals new possibilities in the borrowed words. The opening chapter of *Extension du domaine de la lutte* is set at a party that appears to go on until the small hours of the morning. The borrowed words are a witty and, perhaps mock-heroic, comment on what follows. The metaphorical investment of light and darkness with moral values prefigures an important feature of the novel. Michel's attempt to incite his companion, Raphaël Tisserand, to commit murder takes place at night and the novel ends with at two o'clock in the afternoon, when the sun is at or near its highest point in the sky. This contrast between day and night derives from the epigraph. 'Dépouillons-nous' sounds noble in the writings of the saint but that nobility contrasts with the moment at the end of the chapter when the narrator vomits the food and, principally, drink consumed during the course of the evening – a stripping out of the toxins that make him feel ill.

The phrase 'Dépouillons-nous' echoes throughout this and subsequent novels. It is related to the idea of derivation in that it is a change

---

1   Michel Houellebecq, *Extension du domaine de la lutte* (Paris, J'ai Lu, 2003), p. 5. All subsequent references are to this edition.

accomplished by stripping out or taking away what was originally in place. Thus the phrase (especially given the associations it acquires because of what happens at the end of the chapter) looks forward to the clones in *La Possibilité d'une île*, who have had a functioning alimentary system removed, thus differentiating them from their progenitors. The human waste-disposal system is itself disposed of in order to reach what for the cultists is some presumed essence of what it is to be human. The need to dispose of waste-products is a sign that we are not pure but subject to degeneration – an issue that is to obsess Michel Djerzinski. This is because what we evacuate from the body is, for however brief a time, part of us. It means that we are stripping out part of ourselves, unravelling the notion of the human body as a thing of integrity. It raises the possibility that we may ultimately be nothing more than waste – a suspicion supported by the fact that 'la dépouille' is the human body after death. Just what this means is explored in the grave-yard scene in *Les Particules élémentaires* when Michel Djerzinski contemplates the decomposed body of his grandmother.

The contrast between the tone of Saint Paul's words and the prevailing mood of the chapter, indeed, of the novel, is quite stark. Saint Paul is aware of approaching daylight and seems to relish the fight. His metaphor of struggle does not downplay the difficulties but he hopes that a better future may be won. However, in Houellebecq the predominant tonality is one of despair. Modern life is still a struggle but not in the way envisaged by Saint Paul. His metaphors envisage a threat from without. It is an attack on the body which will need to be strengthened by armour to protect it. Houellebecq's narrator is, at the opening of the novel, incapacitated by what is within him. He feels ill, having drunk too much vodka. His body has been weakened by what he has ingested.

It is at this point that two of his co-workers come and, thinking the room is empty, begin to gossip. Michel is in fact lying down behind a sofa in a quiet room until he feels better. This first episode takes place in a room adjacent to that in which the party is taking place and where darkness and light interact to produce something that depends on both – shadows on a wall:

Aussitôt elles se sont mises à commenter les nouvelles du jour, à savoir qu'une
fille du service était venue au boulot avec une minijupe vachement mini, au ras
des fesses.

Et qu'est-ce qu'elles en pensaient? Elles trouvaient ça très bien. Leurs silhouettes
se détachaient en ombres chinoises, bizarrement agrandies, sur le mur au-dessus
de moi. Leurs voix me paraissaient venir de très haut, un peu comme le Saint-
Esprit. En fait, je n'allais pas bien du tout, c'est clair.

Pendant quinze minutes elles ont continué à aligner les platitudes. Et qu'elle
avait bien le droit de s'habiller comme elle voulait, et que ça n'avait rien à voir
avec le désir de séduire les mecs, et que c'était juste pour se sentir bien dans
sa peau, pour se plaire à elle-même, etc. Les ultimes résidus, consternants, du
féminisme.[2]

The two women speak in 'platitudes' – smooth, well-worn repetitions of
ideas taken from elsewhere. Their judgements are derivative in the worst
sense because they are not developed from what they were. They are cloned
thoughts. Neither woman will say anything startlingly original lest something upset the understanding between them. The passage is a complex
mixture of motivations. Envy, timidity, censoriousness and caution all
have a place.

The women's co-worker has got rid of clothing that she feels to be
out of keeping with her sense of self so that she can now feel 'bien dans
sa peau'. While the ostensible preoccupation may be on what encloses the
body, her clothing, the main concern is what lies inside the skin, the barrier
between inner and outer. Michel, on the other hand does not feel 'bien
dans sa peau' because the effects of the alcohol and whatever else he has
ingested. He is immobilised by his body's temporary inability to stand. He
cannot move himself let alone any objects. Thinking can only be translated
into action with the co-operation of the body just as the body needs to be
guided by thought.

The gossiping shows opinion operating as an instrument of social
control. The parameters of proper dress are being reinforced. The two
women are setting themselves up as arbiters of what is and is not appropriate in the office. They are like CRS (who feature later in the novel)

2   *Extension du domaine de la lutte*, pp. 5–6.

patrolling corridors for signs of disreputable and inappropriate behaviour. In this instance, they are discussing whether or not clothing that might elicit sexual arousal should be allowed into workplace. The two women are policing their colleague's dress because they realize that sexual attraction has a role to play in the power structures of the workplace, structures that give power to men but which are just as much policed by the women they exploit as by the beneficiaries. Nathalie Dumas points to the presence throughout Houellebecq's fiction of 'une conception moderne où la sexualité a été inventée pour la femme mais où les divisions sociales ont été faites pour l'homme blanc hétérosexuel'.[3] Sexuality has been feminised but that does not necessarily redress traditional disadvantages suffered by women. Sexual feelings are exercised in a context that is skewed in favour of traditional male power. Seduction is not just about arousing feelings but about power. However, rather than demonstrate the power of women over men, seduction is in fact the surrender of women to a male desire that they themselves have aroused.

In this scene, Houellebecq subverts the normal conventions of satire. In literary space, satire is a vision that goes from high to low. Satirists look down in judgement. The satirist places himself or herself morally above the object of their criticism. Here, the narrator, Michel is placed lying on the floor. Indeed, he tells us himself that he is aware of the women's voices coming down to him from above. Furthermore the shadows that they cast have been made bigger. His insights may show a thoughtful and well-read person who thinks beyond the trivial but this is someone who is incapacitated because of what he has drunk and who is in a physically inferior position.

Physical sensations cannot be divorced from the way we think. What we ingest, whether it is food, drink or chemical substances, affect our frame of mind. What we perceive acts in a similar fashion. At the party, however, there is also a degree of chaos, engendered by excess – too much stimulation

---

3　Nathalie Dumas, 'Lutte à 99 F: La vie sexuelle selon Michel H et Frédéric B', in *Michel Houellebecq sous la loupe*, edited by Murielle Lucie Clément and Sabine van Wesemael, Collection Faux Titre no. 304 (Amsterdam and New York, Éditions Rodopi, 2007), pp. 215–225, p. 220.

of the body. The well-ordered, clearly demarcated ways of thinking and behaving are disrupted, much as the rigid skeleton of the narrator flops down behind the sofa.

Nevertheless, our minds remain capable of operating in such conditions – unlike computers which simply give up. Indeed, new connections can be made and additional possibilities envisaged. This is reflected in the remarkable contrapuntal quality of Houellebecq's style. Other parts of the novel will echo this scene just as it echoes, in its reference to 'ombres chinoises', the allegorical story of the cave, from Plato's *Republic*. The party is a contemporary version of the original story. Dominic Noguez points out that a feature of Houellebecq's writing is 'des rapports d'un texte donné avec un autre, antérieur (l'hypotexte)'.[4] Texts are not self-standing entities but derive from other texts which preceded them and with which they maintain a meaningful connection. While it is possible to read these texts in isolation, our understanding is enriched if we place them in relation to their provenance.

Effective interpretation depends on grasping what precedents shaped the text. In *Plateforme* the murder of the narrator's father is solved when the detective investigating the crime discovers that the victim had an affair before his death and that the young woman's family disapproved of the match. Even more pertinently, Agatha Christie's *The Hollow*, a novel that *Plateforme*'s narrator analyses at some length, depicts a crime scene whose meaning is changed when the detective uncovers the events that preceded it and which, indeed, shaped it. From Houllebecq's earliest published novel onwards, meaning is established in relation to what went before.

Texts are not limited as to context but can derive from several sources. The scene at the party refers back, perhaps even more pertinently, to Plato's *Symposium*, a text quoted by one of the narrators in *La Possibilité d'une île*. Incidental details are common to both. Houellebecq's scene is a party where there is a couch and a lot of alcohol involved – elements to be found in Plato. Furthermore, Plato's work descends at the end into drunken chaos – as does Houellebecq's first chapter. The subject of the *Symposium* is sexual

4   Dominic Noguez, *Houellebecq en fait* (Paris, Fayard, 2003), p. 102.

attraction, a subject that dominates the thoughts of Michel's co-workers. The verbal sparring of the *Symposium* is updated to the competitive sniping of the two women.

There is also a reference to the Holy Spirit. This does not indicate that Michel accepts the existence of a transcendental spiritual realm. Rather, hearing voices of celestial (or even diabolical) origin is normally a sign of derangement, of a loss of judgement. These particular voices are a harbinger of the mental illness that is to afflict Michel. For the moment, it is physical illness that besets him – though one that has a psychic dimension. His illness affects and is affected by what he the sees and hears and by what he consumes. The alcohol and the food are too much for him. Thus, at the end of the chapter, relief comes when, during unconsciousness, he voids the poisons that have entered his system. Thus he purifies his body. Yet the reality upon awakening is far from reassuring. Michel realizes is that he has lost his car keys. Is this then, what reality is – a sense of loss? The end of illusion is not necessarily positive.

The guidance from the Holy Spirit may be a delusion but it is guidance. Nathalie Dumas argues that Houellebecq's world is one which is rule-based and sees this as a feature of western capitalist society in general: 'Dans la société occidentale, l'individu vit alors, sous le contrôle de l'argent, à travers une multiplicité de codes, de principes, de protocoles et de lois.'[5] This framework may also irk or prove inadequate and even though one may not depart from it, the mere observance of the rules may not bring contentment:

> La difficulté, c'est qu'il ne suffit pas exactement de vivre selon la règle. En effet vous parvenez (parfois de justesse, d'extrême justesse, mais dans l'ensemble vous y parvenez) à vivre selon la règle. Vos feuilles d'imposition sont à jour. Vos factures, payées à la bonne date. Vous ne vous déplacez jamais sans carte d'identité (et la petite pochette spéciale pour la carte bleue!...).
> Pourtant, vous n'avez pas d'amis.[6]

---

5 Dumas, p. 215.
6 *Extension du domaine de la lutte*, p. 12.

This is a passage suffused with wry humour verging on the tragic. Success is defined as meeting the deadline for returning your tax-forms and paying your bills on time. It means travelling with your identity card and having your credit card in a special holder so that you can get at when you want it. However, following the rules does not prevent one being aware of the absence of friends. It does not fulfil our human need to connect with others. Indeed, it suggests that the well-ordered life is in some way responsible. It fills one's life so that there is no room for friends. It is paradoxically a plenitude that is also an absence.

These rules suggest a certain mode of life. The paying of taxes shows the subject as citizen – but not a citizen who is an autonomous participant in the decision-making process but rather who has financial obligations to the state. A further obligation is to carry an identity card when travelling. The subject needs to prove his or her status to the agents of the state, justifying entitlement to be in a certain place. Houellebecq sketches a depressing picture of contemporary life. The narrator is a payer of bills. He may be a consumer but he is one who is depicted paying for, rather than enjoying, what he consumes. In addition, not paying bills, not returning forms to the authorities or not carrying an identity card usually lead to some form of penalty. If nineteenth-century writers, such as Baudelaire, railed against a religious orthodoxy that kept the populace in line by fear of punishment in the afterlife, then modern secular states use rules and regulations – bureaucracy – backed up by penalties to keep contemporary citizens in line.

The phrase 'la petite pochette spéciale pour la carte bleue' reveals the arbitrary nature of this well-ordered world. We are looking at a world of shadows and shapes ('ombres chinoises') created by the mind and not at the real. There is nothing intrinsically special about the 'pochette' that holds the credit card except that it has been so designated. The word 'spéciale' signals not an intrinsic value but one that has been conferred on the object. It is the narrator who has decided that this is to be the specific place where his card will be kept.

The adjective 'bleue' does something similar. The card is blue only because that is the colour that has been used. The card is a credit card or bank card and instead of naming it for its function, as in English, the French use its colour to name it. In like manner, immigrants to the United States seek a green card. This kind of naming is conventional. This bureaucratic world is organised and it runs on rational lines but there is no sense of the rational order being guaranteed in any way. There is no ultimate justification. That is why there is something petty about the lifestyle depicted in this paragraph. Everything works as it should – but to what end?

However, the universe does appear to lend itself to being organised. It has a propensity for organisation that the bureaucratic mind can exploit. Something strange is going on in the phrase 'petite pochette'. The word 'pochette' is a noun deriving from 'poche'. The ending '-ette' is a diminutive. Thus the addition of the adjective 'petite' appears to derive, to spring naturally from a quality deemed to be inherent in the object named. It suggests that there may be some inherent connection, at a level deeper than the surface 'logos' or word that holds the world together. The elementary particle that is '-ette' seems to resonate meaningfully with the adjective.

Making links, even if arbitrary, is something that that the universe lends itself to – and not just as described in this novel. This is reflected metaphorically in the prominence of transport links in Houellebecq – all those, cars, trains and planes that enable the characters to do so much travelling. Things happen when and because the characters travel. The purpose of travel can be seen in a sense not so much as a change of location as a connection between points on the map. To travel is to follow a route. Houellebecq's characters are not fleeing or travelling to new destinations so much as connecting places together, places to which they will return. Julie Delorme speaks of the characters in Houellebecq having a 'propension au *voyage circulaire*'.[7] She characterises this kind of journey as revealing a desire to travel but nuanced by a desire for home when one reaches one's destination – a desire that keeps one from fully identifying with the new people and places when one arrives. The Michel in *Plateforme* travels to the Far East but on holiday and returns home. It is significant that at the end of the novel, it is his staying in the Far East, an interruption of his

7   Julie Delorme, 'Du guide touristique au roman. *Plateforme* de Michel Houellebecq', in Clément and van Wesemael, pp. 287–300, p. 287.

plans and a breaking of his links with his home country, which presages his death. Circulation is necessary to life. The first major journey of Michel in *Extension du domaine de la lutte* is to Rouen where he is to provide training in the use of computer programmes that his company has sold to the Ministry of Agriculture. This trip is a connection. He is taking his expertise from his base in Paris to an outlying city. However, the move is not permanent and the expectation is that he will return to Paris. It is a '*voyage circulaire*'.

He has a companion on this trip, the aptly named, Rafaël Tisserand. The name evokes the angel Raphael, the messenger who comes from (and returns to) God, connecting heaven and earth. It also reminds us of the Holy Spirit of the opening chapter, the person of the Holy Trinity who is the guarantor of the connection between God and his Church. The name Tisserand provides a secular version of this in that the name means 'weaver'. The character's name seems to spring from aspects of his function.

However, there is a countervailing force, one that fosters separation and distinctiveness. The journey, as pointed out above, exemplifies this. Characters may be following a route to connect two points but they are never able to abolish the gap between starting point and destination. They are always aware that the where they have arrived is different from where they set out. Despite his name, Tisserand is someone who is singularly unable to make connections to other people in his private life. The way in which Houellebecq draws this character highlights the fact that human beings are not monolithic but an amalgam of characteristics. We are successful in some areas of our lives and not in others. Rafaël Tisserand is less successful than most. He may function to a certain degree in his work but elsewhere he has serious difficulties. His lack of charisma and lack of appeal make him a particularly isolated individual.

Furthermore, some connections are sanctioned and others not, just as bureaucracy and regulation lay down the lines Michel's life should follow. Controlling movement versus freedom of movement is a key dichotomy in Houellebecq. Cars, planes and trains (particularly the latter) follow pre-approved ways. People are not supposed to leave the beaten path. It is significant that the end of the novel shows the narrator striking out on foot along a route he is forging for himself – something that one of the narrators of *La Possibilité d'une île* also does.

The person who does not travel is stuck in his own private, disconnected space. There is a curious incident later in the novel that illustrates this. The narrator is on his own in Rouen and feeling more and more depressed:

> Le lendemain, je me suis levé tôt, je suis arrivé à l'heure pour le premier train; j'ai acheté un billet, j'ai attendu, et je ne suis pas parti; et je n'arrive pas à comprendre pourquoi. Tout cela est extrêmement déplaisant.[8]

This is a depiction of the depressive who makes a half-hearted attempt to overcome his lassitude by acting. What he is seeking to escape is his feeling of loneliness. He wants to travel, to connect. However, he lacks the energy to follow through, to complete the sequence. It is an interrupted pathway – prefiguring the ending of the novel. Although Michel knows rationally that he needs to do something, there is another part of his psyche that fails him at this point. He is a person whose mind is a site of struggle. This inner struggle leads not, as in Saint Paul, to victory but to immobilisation.

Houellebecq's handling of the dilemma is not simplistic but suffused with his habitual ironic appraisal. The journey out of Rouen may present itself as an escape – which no doubt one part of Michel sees – but on the other hand the train follows a route and timetable set out by someone else. Thus we, and perhaps the part of him that sees the pointlessness, can imagine that this escape is not going to enhance personal freedom but will simply place the narrator within a framework determined by some-one else – it will not give freedom. That is why he does not get on the train. Houellebecq's novels dramatise the struggle between the need to get away, to escape, and the difficulty of getting out of the clutches of the forces that control us. The narrator's dilemma is that connections that bind us to others also limit our freedom.

The computer programmes that Michel installs enables connections to be made and work accomplished but there is also something much more

---

8   *Extension du domaine de la lutte*, p. 72.

sinister. Catherine Lechardoy, an administrator whom he meets in the course of his work, tells him that she is hoping to advance her career by taking classes. This will give her a 'diplôme d'ingénieur.' The qualification suggests that she will learn how to do things. Indeed Michel tells us at this point that he himself has this qualification. So we might expect Catherine Lechardoy to be aiming to be a doer or, like Michel, a facilitator, someone who helps others to do things. When asked which courses she is following, she details them: 'Des cours de contrôle de gestion, d'analyse factorielle, d'algorithmique, de comptabilité financière.'[10] These are subjects that will give her the power not so much to do things as to control and check up on people. Indeed, she sees herself as currently someone who is put upon and used to clear up other people's mistakes but who does not have any decision-making role herself.

Yet she is mistaken in the path she has taken. In seeking to escape, she seems to be rushing towards what she is fleeing from. It will not give her freedom that she achieves. Her new status will simply confirm her role as someone who rectifies the misdoings of others. Indeed, control over others does not mean freedom for herself: 'Souvent le soir elle travaille jusqu'à minuit, dans son studio, pour rendre ses devoirs.'[11] Her learning keeps her in one place, trying to fulfil her homework, her 'devoirs'. Thus in attempting to control others she places herself in a position where she has obligations to others.

Yet just like Michel, who laments not having friends, she realizes that this attempt to master the procedures is not enough – and her realisation echoes his. She knows that things can be different:

> À Paris, on peut crever sur place dans la rue, tout le monde s'en fout. Chez elle, dans le Béarn, ce n'est pas pareil. Tous les weekends elle rentre chez elle, dans le Béarn.[12]

9   *Extension du domaine de la lutte*, p. 27.
10   *Extension du domaine de la lutte*, p. 27.
11   *Extension du domaine de la lutte*, p. 27.
12   *Extension du domaine de la lutte*, p. 27.

The repetition of 'Chez elle' contrasts with 'dans son studio'. Where she comes from is an integral part of who she is. Her Parisian one-bedroom flat – the place where she has ended up – is not home. It is an indication of her isolation, an isolation that is endemic in her experience of the capital and graphically illustrated by the image of the person falling down dead in the street, ignored by the passers-by – a definitively interrupted journey. Catherine believes that her home province is a place where people do connect. Such is the strength of her need to feel a connection that she visits her home province every weekend – a not inconsiderable journey in the train. Thus Catherine is a more complex figure than might appear. Her attempts at control do not depict a very sympathetic personality but her attempts to improve her situation and, particularly, her awareness of a major absence in her life give her a tragic dimension, especially since that awareness does not seem to give her any guidance as to how she might put things right in other parts of her life. Ultimately, Catherine is a fault-finder rather than someone whose insights serve to give her life a new direction.

Catherine's lack of connection is the source of her pain. She can feel the strength of connection to her place of birth but has difficulty connecting with her current circumstances. Disconnection manifests itself in various ways throughout. Michel's client is the Ministry of Agriculture, but this Ministry is about running systems, not growing crops or tending to the animals, something particularly evident at the meeting described in Chapter 9. The people concerned are all administrators of one kind or another. There seems to be little connection between bureaucrat and the thing administered. The head of the Information Technology Department could be working anywhere. He is interested in his role as a manager not in what he is producing. As Michel puts it: 'L'individu semble s'être donné pour mission d'incarner une exagération survoltée du personnage du patron jeune et dynamique.' He dresses and wears his hair in a way that projects the image he wishes to present. The scene makes clear is the extent to which administration, the tertiary sector of the economy, seems to have battened on to other areas. Being a farmer is now about being an administrator. It has little to do with land and animals:

Le quatrième représentant du ministère est une espèce de caricature du socialiste agricole: il porte des bottes et une parka comme s'il revenait d'une expédition sur le terrain; il a une grosse barbe et fume la pipe; je n'aimerais pas être son fils. Devant lui sur la table, il a ostensiblement posé un livre intitulé: 'La fromagerie devant les techniques nouvelles.' Je n'arrive pas à comprendre ce qu'il fait là, il ne connaît manifestement rien au sujet traité; peut-être est-il un représentant de la base. Quoiqu'il en soit il semble s'être donné pour objectif de tendre l'atmosphère et de provoquer un conflit au moyen de remarques répétitives sur 'l'inutilité de ce réunions qui n'aboutissent jamais à rien', ou bien sur 'ces logiciels choisis dans un bureau de ministère et qui ne correspondent jamais aux besoins réels des gars, sur le terrain'.[13]

This man is, we may understand, a representative of the farmers who produce food and as such forms part of the network of representation that runs through the novel. In the first chapter, the Holy Spirit represents God and the shadows on the wall represent people. Michel and Tisserand represent their company. It is not fortuitous that the authorities deal happily not with real people but with their representation. The tax authorities deal with what is represented on the tax returns. The bills Michel pays represent what he has bought and he carries with him not money but a credit card, which represents his financial worth. More tellingly, he needs to have his ID card. It stands in for and replaces the original human being – and does so in a way that allows for the individual to be controlled.

Yet at the same time, it points to a cleavage. The identity card is not identical with the person it represents. There is a gap between it and the being it represents. Thus, here, the farmer's representative is separate from the farmers even when he claims to speak for them – especially when he speaks for them. On the one hand he berates those present for choosing software that does not meet the farmers' needs while participating in the very process. On the other, he complains of unending meetings that get nowhere but is himself the cause of the prolongation of the meeting. Furthermore, his dress is just as important as that of the IT manager. It presents an image rather than being appropriate to the situation. Both men are like

13   *Extension du domaine de la lutte*, p. 35.

the woman who came to work dressed in a mini-skirt deemed too short. She was presenting an image not appropriate for the situation. She was at the office but dressed as though for another venue.

Houellebecq's satire is multilayered and complex. The farmer's representative is dismissed as 'une espèce de caricature du socialiste agricole'. The use of 'caricature' points to a distortion of a distortion: 'socialiste agricole'. One does not immediately associate socialism with the primary sector. Rather it is an ideology that seems to spring from industrial societies. This is perhaps confirmed by the title of the book that the representative places on the table, seemingly for effect. He is a man who is interested in the industrial processes of cheese-producing, the 'nouvelles techniques', rather than in the taste of the cheese or the welfare of the animals. Taken with the purpose of the meeting which is to put in place a computer system that will facilitate administration, this is then someone who manages to have a foot in all three economic sectors – agricultural, industrial and services. He connects all three and at the same time demonstrates that he is an unrepresentative representative. He is also a troublemaker, someone who enjoys disrupting the smooth flow of the meeting and unsettling the processes whereby a coherent strategy can be formed. Indeed, he is a bundle of contradictions.

The phrase 'je n'aimerais pas être son fils' seems to come out of the blue – a comment that is strictly speaking irrelevant to the context. However, it is highly pertinent. It hints that the man might not take proper care of his son. It also tells us something about the narrator and is another illustration that where one comes from is a key element in how one sees oneself. One of the commonplaces of literature is the recognition scene where long lost children are re-united with parents. Michel's statement turns the commonplace on its head. What we have is a misrecognition scene. It is a disavowal of paternity. Michel's statement is an indication of his own lack of connection. He is not someone who, like Catherine Lechardoy, has a sense of belonging to a network of family and friends that could sustain him. He can cope with the demands of maintaining a public persona that can deal with the authorities. But this is not enough. Ways of behaving that are adequate for the public domain are no help in

the private spaces that one must inhabit. There are parts of one's life where
the rules are not enough:

> Cependant, il reste du temps libre. Que faire? Comment l'employer? Se consa-
> crer au service d'autrui? Mais, au fond, autrui ne vous intéresse guère. Écouter
> des disques? C'était une solution mais au fil des ans vous devez convenir que la
> musique vous émeut de moins en moins.
>   Le bricolage pris, dans son sens le plus étendu, peut offrir une voie. Mais rien
> en vérité ne peut empêcher le retour de plus en plus fréquent de ces moments où
> votre absolue solitude, la sensation de l'universelle vacuité, le pressentiment que
> votre existence se rapproche d'un désastre douloureux et définitif se conjuguent
> pour vous plonger dans un état de réelle souffrance.
>   Et, cependant, vous n'avez toujours pas envie de mourir.[14]

The phrase 'temps libre' is resonant. It means not just time for pastimes
but a time which is not structured by those organisations that run one's life
in the public domain. What Michel is faced with is a vacuity that comes
from a lack of connection, an inability to feel. The latter turns out to be
very perturbing, and not just because he generalises from it, projecting
his own inability to feel on all of us by his use of 'vous'. At this point it
manifests itself as an inability to be moved by music. This could simply be
down to overfamiliarity but another possibility is that it could be a sign
of a psychotic personality – the beginning of a psychosis being suggested
already by the way the scene at the party was presented. His personality
is falling to bits. Something within him recognises this and that is why he
is interested in the possible value of 'bricolage'. This is a resonant concept
in Houellebecq. In *Les Particules élémentaires* the word is used to suggest
the filling in of gaps in scientific knowledge. This is not dissimilar to its
use here to indicate the need to fill in the gaps between human beings as
well as the cracks in his persona.

Michel seems, however, resigned to accepting the emptiness of life and
the proximity of suffering. This resignation gives rise not to peace, as in
some belief systems, but to despair. Indeed, with hindsight the juxtaposition

---

14   *Extension du domaine de la lutte*, pp. 12–13.

of this with 'autrui ne vous intéresse guère' is grimly prescient of future developments. In Houellebecq, as in life, hindsight is extraordinarily accurate in its predictions.

Michel experiences life as a malaise. He is not the only one. Characters in Houellebecq's fiction seem not just to be subject to ailments but they do not follow the modern precepts for healthy living. There is a lack of concern for what will happen to them in the future. They smoke, drink too much and consume drugs. Some have a penchant for sado-masochistic sexual practices. The body is abused by its owner and by the process of living. Life is a wearing away of the body. Consequently there is a need for hospitals where a bit of 'bricolage' can be done to try to repair the damage that goes with living.

When Michel collapses in Rouen and goes for tests, the doctor informs him that he has a heart complaint but not one that is fatal:

> Les examens terminés il s'approche de moi et m'annonce que j'ai une péricardite, et non un infarctus, comme il l'avait cru tout d'abord. Il m'apprend que les premiers symptômes sont rigoureusement identiques; mais, contrairement à l'infarctus qui est souvent mortel, la péricardite est une maladie très bénigne, on n'en meurt jamais en aucun cas.[15]

Knowledge is not a matter of facts but is part of a network. Pericarditis is contextualised within a range of heart ailments. It is not fatal, though it has many points in common with the heart attack. Pericarditis is an illness that one lives with.

To be ill is just as much a way of life as being healthy is:

> On s'habitue vite à l'hôpital. Pendant toute une semaine j'ai été assez sérieusement atteint, je n'avais aucune envie de bouger ni de parler; mais je voyais des gens autour de moi qui bavardaient, qui se racontaient leurs maladies avec cet intérêt fébrile, cette délectation qui paraît toujours un peu indécente à ceux qui sont en bonne santé; je voyais aussi leurs familles, en visite. Eh bien dans l'ensemble personne ne se plaignait; tous avaient l'air très satisfaits de leur sort, malgré

---

15 *Extension du domaine de la lutte*, p. 75.

le mode de vie peu naturel qui leur était imposé, malgré, aussi, le danger qui pesait sur eux; car dans un service de cardiologie la plupart des patients risquent leur peau, au bout du compte.[16]

The reader may recognise the situation because it reprises, subtly and with variations what happened in the opening scene of the novel. Michel is lying down, as a result of feeling ill, and is watching and commenting on those who come into a room and who do not take note or are seemingly unaware that he is observing what they are doing. The phrase 'se racontaient leurs maladies' turns symptoms into a narrative, giving illness a structure that makes sense and which can be used as the basis for conversation. Being ill in hospital gives someone something to talk about. It allows human contact to be made, encouraging friendship.

And yet Michel describes the patients' attitude as being 'indécente'. Not only that, he couples it with 'délectation'. The indecent is what goes beyond the bounds of propriety and the patients' interest in their disease goes beyond misery to become a source of pleasure. Talking about one's illness and making it a topic of conversation is transgressive of the norms of a healthy society. In the ward they are the norm.

Yet all is not rosy. The way of life is, the narrator reminds us, imposed on them. Being ill is not something that one chooses. Thus the ill are not free agents. They are in hospital because of external forces that oblige them to be there. Nor can one pretend that this is an equivalent and equally valid form of normality. It is quite different and, if it displays a form of comic camaraderie that is appealing, the narrator is all too aware that, in the cardiac unit, 'la plupart des patients risquent leur peau'. There is an echo with the earlier scene at the party because the word 'peau' echoes 'se sentir bien dans sa peau'. This is a good example of what Hillis Millar calls 'opaque similarities' where meaning is 'generated by the echoing of two dissimilar things'.[17] Here two opposing situations – well-being and illness – are echoed. The patients embrace their situation and work within the framework that illness and hospitalisation imposes on them. The narrator,

16   *Extension du domaine de la lutte*, p. 77.
17   J. Hillis Miller, *Fiction and Repetition* (Oxford, Basil Blackwell, 1982), p. 9.

in his silence, refuses it. He is the participant observer. His gloom contrasts with their relish.

The word 'peau' takes us further, however. The skin is the boundary between inner and outer, between the self and the world. It is the point of contact between the body and the non-body. In making love, it is skin on skin contact that is the expression of attachment and of the limits of that attachment for the skin is a barrier that keeps us separate. The skin holds the body together. Within it lies the structure that connects the various parts of the self and allows them to function. In death that is no longer the case and the skin dissolves allowing our bodily remains to mingle with the earth – something described in *Les Particules élémentaires*. Take away the structure of the body and the self disintegrates – a fate that befalls Christiane, Bruno's lover. Disease in Houellebecq is not something that comes from without – as in Camus's *La Peste*. It is an attack from within. The illness that is most prevalent in *Les Particules élémentaires* is cancer – which leads inevitably to death. In *Plateforme*, on the other hand, the threat to the body is not from illness but comes from without and is a physical attack on the body's framework. The effect, however, is the same. In two cases, that of the murder of Michel's father and the attack on the resort, the violence shatters the body, breaking its integrity and destroying its wholeness and self-sufficiency. In another case, that of the mugging of Michel's co-worker in the metro, the effect of assault on the body is to leave the character psychologically violated and unable to function. The body loses its ability to function and becomes chaotic.

The cheerfulness of the patients should not be seen as an attempt to hide from reality – it is not 'mauvaise foi' – but rather as a way to manage the consequences. If illness, like violence, is an assault on the orderly functioning of the body, then being cared for in hospital is an attempt to find a new structure within which to live. This makes their medical treatments palliative rather than effective so that the treatment is a permanent regime:

> Je me souvenais de cet ouvrier de cinquante-cinq ans, il en était à son sixième séjour; il saluait tout le monde, le médecin, les infirmières ... Visiblement il était ravi d'être là. Pourtant voilà un homme qui dans le privé avait une vie très active: il bricolait, faisait son jardin, etc. J'au vu sa femme, elle avait l'air très gentille; ils

en étaient même touchants, de s'aimer comme ça, à cinquante ans passés. Mais dès qu'il arrivait à l'hôpital il abdiquait toute volonté; il déposait son corps ravi, entre les mains de la science. Du moment que tout était organisé. Un jour ou l'autre il allait y rester, dans cet hôpital, c'était évident; mais cela aussi était organisé. Je le revois s'adressant au médecin avec une espèce d'impatience gourmande, employant au passage des abréviation familières que je n'ai pas comprises: 'Alors, on va me faire ma pneumo et ma cata veineuse?' Ça, il y tenait, à sa cata veineuse; il en parlait tous les jours.[18]

Houellebecq's point is not that this is a repressive regime imposed by force or the threat of force. Rather, the patient is glad to succumb. Faced with the loss of his former structured life, he finds in the ward an alternative to which he gladly submits. He may have lost his freedom but he has the security of knowing that 'tout était organisé'. This is why he is so content. The total breakdown of order that death represents, the destruction of our bodily structures, is such a danger that the order represented by hospital care is welcomed. These new structures devised in hospitals are additional structures to the natural ones that are in danger of failing. The expression 'déposait son corps' suggest a sense of relief at not having to find the strength in one's body alone. One now has the back-up of medical science. The alternative is a loss of self, dissolution. A parallel may be drawn with the possession of an identity card, as described earlier in the novel, because by having one people could be said to be behaving like the patients in the hospital. They are allowing the state to regulate their being. Houellebecq is making the point that we buy into the control that is devised to keep us in our place and that regulates our movements.

The internalisation of this control is demonstrated by the familiarity of the patient and the carers. In a novel like *La Peste* there is a clear hierarchy. The doctor treats the patients but does not fraternise. In *Extension du domaine de la lutte*, the patient and the doctors are bound together by a common language, a structure of communication that allows the patient to feel included but which also excludes those who are not in the know – such as the narrator. Structures work by demarcating what is to be kept in

18   *Extension du domaine de la lutte*, pp. 78–79.

and what is to be kept out. In the dissolution of the grave, the body and the soil, mingle together without hindrance. Thus, 'fraternité' means including some people in one's intimate circle while excluding others. Here, as we saw in an earlier quotation, the narrator feels left out. He has no 'amis'.

The patients' sense of equality is partly the result of the tendency of sufferers to become experts in their own illnesses. They have acquired the knowledge that had been the preserve of the doctors. Nevertheless, this acquisition is not empowering, Knowledge is not necessarily power. On the contrary, what the patient has done is acquire some of the knowledge that the doctor possessed. He is not able to do anything much with it. He cannot – as the questions show – order up his own treatment. He may know what the doctor proposes but he cannot influence it. In fact there is a sense in which knowledge that he has gained comes to possess him. Thanks to it, he is more ready to comply. Knowledge can be a further structure of control. The patient accepts the structured knowledge of medicine because the alternative, not to follow it, is to be allowed to die.

Thus the fear of dissolution leads to an abdication of the will. Patients do not just surrender control of their bodies to the doctors. They also surrender their minds. What we know sets the parameters within which we decide on our actions. By imitating the speech of the doctors, the patients are accepting the knowledge of the doctors and submitting to it. They have been possessed by medical knowledge. They are complicit in their own lack of freedom of action. They are like Michel, unable to get on the bus and leave.

Knowledge of the world is apprehended just as much through the body as through the mind. Similarly, there is no soul outside its physical embodiment. Yet body and mind can be at cross purposes. Illness is one case where the conflict is evident: 'Voir ses jambes comme des objets séparés, loin de son esprit, auquel elles seraient reliées plus ou moins par hasard, et plutôt mal.'[19] The use of the third person to refer to the self is a sign of dissociation. The disjointed phrasing seems to imitate the legs that are somehow responding to the mind but not quite as they should.

---

19   *Extension du domaine de la lutte*, p. 78.

Michel here is a stranger to himself, alienated from his own body. Illness dislocates the body and disturbs the fit between it and the mind.

It also affects the way Michel sees his position in the outer world, exacerbating the lack of harmony between him and others When Tisserand visits him in hospital, Michel does recognise that he is trying to be friendly but Michel himself cannot respond: 'Mon esprit flottait, indistinct, un peu perplexe'.[20] In the struggle for mastery inside and outside, the mind has for the moment given up in perplexity. Such a state leaves one vulnerable. The narrator is lucky in that the doctors are trying to help.

Tisserand, on the other hand, is perhaps less fortunate. Viewed one way he is a success but in another way he is a failure:

> En système économique parfaitement libéral, certains accumulent des fortunes considérables; d'autres croupissent dans le chômage et la misère. En système sexuel parfaitement libéral, certains ont une vie érotique variée et excitante; d'autres sont réduits à la masturbation et la solitude. Le libéralisme économique, c'est l'extension du domaine de la lutte, son extension à tous les âges de la vie et à toutes les classes de la société. De même, le libéralisme sexuel, c'est l'extension du domaine de la lutte, son extension à tous les âges de la vie et à toutes les classes de la société. Sur le plan économique, Raphaël Tisserand appartient au camp des vainqueurs; sur le plan sexuel, à celui de vaincus. Certains gagnent sur les deux tableaux; d'autres perdent sur les deux. Les entreprises se disputent certains jeunes diplômés; les femmes se disputent certains jeunes hommes; les hommes se disputent certaines jeunes femmes; le trouble et l'agitation sont considérables.[21]

Human beings are in competition along a variety of axes. Thus Tisserand is successful in his career but he is not a success with women. Sentences move inexorably, using parallel structures and mirror structures. The reasoning is lucid and clear cut. The parts move forward on seemingly solid ground as an intellectual case is driven home. The conclusions derive inexorably from the premises. The narrator is someone who is able to use language to strengthen his case.

---

20   *Extension du domaine de la lutte*, p. 78.
21   *Extension du domaine de la lutte*, pp. 100–101.

Tisserand's relative success in his work seems not to compensate for his lack of success in sex. As he points out, in a passage shortly before the one quoted above, he can afford a prostitute but he cannot see why he should pay for what others get free '*et en plus avec de l'amour*'.[22] It is not that economic success does not compensate, it is that it is vitiated by his lack of success in love. He is a man who, like Catherine Lechardoy, dwells on what is wrong, on what he needs.

Consequently, Tisserand is an empty shell of a man. He has possessions and a position but he lacks emotional satisfaction and connections to other people. His name points to the business contacts and computer networks that make him a success in economic terms but it also suggest a man who is a skin woven over an inner void. That void demands to be filled. He has successfully struggled to come out a winner on the economic front and is unable to accept that he cannot be a success in the struggle for love. This is indeed how he imagines human relations to be – a struggle. Women are to be subjected to his desires. Love is a struggle where affection is won by subjugating the other person.

This can be seen in the scene in the discotheque. At the start of the chapter, Michel informs us that he bought a steak-knife in preparation for the evening out: 'je commençais à apercevoir l'ébauche d'un plan'.[23] The ambiance in the nightclub is mixture of sexuality and violence: 'Beaucoup de mini-jupes, de bustiers échancrés; bref de la chair fraîche'.[24] The last phrase is particularly disturbing in the light of Michel's purchase. As well as indicating a predatory approach to the person with whom one wants to have sex, it suggests lassitude and a jaded sexual appetite that needs to be stimulated by violence. The struggle is imbued with a violence that is bloody and cruel. The thrill of pain replaces sincerity of feeling.

The party scene, or rather elements of it, is being reprised. The reference to dress and sexual allure is an echo of the conversation overheard by Michel. What is most disturbing is the ambiguity. It is not certain who

22 *Extension du domaine de la lutte*, p. 99. Italics in the original.
23 *Extension du domaine de la lutte*, p. 109.
24 *Extension du domaine de la lutte*, p. 111.

is chasing whom. Women are seeking men and doing so in a certain way that leaves them vulnerable – it is men who have the power to do violence. Dress is presented as bait, a lure for men:

> D'autre part son habillement, d'une grande audace, soulignait sans ambiguïté son intention de trouver un partenaire sexuel: en taffetas léger, sa robe virevoltait à chaque mouvement, découvrant un porte-jarretelles et un string minuscule en dentelle noire, qui laissait le fessier entièrement nu.[25]

The hunters are being hunted. However, this is Michel's view. We are given his perspective just as we are given that of the two women at the party. It is Michel who is interpreting the dress of the woman as an indication of her intentions. He appears to grant the woman autonomy over her sexuality but this does not prevent his projecting on to her his own desires. This is a gaze that seeks to dominate and subject.

Michel's interpretation of the dancer and her intentions is in itself a cliché. Indeed, it is not going too far to see this musing as an example of what the two women were doing earlier – 'aligner les platitudes'. The banality of the depiction, the recycling of pornographic commonplaces, is an indication of a failure of the imagination and of an inability to engage with reality. Michel no less than Tisserand is living in a cave of shadows unable to relate to the reality of human beings – it is little wonder that his attitude to women is Neanderthal.

Later, Michel goes to buy a bottle of bourbon. On the way back he falls:

> ... j'ai entamé la traversée de la piste de danse, ma bouteille à la main; juste avant d'arriver à destination j'ai trébuché dans une caissière et je me suis affalé. Personne ne m'a relevé. Je voyais les jambes des danseurs qui s'agitaient au-dessus de moi; j'avais envie de les trancher à la hache. Les éclairages étaient d'une violence insoutenable; j'étais en enfer.[26]

---

25   *Extension du domaine de la lutte*, p. 112.
26   *Extension du domaine de la lutte*, p. 115.

The scene recalls other situations, such as the party where Michel is similarly in a prone position and feeling unwell, much the worse for drink. There is also the focus on legs which seem to have a movement independent of the bodies to which they are attached, not unlike his experience of his limbs when he was in hospital. Michel's desire to cut them off indicates that his violent urges are pathological. The sentence describing how no-one picked him up when he fell recalls Catherine Lechardoy's complaint about Paris compared to her home province. Hell is a place where no-one helps each other. It is a place of egotists – egotists who clash. The scene is part of a network and is generated by earlier experiences. The way in which it is told relates it to the narrator's past.

The scene is therefore situated within a moral framework, a strong and self-justifying sense of right and wrong. The legs are felt to be a threat and cutting them from their bodies is a defensive action. This is conveyed by the prone position from which they are viewed, the position of the victim and not the aggressor. The next sentence makes Michel's viewpoint unmistakable. The lights are attacking him. He is the one who is suffering – and the torments are the torments of Hell.

However, this is only the narrator's perspective. It arises from his physical position and from his previous history. It could be argued that what is truly Hellish in this scene is the presentation of violent intentions as justified. No doubt Michel's feelings are genuine and, to his mind, justified but, like his disquisition on Tisserand's position, they are only a point of view. The designation of the anonymous woman into whom he bumps is 'caissière'. But how does he know this? A category appears to be a fact but is nothing more than a product of Michel's mind. He supposes her to be a check-out girl – just as he supposes himself to be in Hell and just as he supposes he is right to see a threat from which he should defend himself.

But however much Michel may try to present himself as a victim, he is something more. He becomes the devil himself. The devil uses his powers of language, his skill at weaving a convincing narrative to ensnare Tisserand. The latter's problem, and the reason that he is unsuccessful with women, is that he is ugly and in a world where surfaces count, he will always be a loser. In business situations, he can, like the office manager in the Department of Agriculture, dress the part but he cannot do anything about his face. Among other things, his skin is repulsive: 'Il a exactement le faciès d'un crapaud-buffle – des traits épais, grossiers, larges, déformés, le contraire exact de la beauté. Sa peau luisante, acnéique, semble exsuder une humeur grasse.'[27] The skin is not, in this case, a barrier that separates the individual from the world but is leaking. There seems to be some Platonic ideal, 'la beauté', which Tisserand does not conform to. His features are exaggerated there is something medieval in the reference to the toad and the use of the word 'humeur'. This is a man who does not fit easily into society. He would have been a butt of jokes in medieval times but in our own more sensitive times he is merely cold-shouldered.

A man who has no success in forming intimate relationships, who has no guiding structures in his private life, is left at the mercy of a cunning devil that can provide him with a narrative accounting for his problem and offering a way forward:

> C'est foutu depuis longtemps, depuis l'origine. Tu ne représenteras jamais, Raphaël, un rêve érotique de jeune fille. Il faut en prendre ton parti; de telles choses ne sont pas pour toi. De toute façon, il est déjà trop tard. L'insuccès sexuel, Raphaël, que tu as connu depuis ton adolescence, la frustration qui te poursuit depuis l'âge de treize ans laisseront en toi une trace ineffaçable.[28]

The sinuous, repetitive prose contrasts with the more angular, symmetrical rhythms of Michel's earlier analysis. Whereas there had been some kind of balance before, now there is none. Michel speaks words of concern but they are designed to make the hearer feel worse. The opening remarks seem to promise some sort of explanatory myth of origin, an explanation of the presence of the pain in Tisserand's life. It is that such success is forever denied him because of his very nature. The hurt is untreatable. Tisserand is marked with a 'trace ineffaçable'. He carries with him a mark from the past that continues to determine who is. This is ironic given that in the Old Testament, Raphael is the angel who heals. However, Michel is the devil for whom there can be no redemption and it is in his nature

27 *Extension du domaine de la lutte*, p. 54.
28 *Extension du domaine de la lutte*, p. 117.

to project that thought, to get Tisserand to accept it for himself, thereby ensuring damnation.

Michel suggests that he has a special empathy – this from a man who cannot form friendships. He weaves a story of belatedness and missed opportunity – indeed of opportunities that were perhaps never there to be missed in the first place. He stokes up feelings of thwarted desire by stressing how unattainable they are. It is crucial that we remember that it is not Tisserand who is thinking in this way. It is Michel. Just as he had projected intentions on to the dancer, so he is here creating a situation that he can project on to Tisserand. He is creating his story out of what he has himself experienced. Fiction is woven from what we know of the real world. Thus when Michel speaks of Tisserrand's lack of success, he is also describing himself and his feelings. Tisserand's life is being written from Michel's life or Michel's life is re-written in terms of Tisserand. It is as though Michel is, from the threads of his own experience, weaving a garment for Tisserand to wear, a role for him to assume. The epigraph from Saint Paul with which the novel began is turned in a perverse direction. Tisserand is being offered a garment of darkness to put on. This is a man who does not feel 'bien dans sa peau', who is thin skinned and over-sensitive because of the rebuffs he has suffered. Michel's offer is especially tempting since in his analysis he seems to imply that he alone understands what Tisserand is suffering. Of course he does. He has created this story of pain and suffering.

Like a computer programmer, Michel is trying to download into Tisserand a new set of thoughts. He is acting out his own frustration and rage by proxy. The speech is subtly coercive and because it chimes with Tisserand's mood, it is difficult for him to struggle against it. Michel's speech is an act performed on his listener's mind.

He then proceeds to the next stage:

Il n'y aura pour toi ni rédemption, ni délivrance. Mais cela ne veut pas dire, pour autant, que toute possibilité de revanche te soit interdite. Ces femmes que tu désires tant tu peux, toi aussi, les posséder. Tu peux même posséder ce qu'il y a de plus précieux en elles. Qu'y a-t-il, Raphaël, de plus précieux en elles?[29]

29   *Extension du domaine de la lutte*, p. 117.

In this part of his speech, Michel takes Tisserand to the lowest point. The very use of religious terms, particularly 'délivrance', disempowers Tisserand since it positions him as a passive victim, waiting to be rescued. It also helps that Tisserand feels that he has been treated badly and so in asserting himself he will be achieving justice. The act of violence is not a Gidean 'acte gratuit' but rather 'revanche' the setting right of a wrong. Revenge is powerful motivator and it has the advantage of occupying the moral high ground. Even if we disapprove of the spiral of violence that it might lead to and even if we believe that one should turn the other cheek, there is still an atavistic attachment to revenge as a righting of wrongs and a restoring of balance.

Only one possible way forward is indicated. It is dressed up in the language of power – 'posséder' and 'précieux' are repeated in order to increase their appeal and the use of the Christian name aims to reinforce the feeling Tisserand should have that here is someone who truly understands him. Yet the word 'posséder' is used vaguely. It can mean to possess in the sexual sense but it can also indicate domination, owning the will of the other person, as in demonic possession. Ironically, it is Tisserand who is being possessed. It also means to own as one would own a thing or a person reduced to the status of a thing. Thus the dancer is being reified, reduced from being an autonomous human to being a thing.

Yet the financial aspect of 'posséder' lurks as a shadow, diabolically undermining its own promise. We possess things because we have bought and paid for them. As remarked above, Tisserand had realized that he could use his financial success to compensate for his lack of success in love by purchasing the services of a prostitute. He could thus possess a woman through the power of his relative wealth – but that was what he certainly did not want. The verb 'posséder' and the financial connotations that are also present in 'précieux' point to this shadow. Wealth is a means of exercising the power of the will over another – and Tisserand wants something different. Michel is tempting his victim with something the victim has elsewhere rejected.

The agitation of the legs on the dance-floor or the flopping of limbs in a sick-bed are in sharp contrast to way Michel imagines the forward thrust of the arm as it seeks to cut the life-force out of another body:

Lance-toi dès ce soir dans la carrière du meurtre; crois-moi, mon ami, c'est la seule chance qu'il te reste. Lorsque tu sentiras ces femmes trembler au bout de ton couteau, et supplier pour leur jeunesse, là tu seras vraiment le maître; là tu les posséderas corps et âme. Peut-être même pourras-tu, avant leur sacrifice obtenir d'elles quelques savoureuses gâteries; un couteau, Raphaël, est un allié considérable.[30]

The insistent 'tu' and its attendant forms now speak of empowerment in contrast to the pain that earlier predominated. The switch to the future tense is not just a promise but also gives direction to a movement that the verb 'lance-toi' engages in. Instead of a painful past, Michel engages Tisserand in a future of power and dominance. But this is not the power that comes from constructing and nurturing but from causing fear. Furthermore, this future is an imaginary fantasy, one that flees the present.

What is most disturbing is the way Michel's speech promises pleasure from the suffering of others – a pleasure that has the electric surge of power. It is not just the victims, one feels, who are trembling but also Michel – in anticipation. Worse still is the almost slobbering delectation of 'savoureuses gâteries'. The final flourish is the knife which, in contrast to the reduction of women to objects or things, becomes humanised. Yet the painful truth leaks into the text for all Michel's mastery. He does not have friends. He sees himself as 'un allié'. In the very cry of triumph, the lineaments of isolation and despair can be descried. The tempter never finds companionship.

Michel can only bond with Tisserand by coercing the latter. In the scenario he creates, women will only give Tisserand their companionship by being similarly coerced though that coercion will be physical rather than mental. The physical violence will be at the behest of Michel. Tisserand is acting out his mentor's urges. Thus, the inherent violence of persuasion is brought before us. In its own way, mental coercion is no less a violation of the integrity of the individual than is being ripped open by a knife or raped at knife-point.

30   *Extension du domaine de la lutte*, p. 118.

Tisserand, however, is not just listening to Michel. He is also looking around the club. Sensory impressions come not from a single source:

> Il fixait toujours le couple qui s'enlaçait en tournant lentement sur la piste; une main de la pseudo-Véronique serrait la taille du métis, l'autre était posée sur ses épaules. Doucement, presque timidement, il me dit: 'Je préférerais tuer le type ...'; je sentis alors que j'avais gagné; je me détendis brusquement, et je remplis nos verres. [31]

What is noticeable is the emphasis on the sense of touch in the above description. The couple on the dance-floor experience each other through touch. Tisserand merely sees and the gaze is always distant and indeed unsuccessful in grasping the reality of the other person. The contrast between 'fixait' which means 'to fix' and 'to stare at' and the gentle turning movement of the dancers suggests an inability to reach and possess what one sees. The dancers, however, are holding each other, touching the body in a way that the troubled Tisserand might find particularly painful.

The point of view is supposedly that of Tisserand, the 'il' of the text. However, this is Michel's description of what Tisserand is witnessing. The female dancer is described as 'pseudo-Véronique', a reference to Michel's ex-wife whom she resembles. This is not a reference Tisserand himself could make. It is Michel usurping Tisserand's point of view. The use of 'métis' is another indication. The dysfunctional narrator is not just sexist but also racist. Tisserand, when he speaks directly, refers to the man as 'le type', completely drained of any such connotations.

Michel's intention is that he should kill the girl. Tisserand, however, wants to kill the man who is more successful than he is in love. His words shatter the illusion that the narrator has created. They show that Tisserand is distinct from the narrator and that he has a mind of his own. The triumphant 'j'avais gagné' is only a partial success. Tisserand is indeed moved to kill by Michel's speech – and to that extent he is successful – but Tisserand selects the target. Constrained and coerced though he may be, Tisserand has to a certain extent exerted his own will.

31   *Extension du domaine de la lutte*, p. 118.

Subsequently, as the two set out in pursuit of their prey, Michel remarks: 'À mes côtés, Tisserand tremblait sans arrêt; j'avais l'impression de sentir le sperme pourri qui remontait dans son sexe.' Michel seems to be inside the body and mind of his companion. But again this is Michel projecting on to Tisserand a description of feelings that the latter may or may not have. He implies knowledge of the other's physical being and emotional responses. The trembling can be observed but the rest is speculation. Indeed, it is perhaps Michel who is so excited by the thrill that he is close to orgasm.

However, Tisserand does not kill the couple whom he has followed out on to the sand dunes and observed making love:

> Quand je suis arrivé, ils étaient entre deux dunes. Il avait déjà enlevé sa robe et son soutien-gorge. Ses seins était si beaux, si ronds sous la lune. Puis elle s'est retournée, elle est venue sur lui. Elle a déboutonné son pantalon. Quand elle a commencé à le sucer, je n'ai pas pu le supporter.[32]

These are Tisserand's words and the description of the girl is rhapsodic, almost poetic. It contrasts with the febrile descriptions of the same girl a few pages earlier – but that description was in the words of Michel who brought to his imaging of the girl his memories of his ex-wife. Tisserand does not have these memories to colour his perceptions and hence the more restrained description. Indeed the emotional investment of Tisserand in this particular girl is considerably less than Michel's. Michel's long disquisition in the night-club on how Tisserand must be feeling is a mixture of speculation and his own emotional baggage. Tisserand merely sees an object he desires and who is attractive to him. Where Michel's focus is on the hips, Tisserand focuses on the breasts. The moonlight gives a tender, romantic glow and the images of bare breasts are soft-porn – in contrast with the cruder images of the dancer's undergarments that fascinate Michel. The next sentence does change the mood somewhat. This is a girl who takes the initiative, who begins the sexual stimulation of her partner's penis which

---

32 *Extension du domaine de la lutte*, p. 120.

Tisserand's narrative discreetly refuses to mention. The scene is erotic but not obscene.

However, the observer of the scene is more than a voyeur. He has a knife. There is a tension between the pornographic and the violent, between, as the text puts it, 'sang' and 'sperme'.[33] As does Michel earlier, Tisserand finds relief in masturbation:

> Je me suis retourné, j'ai marché entre les dunes. J'aurais pu les tuer; ils n'enten-daient rien, ils ne faisaient aucune attention à moi. Je me suis masturbé Je n'avais pas envie de les tuer; le sang ne change rien.[34]

The verb 'se retourner' is used but in a different way from the way in which it was used in reference to the girl. Now it means a turning aside not an approach. The phrase, 'Je n'avais pas envie de les tuer' is, significantly, in the imperfect, indicating that in Tisserand's account the lack of desire was not subsequent (or consequent) to the act of masturbation. Tisserand may have had the power ('J'aurais pu les tuer') and he may have relished it but his desire was always fundamentally erotic and not murderous.

Tisserand is not prepared to follow his co-worker or go along with him – hence the importance of Tisserand's departure to Paris without offering to give Michel the usual lift. This is not, however, an optimistic conclusion. Tisserand is killed in an accident when in dense fog he hits a jack-knifed lorry. He may have been able to break free from Michel but he does not have the strength to create his own path, to devise the structures that will shape and give direction to his life. Tisserand breaks away from the path offered but ends up in the fog, his body smashed by a lorry that has been disarticulated. Thus without structures, we are unable to function. There is no natural structure to the events that befall us, to the experiences we have – unless it is given to them.

Events precede their meaning. This we have already seen in the above. Michel's reading of the dancers is a powerful one, one that is fed by his

---

33   *Extension du domaine de la lutte*, p. 121.
34   *Extension du domaine de la lutte*, p. 120.

murderous rage and which in turn feeds it. He succeeds with Tisserand to the extent that he offers him a powerful reading of his experiences of the evening and relates them to his life. His reading shapes events into a narrative and he depends on Tisserand being a willing reader. Writing is but the transmission of a reading:

> Les pages qui vont suivre constituent un roman; j'entends, une succession d'anec-dotes dont je suis le héros. Ce choix autobiographique n'en est pas réellement un: de toute façon, je n'ai pas d'autre issue. Si je n'écris pas ce que j'ai vu je souffrirai autant – et peut-être un peu plus. Un peu seulement, j'y insiste. L'écriture ne soulage guère. Elle retrace, elle délimite. Elle introduit un soupçon de cohérence, l'idée d'un réalisme. On patauge toujours dans un brouillard sanglant, mais il y a quelques repères. Le chaos n'est plus qu'à quelques mètres. Faible succès, en vérité.[35]

The final part of the paragraph with its metaphors of fog and landmarks is a pre-echo of Tisserand's end. It suggests, moreover, that writing is the decipherment of events. It has no creative power. The anecdotes are auto-biographical. They are interpretations not inventions. Writing is reduced to management of the material. It is not the creator of reality but has to work with what is there already.

There is some small psychic relief – even if the 'ne … guère' limits it. The reduction in pain that comes from writing might be compared to the relief experienced by Tisserand after masturbating. Both activities are onanistic in that they are both without issue – 'je n'ai pas d'autre issue'. In other words, writing is perceived has having little impact on the world. It is a dispersal of energy, with no creative potential. It can only retrace what has already been done and it can provide boundaries. In a sense this is what happened on the beach. By masturbating, Tisserand avoided going any further beyond the limits of behaviour. He ceased to transgress and retreated back within the norms of society. He refused to cross the taboo against murder. Tisserand had no other way out, 'pas d'autre issue'. There was no exit – hence his death when he way is blocked by a truck.

---

35   *Extension du domaine de la lutte*, p. 14.

All writing does is allow one to navigate in the fog that is existence. It picks out a few markers but that is all – 'un soupcon de cohérence'. If writing did indeed have the power to change material reality, then the consequence would be truly momentous – something articulated in the next novel, *Les Particules élémentaires*, where one of the two sibling protagonists manages to re-write human DNA and in so doing changes humanity – indeed changes it so much that it is no longer humanity. For the moment, reading has more power:

> Quel contraste avec le pouvoir absolu, miraculeux, de la lecture! Une vie entière à lire aurait comblé mes vœux; je le savais déjà à sept ans. La texture du monde est douloureuse, inadéquate; elle ne me paraît pas modifiable. Vraiment, je crois qu'une vie entière à lire m'aurait mieux convenu.
> Une telle vie ne m'a pas été donnée.[36]

The texture of life, its substance, cannot be changed or altered. We cannot repair its inadequacies. We do not have the power to write our life differently because we do not have the power to control what happens. It is our tragedy as human beings that we cannot just observe our lives.

Reading gives a feeling of absolute control. A life that is read is complete and lies before the reader ready for interpretation. It is like observing the two women at the party, an account of their colleague that rich in interpretative possibility. A banal piece of gossiping at a routine party can be read as reminiscent of important points in cultural history. It can be read as some form of transcendental experience far beyond its seeming triviality. However, the very fact that multiple readings are possible reintroduces the notion of struggle. Often things can be read in a number of ways. Some of these will contradict each other. We may respond by closing down meanings that are incompatible with our interests. Michel reads a dancer's body language and her dress as an invitation to have sex. Because this makes sense to him in that it is coherent with his desires, he will see no alternative reading. The reading that makes sense is the one that we hold on to.

---

36   *Extension du domaine de la lutte*, pp. 14–15.

Many of Houellebecq's characters are readers, in some form or another. Bruno in *Les Particules élémentaires* teaches school children how to read literature (though with limited success) and Michel in *Plateforme* travels with his guide-books from which he quotes or reads. Indeed, even the more writerly Michel in *Les Particules élémentaires* is also a reader – and the importance of his encounter with the *Book of Kells* cannot be underestimated. Houellebecq's readers are not, however, readers who passively absorb what they read but are also interpreters. Things are not just accepted but are used to make meaning, to increase understanding. Indeed, readers decipher the world like the detective and the literary detective (Poirot) in *Plateforme*. Understanding the world is important and, as in the detective story, unravelling the events or providing a reading of the crime scene, breaks the chain of violent events unleashed by the murder. The revelation of the murderer provides the reading of events that shuts off alternative readings.

The novel where Michel's wish is most clearly realized is *La Possibilité d'une île*. The clones do not struggle with life but instead pass their existence reading the life of the original from which they are descended – and adding to a commentary compiled by successive descendants. They do so largely in isolation from each other – so that alternative readings are never brought into proximity and so can never clash. However, the realisation of Michel's desire for 'une vie entière à lire' proves to have its own disadvantages. In foregoing the need to struggle, the need to get involved with other people and events, the clones lose the 'texture du monde'. Life becomes flat and dull.

Struggle is what makes life what it is, for better or worse. When Michel attempts to go to Saint-Cirgues-en-Montagne for the first time, he is stopped by transport strikes:

> La gare de Lyon était pratiquement en état de siège; des patrouilles de CRS découpaient des zones dans le hall d'entrée et circulaient le long des voies; on disait que des commandos de grévistes 'durs' avaient décidé d'empêcher les départs. Cependant le train s'est avéré presque vide, et le voyage tout à fait paisible.[37]

---

37 *Extension du domaine de la lutte*, pp. 129–130.

The style is casual, anecdotal – in keeping with what Michel told us about the nature of the work he is writing. It is an autobiography where anecdotes in succession trace out a life. Yet reading reveals a rich web of complexity. A strike can be portrayed in many different ways but here the choice of words fits into the overall theme to the book – an 'extension du domaine de la lutte'. This is a struggle for control. The hard-line strikers are presented as warriors. There primary aim is to fight, not necessarily to make things better. Thus here the CRS and the strikers are fighting to control the rail network, the communication nexus of the country.

Sometimes it is necessary to be like the detective and read beyond the obvious. Behind the scene at the station lies the phrase that appears on announcements posted at the entrance to stations and metro stops during a strike: 'Circulation perturbée'. Indeed the verb 'circulaient' is used to indicate the movement of the CRS – as though to suggest that maximum disruption calls forth the maximum effort to patrol and control. However, beyond its reference to travel and movement, 'circulation' refers to blood. Such a reading would see the scene at the station as reminiscent of an ailing body. The outlying parts of the country are still connected to the hub but only fitfully so. The CRS patrolling the 'voies' which are 'voies de circulation' – like the arteries in the body – are trying to police the body both to protect it from harm and to ensure that it stays under proper authority. It must be helped 'vivre selon la règle'. The whole scene recalls Michel's limbs spread out in bed, only vaguely connected to his will: 'Voir ses jambes comme des objets séparés, loin de son esprit, auquel elles seraient reliées plus ou moins par hasard, et plutôt mal'.

The strikers want to sever the connections that allow the country to function as a coherent entity. Thus the strike can be seen in two ways. There are two conflicting readings. On the one hand, the strikers are struggling with the forces of regimentation in society, those forces who lay down where one can go and when (a corollary of the train timetable and the network). They disrupt the rigid transport system and prevent it from taking people along the approved routes. On the other hand, their method is to stop all movement, to prevent connections being made. It is significant that what causes Michel to abort his journey is the fact that he cannot get a connection to his destination.

The CRS are a countervailing force to that of the strikers, described in quasi-military terms as though to bring out the equivalence of the two forces. Their role is no less ambiguous in that they can be seen as both controllers and enablers. So, there is no definitive victor in this struggle at the Gare de Lyon. Yet it is in the nature of struggle that is seeks to put and end to itself. Struggle strives for a victory that would render it unnecessary. It is, therefore, in its definition a suicidal word but a suicide that is always promised never accomplished. Struggle sets out for a destination but always sees arrival postponed. It is in the nature of the thing. Struggle can never cease and yet it aims to cease. It is 'la péricardite' and not 'un infarctus'. As long as there is struggle, there is life and connections or the desire for connections, for 'amis' and meanings.

The struggle brings pain and suffering and we long for peace, an exit ('issue') that is 'paisible'. This is the nature of the quest that drives Houellebecq's characters. They are driven by a need to know, by the feeling that there is an answer to the meaning of life, one that will answer all questions and make further struggle unnecessary. They are encouraged by the fact that there are already so many meanings available, so many explanations that this must point to some explanation that is at the root of all of them. Michel is no different. He believes that the location of what he seeks has come to him:

> Vers dix-sept heures une conclusion m'est apparue: je devais me rendre à Saint-Cirgues-en-Montagne. Le nom s'étalait dans un isolement splendide, au milieu des forêts et des petits triangles figurant les sommets; il n'y avait pas la moindre agglomération à trente kilomètres à la ronde. Je sentais que j'étais sur le point de faire une découverte essentielle; qu'une révélation d'un ordre ultime m'attendait là-bas, entre le 31 décembre et le 1er janvier, à ce moment précis où l'année bascule.[38]

This is how he has come to be at the Gare de Lyon. Note that Michel comes to his realisation not through working things out but through reading – just as the later Michel of *Les Particules élémentaires* will have a revelation when

---

38　*Extension du domaine de la lutte*, p. 129.

he looks at the *Book of Kells*. Here, Michel is looking at a Michelin map of the area. Why he has chosen this particular map is a mystery. Michel's role is merely to decipher symbols. Writing is denied any power to figure out the truth or create a sense. Instead it is reduced to representing where things are in relation to each other. It shows the geographical interconnections that allow the reader to navigate through the territory. It gives 'une idée de réalisme'. This time the passage uses expressions of mystical experience and details such as the isolation of the spot – an isolation that is relative – harmonise with this.

There seems to be something special too about the turn of the year, the point where the new year springs from the old. It echoes the time of transition from day to night that lies behind Saint Paul's call to arms. This is a journey which is also a transition. It is a move to a state where no more questioning will be needed. It is the ultimate revelation. The scene at the party where the voices of the two women seem to come from on high is a humorous prophesy of this moment but also it is also a prophesy of the moment's illusory or, rather, delusory nature. Thus to believe that one has or is about to have a revelation is a delusion, a form of madness.

This madness is evident even as Michel thinks he is approaching lucidity:

> J'ai laissé un papier sur mon bureau: 'Parti plus tôt en raison des grèves SNCF.' Après réflexion j'ai laissé un second papier indiquant, en caractères d'imprimerie: 'JE SUIS MALADE.'[39]

Michel tells two stories about why he is absent from his desk. The reader has no way of knowing how they are related. Indeed, they seem to be quite unconnected. A simple explanation is that Michel is losing his grip on reality. He is becoming schizophrenic, a man in two minds and consequently capable of giving two accounts of himself. He represents his activities in two different ways, neither of which is truly him.

As was argued earlier, Michel is not his identity card. This split between Michel and the representation of himself for official purposes is at the

---

39   *Extension du domaine de la lutte*, p. 129.

heart of this illness. The representation does not need to be true. All that is needed is to satisfy the needs of the person reading it. Thus, the need to provide an account of oneself to the supervisors who patrol the office leads to detachment of the self from the truth and, in this case, a schizophrenic multiplication of accounts, each as true or false as the other.

Michel's illness is consistent with the kind of society in which he finds himself. It is a society where people must account for themselves. People are constantly observed, sized up and regulated. Even the strikers seek to do this since they do not appear to have specific aims but are rather seen as people trying to control movement. Those who seek to set out on their own path are in some way delinquent and need to be controlled. The predatory attitude of Michel towards women is not something that can be tolerated just because one disapproves of the prudery that it reacts against. There is an endless struggle between the need for restraint and the desire to be free from constraint.

For all his dissatisfaction with it, Michel is a true product of, and participant in, a society that is based on power relationships – or more accurately power struggles. The male exercises power by force, the power of Mars, while women exercise power through seduction and sexual attraction:

> Il y a un système basé sur la domination, l'argent et la peur – un système masculin, appelons-le Mars; il y a un système féminin basé sur la séduction et le sexe, appelons-le Vénus. Et c'est tout. Est-il vraiment possible de vivre et de croire qu'il n'y a rien d'autre? Avec les réalistes du XIXe siècle, Maupassant a cru qu'il n'y avait rien d'autre; et ceci l'a conduit jusqu'à la folie furieuse?[40]

Men use domination to get their way and their weapons are money and power. Women use seduction. It is the failure of both Michel and Tisserand to keep ahead in this struggle that leads to what Michel calls 'l'état mental contemporain', that is to say: 'l'amertume'.[41] This analysis is the belief system that Michel uses to interpret his life. It is the grammar book he uses when he reads his life. His view of events is formulated according to this prin-

40 *Extension du domaine de la lutte*, p. 147.
41 *Extension du domaine de la lutte*, p. 148.

ciple. His psychotherapist points out that Maupassant's madness was due
to syphilis. There are two explanations, either of which could be the right
one – just as either of Michel's notes could be true.

The therapist's role is to fix Michel. It is to anchor him firmly in a
role where he can function and avoid the mental breakdown that afflicted
Maupassant. It is to re-insert him in the network of rules and regulations.
However, just as with Tisserand, things do not follow the way mapped
out. Michel has his own agenda, a belief system that disrupts the plan
laid out for him. The therapist's opinion that Michel's problems would
be alleviated if he had sex is comically taken by him as an example of the
feminine need to control by use of sexual attraction. This leads to a quick
change of therapist and is the end of her attempts to get him to conform
to her treatment.

However, Michel does not completely get away from her scrutiny.
She continues to read him. She is undertaking a research thesis and he is
one of the case-studies:

> Sans doute est-ce qu'aujourd'hui je poursuis une vague existence dans une thèse
> de troisième cycle, au milieu d'autres cas concrets. Cette impression d'être devenu
> l'élément d'un dossier m'apaise. J'imagine le volume, sa reliure collée, sa couverture
> un peu triste; doucement, je m'aplatis entre les pages; je m'écrase.[42]

This tonally ambiguous passage with its mixture of sadness, peacefulness
and hints of violence provides another example of the sort of split we saw
when Michel left two messages on his desk. There is, however, an important
difference. In the former instance there were two stories about one person.
In this case, there are also two stories, the one that Michel is offering us
and the one that he is continuing to live in the thesis. The 'je' has become
split so that there are now two existences whereas before there was only
one. Michel has reproduced in the manner of a single-cell organism by
splitting in two. The two Michels go their separate ways.

The Michel in the thesis becomes 'une vie entière à lire' – a pre-echo
of *La Possibilité d'une île* – but the tragedy is that this is not given to him

42   *Extension du domaine de la lutte*, p. 150.

but to the therapist. The psychologist is the one who can survey his life, who has ownership of it. This is in contrast to the opening scene of the novel where it was Michel who was the observer. Now his second life is confined within the book, retraced and delimited by the psychologist's writing. Michel's inability to read that writing is an indication of how powerless he now is.

This other life continues independently. There is an undertow of violence, shown by the images of flattening and crushing. This is a second self that has had the freedom crushed out of it. It is fixed like a flower between the pages of a book. It continues, but does not change. All its powers of development have ceased – again, something that foreshadows *La Possibilité d'une île*. The use of the reflexive instead of the passive indicates that the narrator is complicit. He has done this to himself. Tisserand's body may have been smashed in an accident but Michel has crushed himself. In the midst of all this however, there is the verb 'apaise'. It acts as a point of contrast suggesting that despite all the reservations that he has, the knowledge that there is a life of him to be read gives peace. It may not be a life to which he has access but he can imagine it vaguely and that is enough to give him some measure of peace. This is a key moment in the novel and adds an additional twist to Michel's claim that his novel is autobiographic – it is just like the thesis, in which another version of himself continues to have 'une vague existence', preserved like a flower pressed between the pages of a book.

At the end of the novel he leaves the asylum and goes to Saint-Cirgues a second time:

> Je m'avance encore un peu plus loin dans la forêt. Au-delà de cette colline annonce la carte, il y a les sources de l'Ardèche. Cela ne m'intéresse pas; je continue quand même. Et je ne sais même plus où sont les sources; tout, à présent, se ressemble. Le paysage est de plus en plus doux, amical, joyeux; j'en ai mal à la peau. Je suis au centre du gouffre. Je ressens ma peau comme un écrasement. L'impression de séparation est totale; je suis désormais prisonnier en moi-même. Elle n'aura pas lieu, la fusion sublime; le but de la vie est manqué. Il est deux heures de l'après-midi.[43]

43　*Extension du domaine de la lutte*, p. 156.

The verb 's'avancer' is delusional. Michel is advancing towards no goal. The promise of 'sources', an origin that will explain and account for all things, the promise implicit in the hoped-for 'révélation', is no more than the source of a river. Michel loses his sense of orientation. Everything is flattened into a kind of sameness and the pleasant feelings that the landscape seems to promise are denied him. The adjective 'amical' is particularly painful since it recalls Michel's need for friendship and connection with others. Even when he breaks away from the confines of the asylum and goes beyond the beaten track of 'la règle', he still cannot connect but becomes even more isolated. He is breaking out of the restraining and sustaining web that is life.

The word 'peau', used twice in this concluding paragraph, brings echoes of its earlier use. Unlike the co-worker who may have dressed so as to feel 'bien dans sa peau', Michel now experiences 'mal à la peau'. This malaise is the emptiness that he feels within him, an emptiness that he is unable to satisfy. The second use of 'peau' harks back to the image of the skin as the boundary that separates inner and outer, the narrator from the world. In this instance, the separation is very negative. Michel is imprisoned within his skin, aware of what is outside but unable to access it. Moreover, the world is pressing in on him but it is not to absorb him into a greater whole but rather to crush him – intensifying the feelings he had when he thought of the thesis that allowed his other self to carry on. Michel is thus a 'prisonnier en moi-même'. He may have got away from the asylum but he is incarcerated within his own body and he cannot escape.

This is the bleakness of the conclusion. It is enigmatic and yet at the same time exemplary. It is an ending that misses being an ending. The final sentence could easily be taken as a starting point for a story instead of being, as here, a conclusion. This is its enigma. It is not an ending which explains – nor does it start anything. It could be that Michel is struck down by a heart attack – like the man whose death he witnessed in a supermarket. This would fit in with his earlier heart condition. He no longer has the pericarditis with which one can live but now has a fatal heart-attack. The heart no longer beats but is in stasis. The narrator's life collapses into a point in time, two o'clock in the afternoon. The struggle gives way to stasis. But there is at least a peace of sorts. The 'lutte' has lost its 'extension'. It no longer moves. Everything stops.

CHAPTER 2

Les Particules élémentaires: A Tale of Two Humanities

This novel has been translated into English and given the title *Atomised*. According to Richard Holloway:

> The title of Houellebecq's book says it all: we are atomised. Like colliding billiard balls, there is little to hold us together, no common identity that can integrate us into community and its responsibilities.[1]

Holloway's comments are plausible and it would not be hard to find evidence in the text for his claims. Indeed, the novel even describes an incident where two cars hurtle towards each other on an open road as though they were billiard balls about to collide. Atoms stress the singularity and distinctiveness of elements. Iron is an essence that is quite different from gold. The names of the elements indicate marked differences. Atomisation is a belief that the universe can be broken down into its discrete components.

However, if what Holloway says is true, it represents a radical departure from the kind of world depicted in *Extension du domaine de la lutte*. There life was a web and it was the separation of the individual from that web, which led to crippling, if not deadly, isolation. The problem with Holloway's analysis is that it ignores Houellebecq's more complicated vision of the human condition. In part it does this because of the title in English: *Atomised*. However, the title in French is *Les Particules élémentaires*. This emphasizes the fact that matter is derived from small, sub-atomic particles. If, as Holloway believes, the title says it all, then using the original title gives a quite different perspective.

---

1   Richard Holloway, *Looking in the Distance* (Edinburgh, Canongate Books, 2004), p. 96.

One of the central themes of the book is the tension between those forces which tend towards building coherence out of particles and forging links betweens individuals – 'particules' and 'particuliers' in French – and those forces that lead towards the disaggregation of matter into its constituent parts and which break down the bonds that unite individuals. Yet Houellebecq also explores the extent to which these are not necessarily opposing forces but rather competing or even cooperating forces. The complexities of the 'domaine de la lutte' of the first novel are developed and further extended in this one.

Houellebecq is interested in what results when we combine elementary particles, in what holds them together and in what drives them apart. The functioning of elementary particles is a metaphor that he develops beyond its application to scientific facts. Thus the way a family is formed and split up only for the constituent parts to form new and different groupings turns out to be a reflection of the fundamental laws of matter. Reality is not the smooth surface that we can see and touch but is the result of a combining of smaller constituent parts that have come together to form a unity but which can also split apart over time in a variety of ways. A family is a unity made up of individual members who may drift away in time, who may turn against the other members – much as David di Meola does.

No structure is permanent – but by the same token, that also facilitates the construction of new ones by the forging to new links and fitting elements that belonged to one structure into a new framework. Fiction, particularly the works of Houellebecq, also exemplifies such processes. The elements that are incorporated into his works are multiple, resulting in structures that are complex amalgams. This means that attempts to classify his fiction come up with many competing answers, no single one of which will suffice. Houellebecq's works tease the reader by playing with the conventional arrangements of genre. His novels combine bits in different ways to produce something that is *sui generis*. Jacob Carlston sees Houellebecq continuing the traditions of Menippean satire.[2] Bruno Viard sees

---

2   Jacob Carlston, 'Écriture houellebecquienne, écriture ménipéenne?', in *Michel Houellebecq sous la loupe*, in Clément and van Wesemael, pp. 19–30.

him as belonging to the tradition of Balzac with his panoramic depiction of society.[3] Sandrine Rabosseau argues that Houellebecq provides an updated version of Zola's 'roman experimental'.[4] All of these are true. It would be a mistake to make one of them the single determining producer of the work before us. Houellebecq's novels are not clones – faithful reproductions of their predecessors. Simon St-Onge speaks of the 'caractère hybride' at the heart of Houellebecq's style, 'un lieu de cohabitation d'antagonismes'.[5] St-Onge's oxymoronic phrase is important because it underlines the fact that this is a 'textualité paradoxalement segmentée et à la fois unifiée par divers espaces de discours'.[6]

Les Particules élémentaires is no exception in that it knits together a variety of writing styles and traditions, exemplifying what Carlston the 'caractère autofictionnel' of Houellebecq's novels.[7] These writing styles are not limited to those which refer to other types of fiction. Houellebecq incorporates elements appropriate to scientific writing. Other passages have a documentary feel – a description of a walk down the Boulevard Saint-Michel in the mid-seventies provides accurate information about the shops and business that were there at the time. These resemblances are knowing: Houellebecq's novels are always 'conscients d'eux-mêmes'.[8] Carlston finds this curious in an author 'qui avait jugé dans *Rester vivant* qu'une représentation naïve du monde était déjà un chef d'œuvre'.

But this paradox is the key to understanding the way Houellebecq's style functions. Floriane Place-Verghnes puts it differently: 'on peut très bien comprendre la prose houellebecquienne sans avoir lu un traître mot

3   Bruno Viard, 'Faut-il en rire ou faut-il en pleurer? Michel Houellebecq du côté de Marcel Mauss et du côté de Balzac', in Clément and Wesemael, pp. 31–42.

4   Sandrine Rabosseau, 'Houellebecq ou le renouveau du roman experimental', in Clément and Wesemael, pp. 43–51.

5   Simon St-Onge, 'De l'esthétique houellebecquienne', in Clément et Wesemael, pp. 67–80, p. 70.

6   St-Onge, p. 70.

7   Carlston, p. 24.

8   Carlston, p. 24.

des auteurs précités'.⁹ That is, it can be read naïvely. The novels make sense. However, that simplicity is built on the author's profound grasp of the complicated structures that lie beneath the surface presented to the reader. In other words, the 'représentation naïve' is a construct, something that has been arrived at by a careful combination to create the impression of naturalness.

The same is true of the world that fiction represents. The fundamental particles of the title provide a repertoire of constituent parts that can be combined to form the matter in the universe. Yet the matter which they constitute appears stable despite being at its fundamental level packets of energy. The stability of matter depends on the cohesion of those minuscule particles that make up the universe. Particles are not specific in the way atoms are. There are no such things as oxygen quarks or neutrinos in the way that there are atoms of oxygen. Particles do not exist independently but connect to make a whole. An atom is a community of fundamental particles. All matter is a web.

This also applies to our sense of identity. *Les Particules élémentaires* explores the fundamental particularities of being French. Frenchness is not atomic, in the sense that oxygen is. It may rather be said to be particular – an assemblage of particles. Humanity has what St-Onge might call a 'caractère hybride'. One can be French in different ways – someone from Strasbourg will not be the same as someone from Angers, and an eighteenth-century French woman will not be the same as one born in the twentieth century. Thus, as the name Michel Djerzinski suggests, to be French is to be an assemblage, an interconnection – but an interconnection that is always dynamic, never static. The human being is always a descendant, always coming from somewhere. Being nomadic rather than settled is a particularly strong mark of contemporary life. The ancestry of Bruno is as complex as his brother's – added to which is the fact that he was not born in France itself but in the overseas territory of Algeria. In a sense, to be French is not an apparently simple quality, one which apparently conveys unity, but contains already what is other, what might be characterised as

9   Floriane Place-Verghnes, 'Houellebecq/Schopenhauer: Souffrance et désir gigognes', in Wesemael and Clément, pp. 123–132, p. 126.

non-French. Michel Djerzinski is a Frenchman who also has in his genetic make-up the non-French genes inherited from his father.

Furthermore, Frenchness goes beyond genetics. Bruno's comments regarding the relevant places of Snoop Doggy Dogg, Bill Gates and the Duchesse de Guermantes in the French cultural value system are in indication that the vision of French culture presented in the novel is far from being purist. The range of references would be familiar to many if not all:

> La Duchesse de Guermantes avait beaucoup moins de *thune* que Snoop Doggy Dog [*sic*]; Snoop Doggy Dog avait moins de *thune* que Bill Gates, mais il faisait advantage mouiller les filles.[10]

Linking the references in this way shows the complexity of the contemporary French cultural field. There is humour in comparing the elegance of Proust's duchess with the rap singer and in grounding the comparison between Snoop Doggy Dogg (now known as Snoop Dogg and originally called Cordozar Calvin Broadus, Jr) and Bill Gates in sexual attractiveness. The point is that there is nowadays no fixed hierarchy with its intricate rules of precedence and order but rather a series of inter-related positions of value. Indeed it is impossible to say which of the two, Bill Gates or Snoop Dogg is the leader. They are like particles whose position can be mapped but their relative position will depend on that of the observer. All that does appear certain is that the Duchesse de Guermantes is less important than the other two on both counts. It may be objected that she is a fictional character, living only in Proust's novel but the majority of people know Snoop Dogg or Bill Gates not directly but through the medium of writing. So, they inhabit our thoughts on just the same terms as she does. The Bill Gates that we think we know is an amalgam of writings about him.

The Duchesse de Guermantes is quite unlike the other two in that her worth and pre-eminence lie in a paring away of all that is ignoble, of what is likely to degrade and bring low. In short, she is seen as a higher sort of human being:

10   Michel Houellebecq, *Les Particules élémentaires* (Paris, J'ai Lu, 2003), pp. 192–193. All subsequent references are to this edition.

La pureté d'un sang où depuis plusieurs générations ne se rencontrait que ce qu'il
y a de plus grand dans l'histoire de la France avait ôté à sa manière d'être tout ce
que les gens du peuple appellent 'des manières', et lui avait donné la plus parfaite
simplicité.[11]

The phrase '*la plus parfaite simplicité*' contrasts with St-Onge's description
of Houellebecq's work, with its 'caractère hybride'. It also looks forward to
the simplification of the human body that is part of the cloning technology in *La Possibilité d'une île*. The Duchesse's simplicity is, however, something of an illusion, a naivety that conceals complexity. The Duchesse de
Guermantes is the representative of the ideal of her class but her unsullied
and unforced simplicity turns out to be the result of careful breeding. The
adjective 'parfaite', from 'faire' is a hint that this perfection is a work of art
that conceals its artfulness.

The above quotation is used by Bruno in a class he is teaching and the
seeming lack of comprehension on the part of one of his pupils leads Bruno
to the reflection on competing cultural values cited above. The reaction of
the student, Ben, as viewed by Bruno, could not be more different:

Je regardais Ben: il se grattait la tête, il se grattait les couilles, il mastiquait son
chewing-gum. Qu'est-ce qu'il pouvait bien y comprendre ce grand singe?[12]

There is a disagreeable element of racism in the characterisation of Ben by
Bruno. Earlier the former had been described as a 'babouin'. The implication is that this student of African origin does not quite qualify as human.
He is lower down the evolutionary chain – he has travelled lest far from
or ape-like ancestors. The rendering of 'Dogg' as 'Dog' also fits into this
pattern – though the slip may be accidental. Bruno's racism stems just as
much from sexual rivalry, the impulse to pass on the genes, as from race
phobia. Ben and his teacher are, in the eyes of Bruno at least, in competition
for the affections of the female students in the class, and one in particular.
Ben appears to be winning – he has something of Snoop Dogg's sex appeal

11   *Les Particules élémentaires*, p. 192.
12   *Les Particules élémentaires*, p. 192.

and Bruno's suppositions about the size of the young man's penis are an unequivocal expression of envy.

There is another way of looking at this episode. It is Bruno who is reading Ben's physical gestures as indications of incomprehension and conventionally scratching the head is a sign of lack of understanding. However, he also scratches his testicles, drawing attention to his penis. This could be interpreted as preening. Ben, whom Bruno is characterising as an ape, is grooming himself in the presence of an attractive female – even if that presence is only in the imagination. If Bruno sees in the Duchesse de Guermantes the expression of what is uplifting and noble in French womanhood, Ben sees her as someone he would like to have sex with.

Interpreting the scene this way re-positions the Duchesse de Guermantes in the tripartite comparison. Suddenly, the Duchesse acquires something of the sex-appeal of Snoop Doggy Dogg, able to arouse carnal desires in the opposite sex. Her 'simplicité' is taken less as a sign that she is out of reach than as something that makes her desirable. In this context, she is less disadvantaged in comparison to Snoop Doggy Dogg and Bill Gates. She is presented as a creature whose power can be felt by both Bruno and Ben.

This power is analogous to the attractiveness of the youthful body: 'Le désir sexuel se porte essentiellement sur les corps jeunes [...]'.[13] It is not just that young people are more appealing but rather that the freshness of their bodies is new territory to be conquered, new lands to be despoiled. Their power to attract becomes their vulnerability. The sexual act allows the male to leave a trace in or on the body of the woman. It is an act of pollution that is also an expression of possessive territoriality. Not surprisingly, jealousy is a powerful force in Houellebecq, animating such disparate characters as Tisserand, whose jealousy is all the more acute for not actually possessing the beloved object, and Daniel1, in *La Possibilité d'une île*, who ends his days as a stalker of the woman who has escaped his clutches. Sex and power are linked motifs and, in *Plateforme*, reach their most disturbing expression in the paedophiliac attachment of the rich, successful businessman, Jean-Yves, for his children's babysitter.

---

13   *Les Particules élémentaires*, p. 106.

As can be seen from the above, to be French is more that just a question of genes for the mixture of real and fictional, high and low, American and French, entrepreneur and aristocrat, titled and untitled, pseudonym and real name speaks of a France that is a site traversed by different cultural forces rather that a clearly defined, pure cultural entity. France has a global dimension. It is not a self-contained entity with characteristics peculiar to itself. 'La particularité française' is something else entirely now, not a declaration of independence or uniqueness, but an indication that it is a composite of various component parts or particles, a field subject to powerful forces. Like particles, France is part of an interconnected system. It is not an individual atom, autonomous and distinctive. The 'simplicité' of the Duchesse de Guermantes is an outmoded vision that has been swept away. Nevertheless, she has a place in the new vision even if she is no longer pre-eminent. She is not excluded.

We live inclusively in a world of subtle and sophisticated interconnections. This is not just a question of being open to influences from outside but rather of being a member of a global network of shared values. France is a participant culture – not a submerged one. It receives but it also exports influence. It is not alone in being subject to forces outside itself but can itself be a force influencing others. When Michel takes Xanax, it is a brand that is recognised inside and outside France, a product on sale in different countries. When he mentions Aspect, on the other hand, he is referring to a French scientist with an international reputation, someone who has helped shape thinking outside France as well as inside. Houellebecq's world is a world of mutuality. Indeed, the heterogeneous parts of this world are held together in a tension that is competitive and yet in dialogue.

If it is impossible to identify and isolate a stable essence of the self, it becomes equally difficult then to have a clear and simple sense of the Other. There are so many phenomena that impinge on our lives. They are part of the way we live and so cannot truly be called strangers. Familiarity, however, does not necessarily mean ease. Bruno's racism testifies to that. Alienation in Houellebecq is still an important if much more complex phenomenon – more subtle, ambiguous and insidious. It is true, as Rabosseau reminds us, that Hoeuellebecq's characters belong to 'la classe moyenne tout aussi aliénée' as the workers depicted by Zola.[14] She attributes this to the conditions under which they are forced to labour. This is true. As we saw in *Extension du domaine de la lutte*, the workers in the Ministry of Agriculture are divorced from any contact with the land and Catherine Lechardoy feels particularly ill-at-ease way from her native Béarn. Alienation is part of our experience. It is inseparable from our lives. We cannot but participate in it.

However, alienation is not the essence of the human condition but only one constituent factor. Both Michel and Bruno may be at odds with the society in which they live. They are, in their own ways, outsiders just like Meursault in Camus' *L'Étranger*. Indeed Bruno, like Meursault, is born in Algeria. Yet both brothers are participants in society. They share the same reference points. They are members of groups – Bruno in his sex clubs and Michel with his research team. The question is: what does it mean to be alienated? No longer is it enough to be a loner, outside conventions. Both brothers are insiders and outsiders, aliens in their own land.

The theme of alienation was an important theme in *Extension du domaine de la lutte* where the related theme of aliens from outer space also appeared. What connects the two themes is the feeling of not belonging to Earth. Our own world seems strange to us, its inhabitants, just as it would to beings from outer space. *Les Particules élémentaires* makes further use of elements normally found in science fiction. However, it is not a pure science fiction novel but something much more complex. Indeed it incorporates elements that are alien to science fiction, navigating genres and situations that we might prefer to avoid. Many readers might be alienated by the following, which owes more to hard core pornography than to more respectable writing styles:

> Au matin, il [Bruno] essaya de pénétrer Christiane, mais cette fois il échoua, il se sentait ému et nerveux. 'Jouis sur moi' dit-elle. Elle étala le sperme sur son visage et sur ses seins.[15]

---

14 Rabosseau, p. 45.
15 *Les Particules élémentaires*, p. 149.

Indeed, there are many similar passages which seem to be taken from that category of books known as 'livres qu'on lit d'une main', books written for a certain kind of male readership. Episodes of sexual activity, graphically detailed, are frequent and Bruno, one of the central characters, is a consumer of pornography. The spreading of sperm over the face and breasts of the woman is a detail intended to titillate and arouse desire. It is also suggestive of the sullying of the female by the male during sex. Pornography is an ambivalent form, arousing some people and disgusting others. It taps into visceral, if ambivalent, feelings about sex.

However, this is not enough to settle the meaning of this passage. It can be seen as an example of the male making his mark on the female body in order to take possession of it. Against this, must be set the fact that it is Christiane herself who rubs the fluid over her body suggesting that she enjoys this and finds as much sensual pleasure in the act as the voyeuristic Bruno or the reader. The latter may wonder if the enjoyment is to be taken as no more than that or if Christiane is merely fulfilling the male fantasy of the woman pleasuring herself – she exists as an object to be gazed upon. It may also be possible to see the incident as demonstrating that sex does not have to be penetrative to be enjoyable or that non-penetrative sex is possibly more pleasurable for women. Yet again, it is possible to see this episode as an affirmation of the passivity of women. Christiane is the receptacle of the male ejaculate. Her body might additionally be seen as a page inscribed by sperm from the pen-like phallus. Her action invites a multiplicity of interpretations.

Significance and value are not features of the text but are attributed by the interpreting gaze. Reading is like sex – particularly like the act described above. Both parties (reader and authorial text, Bruno and Christiane) bring different individual experiences to the act. The reader's interpretation is not a penetration of the mystery of the text but something that originates in the reader as a response to the text and which can be spread over the text and absorbed into it.

Meaning is not located in the text but is a response to it. There is no single, god-like perspective from which a single truth may be established. Instead the text may be viewed in a multiplicity of ways. There is an interdependence of text and reader such that a change in the latter's point of view will entail a change in the interpretation of the former. The reader can see the above extract as an example of pornography but alternatively may also (or only) be conscious of the gap between sexual fantasy and the reality of a body that will not perform. The erotic image of Christiane spreading sperm on her erogenous zones, the sites of male desire, is undermined by the failure of Bruno to achieve full sexual congress. In the world of pornographic stereotypes men are studs who always perform. Bruno is a sexual inadequate, suffering from the kind of anxiety that leads his brother to consume Xanax. However, there is also a tenderness and consideration that is alien to pornography. Christiane shows an understanding of Bruno's needs that indicates that she treats him other than as a sexual performer. What is outside the genre is brought within it, alienating it from itself.

Houellebecq is not seeking to titillate but to enlighten. There is a refusal to ignore the more sordid side of experience. There is also a metaphorical richness. Houellebecq acknowledges the animal and instinctive side of our nature. There is something dirty about the human experience, expressed in the sullying of Christiane's skin. Yet humanity seeks to escape that side. Bathing and swimming pools are important features of this novel and others. Christiane and Bruno first meet in a Jacuzzi – where they have sex.[16] This is an image of cleansing, an attempt to purify the sex act. There is something dirty about the way that we reproduce, something that contaminates our species – and which preoccupies Bruno's brother, Michel, who sees our DNA as 'un peu n'importe quoi', hopelessly compromised by the inclusion of redundant features.[17] No less than the aristocracy, Michel seeks to perfect humanity by stripping away anything that might sully it and compromise its purity.

Yet that side of experience cannot be denied. The visitors to the Lieu du Changement may be looking for a something more spiritual but the bestial side of humanity cannot be washed away. The contamination of the body is a sign of our mortality, perhaps nowhere more so than in the grave

---

16   *Les Particules élémentaires*, pp. 138–139.
17   *Les Particules élémentaires*, p. 272.

where the dirt mingles with our remains, as illustrated when the grave of Michel's grandmother is re-opened and her remains disinterred.[18]

Generally, Houellebecq avoids the scatological – perhaps the ultimate in human impurity for it is pollution of the self by the self or by others. One significant exception to this (another occurs in *La Possibilité d'une île*) is the scene early in the novel where Michel's father finds him in Janine's house: 'Son fils rampait maladroitement sur le dallage, glissant de temps en temps dans une flaque d'urine ou d'excréments.'[19] Helplessness, vulnerability, pollution are all combined in this image. Mess is limiting. There is also a sense in which the elimination of waste products, themselves expelled from the human structure, are associated with a wider breakdown in social structures – in this case the family. His brother Bruno has a similar experience of childhood which he recalls when he re-visits his school in Meaux: 'd'autres garçons m'avaient frappé, humilié, ils avaient pris plaisir à me cracher et à me pisser dessus, à plonger ma tête dans la cuvette des chiottes.'[20] There is something deeply disturbing about this passage not just because it goes beyond the cruelty inflicted on Michel. That was the result of neglect. This is the result of cruelty, cruelty from those who are supposed to be innocents – other children. Their actions are reminiscent of gang-rape, but without the sex. Essentially this is about power and domination. Bruno's humiliation is signalled by the other boys making marks that pollute his body. Like dogs, they urinate on him to mark him out as theirs. Sticking his head down the toilet pan is a parody of baptism – desacralising what is intended to wash away the evil in our souls. It parodies the scenes of bathing elsewhere in Houellebecq.

Being left in his urine and excrement is the low point of Michel's life. The mess of his childhood seems to be something that he is determined to flee but which returns to haunt him again and again. Michel is driven by a belief that humans are more than just animals with instincts based on self-gratification, territoriality and domination – animals with brief spans whose bodies end up as dirt. Ironically, his mother and father, both

18   *Les Particules élémentaires*, p. 230.
19   *Les Particules élémentaires*, p. 30.
20   *Les Particules élémentaires*, p. 190.

in different ways, have a similar view but the more his mother in particular seeks to rise above human weakness, the more it manifests itself in her surroundings. The squalor of Michel's living conditions and the savagery of the di Meolas are just two examples of this.

It is to science rather than to religion or New Age practices that people should look to deal with the complex mess that life can degenerate into. Houellebecq has complained of the failure of writers and intellectuals to engage with issues that are of interest to a contemporary readership. He is particularly concerned with the failure to incorporate the insights of science, preferring instead commitment to a political struggle to change society:

> Il faudrait encore citer Ballard, Disch, Kornbluth, Spinrad, Vonnegut et tant d'autres qui parfois en un seul roman, voire en une nouvelle, ont plus apporté à la littérature que l'ensemble des auteurs du *nouveau roman*. Sur le plan scientifique et technique, le XXe siècle peut être placé au même niveau que le XIXe. Sur le plan de la littérature et de la pensée, par contre, l'effondrement est presque incroyable, surtout depuis 1945, et le bilan consternant: quand on se remémore l'ignorance scientifique crasse d'un Sartre ou d'une Beauvoir, pourtant supposés s'inscrire dans le champ de la philosophie, quand on considère le fait presque incroyable que Malraux a pu – ne fût-ce que très brièvement – être considéré comme un *grand écrivain*, on mesure le degré d'abrutissement auquel nous aura menés la notion d'*engagement politique*, et on s'étonne de ce que l'on puisse, encore aujourd'hui, prendre un intellectuel au sérieux; on s'étonne par exemple de ce qu'un Bourdieu ou un Baudrillard trouvent jusqu'au bout des journaux disposés à publier leur niaiseries. De fait, je crois à peine exagéré d'affirmer que, sur le plan intellectuel, il ne resterait rien de la seconde moitié du siècle s'il n'y avait pas eu la littérature de science-fiction.[21]

For Houellebecq, only literature that is in touch with science will be meaningful not just because it is tackling an important feature of twentieth-century life but also because it is a kind of writing that masses of people find interesting.

---

21   Michel Houellebecq, 'Sortir du XXe siècle', *Nouvelle Revue Française*, no. 561 (April, 2002), pp. 117–121, p. 120.

His stance in the above quotation is robust and his lack of respect for intellectuals of a certain stamp shows through in his dismissal of Malraux and in his contempt for what he believes is Sartre's lack of understanding of science. The use of 'on' generalises a personal point of view. It is thereby suggested that more people than he are contemptuous of the adulation afforded to Bourdieu and Baudrillard in the press. Above and beyond this, it is implicit that Houellebecq himself prizes novels that have a scientific content, that contain within them elements of science fiction.

Houellebecq's polemic points to what he sees as a breach between intellectuals and the masses. What Houellebecq is arguing, if it may be put in less incendiary (and less entertaining) form, is that intellectuals will find that the reading public will more readily understand the problems of modern society if the analysis is done in terms derived from science rather than if the analysis is purely political or philosophical. The public has knowledge and interests that are different from the intellectuals and the writers and it is they who must speak to the public by using forms that the public will respond to. The implication is that it is just as legitimate, if not more so, to expect readers to grasp scientific concepts as it is to expect them to understand the philosophical and political language of the intellectuals.

Houellebecq wants us to take science seriously. His novel has affinities with the subgenre known as hard sf [science fiction]. Kathryn Cramer defines it thus: 'hard sf is science fiction that gets the science right'.[22] More importantly she also points out that the science has a literary dimension: 'What science gives to hard sf is a body of metaphor that provides the illusion of both realism and rationalism'.[23] The rationality and realism are only an illusion because the 'science is used as a mythology'.[24] Thus science is a belief system – just like the obscurantist religions it supposedly replaced. The alliance with the New Agers at the end of the novel is not really a sur-

---

22 Kathryn Cramer, 'Hard Science Fiction', in *The Cambridge Companion to Science Fiction*, edited by Edward James and Farah Mendlesohn (Cambridge, Cambridge University Press, 2003), pp. 186–196, p. 188.
23 Cramer, p. 188.
24 Cramer, p. 188.

prise. Indeed the link between advanced scientific research and the cultists in *La Possibilité d'une île* is, in such a context, eminently plausible.

Houellebecq incorporates the language of science into the novel, just as he does the language of pornography. Both provide rich sources of illuminating metaphors for the uniqueness of the human condition. If pornography allows a sophisticated presentation of the baser elements in our make-up, then science allows an exploration of that within us which seeks to go beyond our limitations. Aliens are explorers. Science deals with that part of our experience that is less concerned with marking frontiers than with going beyond them or with discovering new and strange structures:

> Le 14 décembre 1900, dans une communication faite à l'Académie de Berlin sous le titre *Zur Theorie des Geseztes der Energieverteilung in Normalspektrum*, Max Planck introduisit pour la première fois la notion de quantum d'énergie, qui devait jouer un rôle décisif dans l'évolution ultérieure de la physique.[25]

As it turns out it is not just physics whose evolution is affected but humanity's. Wesemael sees passages like this as one of Houellebecq's 'pastiches'. She describes *Les Particules élémentaires* as 'une critique caricaturale de la science'.[26] Carlston concurs, saying that Michel's researches are 'd'un haut comique'.[27] Rabosseau similarly dismisses those same researches, calling them 'piètres'.[28] These comments would seem to argue that Houellebecq's treatment of science lacks the respect identified by Cramer as being a feature of hard sf. Michel's thoughts are, as Wesemael puts it: 'une démonstration scientifique et philosophique burlesque'.[29] Wesemael is right to see a desire not to spare any particular set of beliefs. Bruno's critique of Proust is burlesque literary criticism. Nothing is spared debunking: 'Chez Houellebecq, la désacralisation n'épargne rien'.[30] However, where is the burlesque in the

---

25   *Les Particules élémentaires*, p. 16.
26   Sabine van Wesemael, *Michel Houellebecq: Le plaisir du texte*, Approches Littéraires (Paris, L'Harmattan, 2005), p. 201.
27   Carlston, p. 25.
28   Rabosseau, p. 50.
29   Wesemael, p. 201.
30   Wesemael, p. 200.

above quotation telling us of Planck's paper? It is expository and factually accurate. If it is pastiche, it is remarkably close to its original source.

Subsequent examples depart more and more from scientific knowledge as it currently exists. By the end of the novel we are most definitely in the territory of cod science. The pastiche is evolutionary. Thus Wesemael is not far from the truth when she says of Michel: 'Il puise ses idées dans un catalogue 3 Suisses et dans les *Dernières Nouvelles de Monoprix* et dans le *Book of Kells*.'[31] This wickedly funny comment correctly points to an important characteristic of Michel's science – it is the science of a consumerist society. His researches are not a disinterested pursuit of knowledge but seek to satisfy its needs. It is about lifestyle and the way we live – and this is indeed where his discoveries have most impact. Furthermore, the reference to the *Book of Kells* hints perhaps that his investigations have all the genuine insight of a tourist visit. Thus, Houellebecq's use of scientific terminology captures the seductiveness of its attempts to explain the world. Science has to be just as attractive as an item on sale – and just as available.

Nevertheless, Houellebecq maintains, as Cramer put its, the 'illusion of realism and rationalism'. In the above, he explains how Planck's paper revolutionised scientific thought. He describes the moment when the mechanical model of the physical universe was no longer sufficient as a description of reality. The quotation refers to Planck's argument that energy is not a continuum but rather occurs in discrete packets, quanta. The implications of Planck's theory are important not just in terms of the extract discussed but for the form of the novel as a whole. The notion of quanta fits into a new conception of how the universe behaves. The fundamental characteristic of matter is that it is made up of discrete packets of energy. That matter appears to cohere is an impression that we have. The word energy is important because it indicates that the fundamental building blocks are not so much things but movement. Without movement, there would be no time, no change and no life. Science seeks to establish the laws that govern existence – at all levels. These laws are a set of universal beliefs. They have an explanatory force that goes beyond their original context.

31   Wesemael, p. 201.

Houellebecq establishes common ground between the language of science and the language of literature. The two can co-exist within one intellectual framework. In another passage from *Les Particules élémentaires*, he describes how Bohr was able to discuss a wide range of topics:

> Il aimait inviter ses étudiants à le rejoindre dans sa maison de campagne de Tis-vilde; il y recevait des scientifiques d'autres disciplines, des hommes politiques, des artistes; les conversations passaient librement de la physique à la philosophie, de l'histoire à l'art, de la religion à la vie quotidienne.[32]

What evenings at Tisvilde exemplify is the principle that science is not divorced from the other spheres of existence, and certainly not from literature. It is not separated into its own ghetto to which access is reserved. Rather it is part of the exchange of ideas that any interested person may participate in. Crucially, the various subjects that constitute conversation, the elementary particles of their discourse, combine, separate and re-combine ('passait librement') in a way that exemplifies the way the universe structures and re-structures itself as it evolves over time.

That, however, fails to do justice to the tone of the passage. If *Extension du domaine de la lutte* showed that the Darwinian struggle for the survival of the fittest has spread to all aspects of life, Tisvalde provides that the competition of ideas and opinions can be positive and enjoyable. These scientists make progress, not through vanquishing the opposition but through encountering difference and by learning from it – the find the familiar in the alien, alternative modes of knowledge. There is also something festive about these meetings. It is like a party with guests circulating freely, striking up new acquaintanceships. There is something almost casual about the use of the word 'conversations'. This is not a structured or purposeful debate but something much more haphazard. Yet out of this new ideas and ways of thinking were to come, revolutionising the scientific view of the world.

There is something of the utopian about this vision. It is as though Tisvalde is a lost paradise. Djerzinski fails to recreate its spirit in the present:

---

32   *Les Particules élémentaires*, p. 17.

L'ambiance au sein de l'unité de recherches qu'il dirigeait était, ni plus ni moins, une ambiance de bureau. Loin d'être des Rimbaud du microscope qu'un public sentimental aime à se représenter, les chercheurs en biologie moléculaire sont le plus souvent d'honnêtes techniciens, sans génie, qui lisent *Le Nouvel Observateur* et rêvent de partir en vacances au Groenland.[33]

Instead of a freewheeling exchange out of working hours, we have an 'ambiance de bureau' with its overtones of mundane routine, strict timetables and deadlines, diligent procedures that seek to check and cross-check findings so as to eliminate mistakes. This is research that fills in the gaps in knowledge but which does not seek to change paradigms. It is very limited and seems to have no concern for what lies outside its narrow domain.

Djerzinski's team is working in an environment that is not conducive to the kind of discoveries Rimbaud represented. It is not that the team is hostile to change. It is that they are not prepared to be truly adventurous. They advance knowledge but in a well-behaved manner:

> La recherche en biologie moléculaire ne nécessite aucune créativité, aucune invention; c'est en réalité une activité complètement routinière, qui ne demande que de raisonnables aptitudes intellectuelles de second rang. Les gens font des doctorats, soutiennent des thèses, alors qu'un Bac + 2 suffirait pour manœuvrer les appareils.[34]

There is a sense in which these are people not just of limited horizons but also people who are boxed in, confined within roles for which they are over-qualified. They live in a social context where people are not achieving fulfilment. Furthermore, thinking is reduced to a purely mechanical process, one dominated by machinery which can do the sort of thinking current science needs – mere calculation. People are reduced in status, serving only to regulate machinery. In a sense, they are no longer the masters, but the servants of a mechanical process. As Desplechin, Michel's boss puts it: 'On décrypte, on décrypte.'[35] He goes on to dismiss the activity as:

33   *Les Particules élémentaires*, p. 17.
34   *Les Particules élémentaires*, pp. 17–18.
35   *Les Particules élémentaires*, p. 18.

'Du bricolage, de la plaisanterie'. This is low-level fixing not creative. The word 'plaisanterie' contrasts with the atmosphere Bohr had around him. This is a dismissive humour not a companionable one. Indeed, Rabosseau's use of 'piètre' could more accurately be applied to these scientists rather than to Michel who is chafing against the mediocrity that surrounds him.

The above themes climax in the musings of Desplechin at the end of the second chapter:

> Il demeurait de vrais problèmes en biologie fondamentale. Les biologistes pensaient et agissaient comme si les molécules étaient des éléments matériels séparés, uniquement reliés par le biais d'attractions et de répulsions électromagnétiques; aucun d'entre eux, il en était convaincu, n'avait entendu parler du paradoxe EPR, des expériences d'Aspect; aucun n'avait même pris la peine de s'informer des progrès réalisés en physique depuis le début du siècle; leur conception de l'atome était à peu près restée celle de Démocrite. Ils accumulaient des données, lourdes et répétitives, dans le seul but d'en tirer des applications industrielles immédiates, sans jamais prendre conscience que le socle conceptuel de leur démarche était miné.[36]

This passage links biology (like the novel, the study of living forms) and physics. Desplechin's point is that that the concept of the atom as conceived by Democritus and which served well for centuries is now outmoded. Atoms are no longer the fundamental building blocks of the universe, governed by the laws of attraction and repulsion. Electromagnetic charges on the surfaces of atoms accounted for these forces of attraction and repulsion. Scientific developments have overtaken such a conception. Now, the discovery of fundamental particles shows that what we took to be indivisible – the atom, as its name indicates – is in fact a relationship. It is a combination not a singularity. This does not abolish atoms. Nor does it suspend the laws of attraction and repulsion. Rather it shows that such concepts are only of limited usefulness. Desplechin, and later Michel, wants to apply the same insights to humans. Humans are social beings.

---

36 *Les Particules élémentaires*, p. 20.

We can read the scientific passages metaphorically, applying their insights to the way we relate to one another. Like molecules, human relationships can no longer be seen simply in terms of attraction and repulsion – as in the classical novel – but must take into account other forces, unknown or unrecognised by previous writers. There are deeper forces at work, forces beyond the surface. Of course, attraction and repulsion are still important factors. It is not without significance that Bruno's father enjoys considerable success as a plastic surgeon – until he is out-classed by the competition. That is because he is able to enhance the attractiveness of women, their powers of attraction. There are, however, other ways of relating to each other and the relationship between the two brothers exemplifies links that go beyond attraction and repulsion.

Houellebecq shows that engagement with science is just as worthwhile a way of confronting the problems of humanity as engaging with philosophy or politics. These different modes of knowledge are not mutually exclusive. The problem for the research teams, as Desplechin sees it, is that exclusivity will thrive. Just as the philosophical novel may, in Houellebecq's view, overlook, evade or discount other approaches or even subordinate them to its own vision, so knowledge workers may limit themselves or feel themselves limited to just one small area.

Collection of data may be a necessary precursor to interpretation but, Michel believes, that is a routine matter that does not require much advanced expertise. More useful is the kind of knowledge that arises from the way facts can be related to other facts and to a whole. New interpretations can arise from the struggle between competing conceptions, which allows new ways to thinking to appear. Knowledge evolves. New paradigms, descended from previous ones, can suddenly appear and are then slowly developed by the collectors of data.

In any revolution, the consolidators (those who are happy with the collection of confirmatory data) will resist dramatic revolutionary change. This is the point about the EPR paradox, named after the scientists Einstein, Podolsky and Rosen. The paradox that they identified concerned the way a sub-atomic system might be influenced by a force operating on an equivalent system at a distance – even though there was no channel transferring the force between the two systems. It is as though one system knew what was happening to its pairing – even though there was no identified way by which it could know. Since quantum mechanics could not account for this apparent absurdity, Einstein and his two colleagues believed that the theory must be in some way deficient. The basis on which they arrived at this conclusion was reasoning. Alain Aspect, born in the Parisian suburb of Cachan in 1947, was able to show that the EPR paradox postulated by Einstein and the others could in fact be demonstrated by experiment. Action at a distance did appear to take place in a way that could not be accounted for.

These findings originate in the field of sub-atomic physics. Desplechin and Djerzinski are dismayed that the implications of developments in one field of study are not being taking into account in another:

> Djerzinski et lui-même, de par leur formation initiale de physiciens, étaient probablement les seuls au CNRS à s'en rendre compte: dès qu'on aborderaient réellement les bases atomique de la vie, les fondements de la biologie actuelle voleraient en éclats.[37]

They are the only ones to realize that what is true in one area could well be applicable in other areas. Biologists are not factoring in the implications that new concepts in the physical sciences, such as the notion of action at a distance, might have for their fields. This might be considered an example of how action at a distance functions. A discovery concerning sub-atomic physics means that biology should no longer consider its own fundamental concepts in the same way as before. A change in the concepts underpinning physics also means that there is an equivalent change in what underpins biology – even though these are supposed to be two discrete fields of knowledge and there is no demonstrable channel of communication or contact between the two. The fact is that biology cannot be pursued in the same manner as before and still hope to be adequate to the establishment of truth.

---

37 *Les Particules élémentaires*, p. 20.

Discoveries in science must have an impact on how we think about the world and how we deal with it. Midgley argues that Democritus' concept of the indivisible atom had far ranging consequences beyond the scientific:

> For Lucretius did not see atomism primarily as a solution to scientific problems. Following Epicurus, he saw it as something much more central to human life. For him it was a moral crusade – the only way to free mankind from a crushing load of superstition by showing that natural causation was independent of the gods.[38]

This was because it placed causation as the motive power in the world. Things happened not by the will of the gods but because there was an identifiable cause. Through the work of Lucretius, the implications, already identified by Epicurus, were given wider currency. Atomism is a view of the physical world that has implications for those who live in it. It has a moral dimension. If events are the result of the principles of causation, then it invites us not to trust in some divine intervention but rather to assume responsibility for our lives.

As Holloway's remarks show, how we view the structure of the universe matters. Seeing the world as being made up of separate atoms, rushing around, crashing into each other, will be different from seeing a world constituted by interrelated particles. A cursory, incurious reading might suggest that the view of the universe it proposes is atomistic. One might see the various characters as separate atoms, bumping into and off each other. However, closer examination reveals that they interact in a more complex fashion. Collisions are not what they seem. They can turn out to be more like the sex act between Bruno and Christiane, where sympathy, the mutual exchange of emotional support across a gap, is just as important as physical contact. There are other forces operating in the universe besides causation:

> Bruno perdit le contrôle de son véhicule peu après Poitiers. La Peugeot 305 dérapa sur la moitié de la chaussée, heurta légèrement la glissière de sécurité et s'immobilisa après un tête-à-queue. 'Bordel de merde! jura-t-il sourdement, bordel de

38   Mary Midgley, *Science and Poetry* (Abingdon, Routledge Classics, 2006), p. 30.

Dieu!' Une Jaguar qui arrivait à 220 km/h freina brutalement, faillit elle-même percuter l'autre glissière de sécurité et repartit dans un hurlement de klaxons. 'Pédé! hurla-t-il, putain de pédé!' Puis il fit demi-tour et poursuivit sa route.[39]

This is a seemingly small incident that is just one of many misfortunes that befall Bruno. The incident begins dramatically with Bruno losing control, a small but telling detail that indicates a lack of intentionality. Bruno is not master of the situation. The scene points to a theme in Bruno's life, the lack of influence his will has not just on the lives of others but, more crucially, on his own. However, Bruno is not quashed or destroyed (as would have happened had the crash taken place). Rather, his lack of strong willpower means that he is like the tree that bends before the wind and whose pliability saves it from destruction.

The paragraph is physically isolated by a space in the text from what follows. Houellebecq orchestrates the visual details in a way that is cinematic. The reader sees bits of the action in close up, as it were, and then has to fit them together or rather see how they fit together coherently. The narrative particles bind together to form an incident. Forces of attraction and repulsion are clearly present as Bruno and the other drive hurtle towards each other but then miss, but in such a way that Bruno's car appears to have been pushed aside. A casual reading might simply see Bruno crashing the car. The point, however, is that he does not. The two cars do not collide. He has a near-miss on his way to stay at the Lieu du Changement resort. It is important to note that Bruno changes course (his car spins round and ends up facing in the opposite direction) without touching or being touched by the other car. This is not one object striking another and causing it to move in a certain direction. It is like two identically-charge particles being shot at each other but being unable to collide because the similar charge that each carries prevents it. The similar charges repel each other.

On one level, the scene accentuates elements that bring it close to something from a science fiction film. By suppressing the human agent, the driver of the other car, it makes the encounter seem like a clash between a human being and a robot, an autonomous machine. There is another perspective that one can take, one that is historical rather than future-orientated. The car seems to challenge Bruno's right to continue his journey – not unlike what happens in a medieval epic. Indeed, the fact that there are crash barriers and also that both drivers are encased in the metal of their car only adds to any impression one might have of knights jousting. This is a confrontation, not a meeting or exchange.

So far, the incident seems to confirm classical physics. Two objects are subject to the laws of attraction and revulsion. However, it is not just the visual aspect of the scene that is important. Houellebecq also orchestrates its sounds. He avoids the obvious. There is no squealing of brakes or sound of metal on metal. What he does concentrate on describing is sound on or over the limits of communicability. These are sounds that are supposed to convey messages. First, we have Bruno's thoughts that appear to be insults hurled at the other driver. However, these are unvoiced – 'sourdement'. Is this communication or not? Is the second sound, the blaring horn of the Jaguar, a response or not? It would appear to be except that it could not be caused by Bruno's silent imprecations. It appears to be a conversation that is happening at a level beyond normal. Bruno then responds by shouting after the car – but not towards it, as in a normal conversation. Furthermore, the actual meaning content is minimal. The sound of the horns has no semantic value and Bruno's expletives are more an expression of emotion beyond words. It is as though the two drivers are in touch at a level beyond the physical. As well as the forces of attraction and repulsion, there is something that connects them – a force that is all the more mysterious as the other driver disappears never to be referred to again.

This brief incident is typical of the way the novel works out the implications of what the changes in physics mean for our belief systems, which in turn determine how we cope with life. Events in the world are related in ways that exceed what we would expect if natural causation was the only predominant force. What Houellebecq seeks to describe is the world as science now conceives it. Indeed the very anxiety that seems to pervade the lives of so many characters, the sense of threat, stems from the fact that they are seeking to come to terms with a world which does not obey predictable laws of cause and effect. The violence of a David di Meola is a lashing out at a world that does not conform to his desires, that he cannot make conform to his aspirations. Effort does not lead to the desired outcome. The world does not behave as he expects. Simple causation is no longer a sufficient guide for action.

Thus the major characters in the novel are all searching. This is true of those who are staying in the Lieu du Changement – as the name of the resort implies – even though Houellebecq may have fun at their expense. That is more because they are looking for ready-made answers – at least they have an awareness that their current conceptions are in some way deficient. They know that the world that they live in does not conform to conventional wisdom. Similarly, the mother of Michel and Bruno is, in her adoption of what might be labelled an alternative lifestyle, seeking for a different way of knowing the world – because that is what it means to be alive. This does not mean that she or anyone else will be successful. Her cult of youthfulness seems to be particularly pointless and poignant.

The novel's structure and content reflect the ideas that Desplechin and Michel draw attention to in the second chapter. The story is of two brothers, Michel and Bruno, born to the same mother but of different fathers. It is possible to see them as negative and positive versions of same being – like matter and anti-matter. Such a conception has much to commend it and there are ways in which the brothers are opposites, the most obvious being that Bruno is an extrovert and Michel an introvert.

However, we can see them also as two different but equivalent systems, a sort of illustration of the Aspect experiment, at times in contact with each other and at other times living apart. The way they interact is illustrative of action at a distance. The brothers are always in a relationship one to the other – even when they are not in proximity. The way their lives impinges on each other goes beyond mere causation. These characters of similar biological origins have very different upbringing and develop very different interests and life experiences – and yet their lives are intertwined like the double helix. One becomes a scientist and the other a teacher of literature. What they know of the world is very different. Thus they experience it and deal with it in differing ways. However, these differences are inter-related. What happens to one brother is not unrelated to what happens to the other. They cannot act totally independently of each other:

> Bruno commença à manger. Il se stabilisa rapidement autour d'un parcours ali-
> mentaire qui descendait le boulevard Saint-Michel. D'abord il commençait par
> un hot-dog, dans l'échoppe au croisement de la rue Gay-Lussac; il continuait
> un peu plus bas par une pizza, parfois un sandwich grec. Dans le McDonald's
> au croisement du boulevard Saint-Germain il engloutissait plusieurs cheese-
> burgers, qu'il accompagnait de Coca-Cola et de milk-shakes à la banane; puis
> il descendait en titubant la rue de la Harpe avant de se terminer aux pâtisseries
> tunisiennes.[40]

This looks like a straight-forward description of a period in Bruno's life
when he took to eating as a means of distracting himself from his emotional
problems occasioned by his lack of success with the opposite sex. It is a
psychological study of compensatory behaviour and is mildly humorous if
somewhat lacking in pity. The image of Bruno staggering down the Rue de
la Harpe in search of yet more food is a picture of pointless excess.

However, the passage is much more complex. It is significant that
the food is not French. It seems to parallel the mongrel origins of the two
brothers and mocks the notion of purity. The food comes from around
the Mediterranean and the United States. This is globalization. It takes us
back to the question, raised earlier, of what it means for something to be
French. This food is in France but not of the country. Is it then French?
Looked at another way, is the eating of food of foreign origin indicative of
the undermining of an important part of the French way of life? Indeed,
it is what many would consider to be poor quality food, high in carbohy-
drates and saturated fats.

Bruno's movement is also an illustration of how in physics forces act
on a body in movement. To begin with, the passage humorously illustrates
the principle that a particle only acquires mass when it is in movement.
Bruno's progress through the take-aways of the Boulevard Saint-Michel
and the Rue de la Harpe is a demonstration of this principle since thereby
he acquires bodily mass.

Furthermore, if Bruno's daily route is traced on a map, he first moves
in a straight line down the Boulevard Saint-Michel but when he reaches

40   *Les Particules élémentaires*, p. 150.

the Boulevard Saint-Germain, which crosses the Boulevard Saint-Michel at right angles, he does not continue straight on down the Boulevard Saint-Michel until it ends at the Seine but rather turns down the Rue de la Harpe, a smaller street which almost bisects the right angle made by the two major boulevards. In other words, the trajectory resembles that of an object travelling in a straight line until it meets a force at right angles causing it to change course by an amount determinable by a mathematical formula. This is Newton's First Law. Bruno appears to be a body upon which external forces act.

However, there are no readily discernible physical forces. No bus comes careering along the Boulevard Saint-Germain, knocking Bruno off his trajectory. Whatever is acting on him is not physical. Something makes him decide to take the route he does. This is not to say that he is a pawn, moved around at some-one else's will but rather that his actions are subject to influence – or he lets himself be influenced. The attenuation of his will can also be seen in the tense structure of the extract above. The past historic gives way to a series of imperfect tenses. This is a routine, a path that Bruno follows by force of habit rather than by forceful decision. The iterative nature of the movement, combined with the resemblance of the trajectory to the movement of a particle diverted by a countervailing force, serves to diminish the degree of intentionality. Bruno is not in full control of his movements. It is not unlike the earlier encounter with the Jaguar which also caused him to veer off course – though there is less feeling of antagonism.

A clue to what is going on here is provided by the names of the boulevards. The first is called Saint-Michel, a possible reference to Bruno's brother and symbolic of the deep empathy between the two despite their separation by circumstances. Furthermore the Boulevard Saint-Germain is a further reference to his brother since etymologically 'Germain' means 'of the same blood'. Bruno, the less forceful of the two brothers generally, is thus moved across this part of Paris but not solely under his own will.

Again one should be wary of being too simplistic. It is clearly not the case that one brother controls the other. Bruno is not to be considered a machine that is remotely controlled by his absent brother. There is rather a sense in which he is somehow sensitive to, co-operative with, the will of others. The brothers are, even though apart, indivisible. It is a though one brother's willpower can increases as the other's diminishes – even over a considerable distance. In this respect, Houellebecq is taking on board the implications of the EPR paradox for the writing of his parallel lives. The mundane hides the intricate workings of the universe.

The two brothers are bound together at some level beyond the merely physical. They seem to have a sharing so that what one has is always at the expense of the other. It is as though they were one human being in two bodies. We can see this in the passage analysed above but it also occurs at various other points. For example, it is at the point that Bruno loses Christiane that Annabelle re-enters Michel's life. But it happens at various other points:

> Avant de rentrer, par un réflexe de pur désespoir, il [Bruno] interrogea son répondeur. Il y avait un message. 'Tu dois être parti en vacances ... énonçait la voix calme de Michel. Appelle-moi à ton retour. Je suis en vacances aussi, et pour longtemps.'[41]

Bruno's despair is matched by Michel's calm. One is experiencing turbulence while the other is more detached. Bruno is questioning while Michel is answering. There is also the suggestion, implicit in 'dois', that Michel seems to know what Bruno is doing. In short, the two brothers are a symbiotic unit. What one has, the other is somehow denied. This should be seen as a balancing of two parts of an entity, a state of equilibrium as well as a struggle. They are like two sub-atomic systems that exemplify the EPR paradox, with a change in one entailing a corresponding and compensatory change the other. The two brothers are curiously united in competition – an 'extension du domaine de la lutte', but one that indicates a bonding that runs very deep.

So far, the image that emerges from the above examples is of a relatively benign universe. The influence of one brother on the other stems from a deep, hidden and unspoken sympathy. However, the universe has its dark

---

41   *Les Particules élémentaires*, pp. 118–119.

side as well. There are other forces at work, ones which are destructive. Structures are created only to be torn down and reformed. Even as we live, we are subject to forces that lead not to a sense of cohesion and connectedness but to breakdown and dissolution of the self. Michel's mysterious disappearance into the sea is but one example of this. It is rendered poetically, in a landscape where, according to his own notes: 'le ciel, la lumière et l'eau se confondent'.[42] The dissolving of the Irish landscape in the mist of sky, light and sea seems to provide an easy exit from existence. However, it is not always so easy.

Death in this novel is rarely so beautiful. The human body is destined to decay. Christiane has a spinal illness that ends up paralysing her:

> Le diagnostic était simple: la nécrose de ses vertèbres coccygiennes avait atteint un point irrémédiable. Elle s'y attendait depuis plusieurs mois, cela pouvait arriver d'un moment à l'autre; les médicaments avaient permis de freiner l'évolution, sans toutefois la stopper. Maintenant la situation n'évoluera plus, il n'y avait aucune complication à craindre; mais elle resterait définitivement paralysée des jambes.[43]

Her brief period of happiness with Bruno has come to an end. Indeed it is part of the human condition that things change – and not always for the better. The use of 'évoluer' and 'évolution' points to the fact that human life is a process in itself and is also part of a larger process – evolution. Everything is part of the process of change – even death. The noun 'nécrose' sees death as a process not a state and this is underlined by the use of 'atteindre'.

This is not to claim that states do not exist or are not possible. However, states are not permanent but are rather stages in a process. There is evolution is from state to state. Christiane's paralysis is a new stage that will represent stability – at least for a while. Like Bruno's circuit of comfort-eating in the fast-food joints along the Boulevard Saint-Michel and the Rue de la Harpe, there is an element of routine indicated in the case of

---

42 *Les Particules élémentaires*, p. 304.
43 *Les Particules élémentaires*, pp. 246–247.

Christiane by the 'n'évoluera plus' and in the case of Bruno by 'se stabilisa'. Yet this stability is only temporary. What we think of as being permanent and secure – even the bad things that we may cling to – is fated to change, something that places a question mark even over the placid routine of Michel's fellow researchers. Their secure regime can no more last than did the edenic Tisvalde. States are temporary. In science, orthodoxies succeed each other. Every so often – as happened, according to the novel, in 1900 when Planck gave his paper – there is a paradigm shift. After such a seismic shift in thinking, there is a resumption of steady progress, accumulating new pieces of knowledge to fit into the current scheme of thinking, until there comes a point when the paradigm shifts once more. This is about to occur again.

Christiane's body undergoes a similar process. It is changing and contains within it the seeds of its own decay, in this case a genetic malformation unnoticed at first but which manifests itself later on, destroying the host. This process is one in which the human will has limited rather than a determining role. Christiane is aware of what is happening – and has been for some time. All that is under her control is how she responds to what is happening within her body. Her will-power cannot influence the disintegration of the root of her spine. Nor can drugs can hold the inevitable at bay for long. Again, a comparison can be made, this time with Michel who consumes Xanax in an attempt to keep anxiety under control. Medicine is not a solution. Like Bruno's eating or indeed his consumption of alcohol is merely a means of attenuating the symptoms of human malaise. It is not just the shattering of the base of Christiane's spine that is 'irrémédiable'.

If previous generations might have accepted the ineluctability of decline, things are different in our modern age, obsessed as we are with the quality of life:

Jamais, à aucune époque et dans aucune autre civilisation, on n'a pensé aussi longuement et aussi constamment à son âge; chacun a dans la tête une perspective d'avenir simple: le moment viendra pour lui où la somme des jouissances physiques qui lui restent à attendre de la vie deviendra inférieure à la somme des douleurs (en somme il sent, au fond de lui-même, le compteur tourner – et le compteur tourne toujours dans le même sens). Cet examen rationnel des jouissances et des douleurs, que chacun, tôt ou tard, est conduit à faire, débouche inéluctablement à partir d'un certain âge sur le suicide. Il est à ce propos amusant de noter que Deleuze et Debord, deux intellectuels respectés de la fin du siècle, se sont l'un et l'autre suicidés sans raison précise, uniquement parce qu'ils ne supportaient pas la perspective de leur propre déclin physique. Ces suicides n'ont provoqué aucun étonnement, aucun commentaire; plus généralement les suicides des personnes âgés, de loin les plus fréquents, nous paraissent aujourd'hui absolument logiques.[44]

Death is not just the end of life but also the end of human decline. Paradoxically, the culmination of the process is also its end. Bruno's thoughts are built up logically and ineluctably. They begin with a meditation on the human condition as it is at the end of the twentieth century. The viewpoint is very utilitarian. What is the use of living, if one cannot enjoy it? The weighing of options is one that leads inevitably to our considering death. The example of two eminent philosophers is invoked. They are role models whose deaths seem, if not to justify the taking of one's own life, then at least to indicate that it is now within the framework of conventional norms of behaviour. Indeed, the fact that old people are the most likely to commit suicide seems to confirm this position. It is normal and therefore right. This is a form of morality based on the conventional. There is no sanction for behaviour beyond use and custom – and no justification beyond pleasure.

Bruno's thought processes, here as elsewhere, are governed by the kinetic. Thoughts are like physical movement – the examination of one's life is a contemplation of 'perspective' (used twice) and it leads to ('débouche ... sur') suicide. Suicide is the end result of a mental journey. Even the word 'déclin' is a part of this pattern with its suggestion of falling movement – a metaphor that is actualised in the suicide of Christiane as she hurls herself down the stairs in her block of flats. Similarly, Deleuze threw himself out of a window. These forms of movement all involve direction. So does 'le compteur tourne toujours dans le même sens'. Here the phrase 'toujours dans le même sens' conveys the expected inevitability of time. However, the turning of the counter indicates a circular movement, one that goes round and round but leads nowhere. It is a metaphor for the pointlessness of the movement. It accomplishes nothing even as the numbers on it increase.

Furthermore this counter, like the milometer inside a car, is inside us, inviting a comparison between humanity and machinery. The equivalence of humans and machines was a feature of the car episode examined above – and it is a model put forward in the later novel, *La Possibilité d'une île*. It emphasizes the calculating, rational side of what we are. Nevertheless, the organic side of our humanity, the animality cannot be denied. Just as some religions would place us between the angels and the beast, so the modern way of conceiving of humanity places us between the animal and the computer. Machines are renewable. Parts can be replaced. Humans, however, decay and cannot be renewed.

Bruno's musings on suicide appear to offer a way of coping with our mortality. Death will destroy our bodies. It is already at work even as we are most alive. Christiane is struck down during sexual games. Yet, Bruno's thoughts seem to show, if we accept the finality of death as Deleuze and Debord did, we can halt the process of decay. Death defeats its own processes.

This embracing of the tragedy of our lives appears an attractive and indeed courageous option. By committing suicide, we take control. So, even if the outcome is defeat, it is still an affirmation of the will. Furthermore, it is also a defeat for death. Nothing can harm us any longer. Yet should we accept this? Bruno's thoughts are in a seemingly ineluctable sequence. We follow them as he followed the Boulevard Saint-Michel until he turned into the Rue de la Harpe. Yet this is the man who thought of Ben as a 'babouin' – a nasty comparison. Wesemael notes that Houellebecq's characters frequently indulge in 'des analyses souvent rieuses, moqueuses'.[45] However, it is also noteworthy that these analyses are frequently very cogent and highly persuasive: 'Il est souvent difficile de faire le départ entre ce qu'il y a de vrai et ce qui se relève de la tendance à l'exagération et à la provocation'.[46]

45   Wesemael, p. 201.
46   Wesemael, p. 201.

Houellebecq's skill lies in treading a very fine line and it behoves the reader to tread carefully.

Thus Bruno's view of death and can be set beside an earlier scene which is less comforting. If anything, this vision is bleaker. Where traditional Christianity could frighten souls with the prospect ('perspective') of eternal suffering in Hell, Houellebecq has his own version of the afterlife to show that while Bruno's thoughts may be rational and ineluctable, they are not a complete and final response.

A few pages earlier, Michel, had been summoned to the graveyard in Crécy where his grandmother hand been buried. Significantly, this powerful episode occurs in the novel before Bruno's musings on suicide and the reader's thoughts cannot but be influenced by what happens here. His grandmother's remains are to be transferred to another part of the cemetery to make room for an enlarged bus station. This detail, illustrative in itself, goes beyond the mere verisimilitude which is its starting point and emphasizes the importance of movement and the link between movement and life. Indeed, the 'arrêt de bus' manages to combined the tension between life and death and the encroachment of one on the other. The buses will be stopping where graves used to be. It is impossible to say whether life or death is the stronger force. Will the buses continue on their way or is this the terminus? The spot is an ambiguous place, between two realms.

Michel, who is required to oversee the process, is met at the entrance by the gravedigger, a moment that recalls Orpheus meeting Charon at the Styx (the frontier he has to cross with the ferryman's help). The gravedigger here tells Michel that he is not obliged to look: 'Vous êtes pas forcé de regarder'.[47] The spectacle is not one that anyone has to look at. We have a choice about our level of engagement. What is placed before us is not necessarily something that we can easily take in:

> La mort est difficile à comprendre, c'est toujours à contrecœur que l'être humain se résigne à s'en faire une image exacte. Michel avait vu le cadavre de sa grand-mère vingt ans auparavant, il l'avait embrassé une dernière fois. Cependant, au premier regard, il fut surpris par ce qu'il découvrait dans l'excavation. Sa grand-mère avait

été enterrée dans un cercueil; pourtant dans la terre fraîchement remuée on ne
distinguait que des éclats de bois, une planche pourrie, et des choses blanches plus
indistinctes. Lorsqu'il prit conscience de ce qu'il avait devant les yeux il tourna
vivement la tête, se forçant à regarder dans la direction opposée; mais c'était
trop tard. Il avait vu le crâne souillé de terre, aux orbites vides, dont pendaient
des paquets de cheveux blancs. Il avait vu les vertèbres éparpillées, mélangées à
la terre. Il avait compris.[48]

Some readers, pertinently in view of what is found in the grave, will also
be reminded of the scene between Hamlet and the gravedigger – where
the discussion touches on how long the body will last. Houellebecq faces
us with the reality of death. Although this is a scientific, materialist vision,
like painters of the medieval period, he depicts a scary picture of what happens after death. The body is dispersed, no longer a body exactly. This is
the horror. The framework of the body is broken. The coffin that houses
that human frame (like a car round the driver) is likewise dispersed. The
beloved grandmother that Michel kissed is no longer an identifiable body
but a collection of scraps to be shovelled into a plastic bag – its very plastic-
ity denying form to the remains. This detail is one of the most distressing.
The way a society treats dead bodies says something important about that
society. The reverence that Michel shows in kissing the corpse contrasts
with the way the gravedigger, a functionary, treats the remains. His lack
of respect is exceeded only by that of a public authority that prioritises the
building of a bus station over leaving the dead in peace. There is something
profoundly wrong with a society that cannot honour its dead.

Yet the body undergoes worse treatment from natural forces. The last
words of the paragraph are ambiguous. They could be taken as showing
that Michel understands why the gravedigger warned him not to look.
Or, they could indicate that Michel grasps the reality of death. The body
continues to decay. Indeed, death gives decay the ultimate victory. Life, like
the medicines Christiane was taking, held the decay in check, the renewal
of our cells retarding the decay even if it could not definitively halt it. Now,

there is nothing to stop the dispersal of the body – a form of motion that mocks the movement associated with living.

The dead are moved by forces outside themselves and which are not under their own control. This being so, Bruno's trip along the Boulevard Saint-Michel acquires a sinister tinge. By not using the power of his will, Bruno is not living fully. His actions are a habit. However, seeking to be always in control also has negative consequences. Being in a constant state of alertness leads to anxiety – hence Michel's use of Xanax and his suppression of emotional attachment. The brother with the stronger will is the one more prone to anxiety.

Michel's parents have quite a different relationship to that of the two brothers:

> Et malgré tout certains êtres quoi qu'on en dise jouent un rôle fondamental dans votre vie, lui imprime bel et bien un nouveau tour; ils la coupent positivement en deux. Et pour Janine, qui s'était fait rebaptiser Jane, il y avait eu un *avant* et un *après* le père de Michel. Avant de le rencontrer elle n'était au fond qu'une bourgeoise libertine et friquée; après la rencontre elle devait devenir quelque chose d'autre, de nettement plus catastrophique. Le mot de 'rencontre' n'est d'ailleurs qu'une manière de parler; car de rencontre, il n'y en avait réellement pas eu. Ils s'étaient croisés, ils avaient procréé, et c'est tout. Le mystère qui était au fond de Marc Djerzinski, elle n'avait pas réussi à le comprendre; elle n'avait même pas réussi à s'en approcher. Y pensait-elle en cette heure où prenait fin sa vie calamiteuse?[49]

It is perhaps worth noting that the portrait of Janine is the negative of that of the Duchesse de Guermantes. Instead of the refined manners of the aloof aristocrat, Janine is 'une bourgeoise libertine et friquée'. The one thing they do have in common is money – a feature that serves to point up the other differences between them – though it is probably safe to assume that Janine has less.

Unlike the brothers, Janine and Marc are most certainly not of one mind. Each one's thoughts are closed to the other. Janine seems to want

---

49   *Les Particules élémentaires*, p. 256.

to reach out to her partner, to understand him. However, she is unable to do so though it is not made clear whether the failure lies with her or with Marc. Not only does he remain a mystery but he shows no inclination to even try to understand her. The use of 'se croiser' recalls the incident on the road. The verb indicates not just a meeting but a continuing on their separate ways afterwards – just as happened between Bruno and the other driver. In that case, the pair of drivers did not actually touch. Like Michel's parents, they did not get really close.

Yet, there is an effect. Janine's life is changed and Bruno is forced off the road. The encounter also recalls the walk down the Boulevard Saint-Michel, where Bruno's turning down the Rue de la Harpe could be seen as the result of a moving body being hit by a force at right angles, causing him to continue on his way but on a different course. Thus, Janine may not fully penetrate the secrets of Marc's innermost thoughts – just as Bruno fails to penetrate Christiane – but the course of her life is altered and not for the better. Her life becomes 'catastrophique'. If Bruno escapes a car-crash, Janine seems to have to suffer the complete wreaking of her life. The change in name indicates not only the lack of a stable identity but also seems to signal a diminishing of Janine's stature. It is as though she emerges from the encounter having lost something – something that is connected to procreation. It is significant that it is Marc, Michel's father, who enables this change. It foreshadows the act of his son who effects a radical transformation in humanity.

Is the fact that Janine's change is 'catastrophique' an oblique challenge to the value of Michel's breakthrough? Certainly, other aspects of the book make us wonder if the future is one that we might desire. For one thing, the price paid by Bruno is very high. The last we see of him is when he is dancing round and round on the eve of the millennium, his mind dulled and quiescent under the influence of drugs. Indeed as Bruno's mind becomes less and less active, so Michel's mental capacities seem to increase. It is as though across the distances that separate them, the faculties of one are being leeched by the other. The brothers are truly of one mind – a single, formidable intelligence shared between two people which unites Bruno's literary orientation and Michel's scientific one. This becomes a modern equivalent of what happened at the parties in Tisvalde. Michel takes nourishment from Bruno's mind, leaving his brother little more than an automaton. It would be hard not to feel sympathy for Bruno despite his faults and failings.

Furthermore, as we have seen, even Michel himself is not allocated a place in this brave new world. He disappears off the coast of Ireland, leaving his writings behind him. What results is a religion for the modern age, one that takes into account science. Desplechin proves prescient when he remarks:

> J'en suis venu à penser que les religions sont avant tout des tentatives d'explication du monde; et aucune tentative d'explication du monde ne peut tenir si elle se heurte à notre besoin de certitude rationnelle. La preuve mathématique, la démarche expérimentale sont des acquis définitifs de la conscience humaine.[50]

One of the things that science and religion have in common is that they explain. Faced with a teeming universe that seems to evolve by chance rather than design, they weave narratives that seduce us into belief by the power of those explanations. Indeed, etymologically, religion is a tying together, a network of beliefs that link the here and now with some transcendent system of values. This is how it imbues the world with meaning. The universe is not, as it might appear, random and chaotic but patterned in ways that make sense, if we could but discern what purpose was being worked out. Science provides a different but equivalent awareness of how the different parts to the universe are tied together. This allows humanity to discern its role in it and to make sense it. What follows Michel's death is a new set of explanations (or beliefs), ones that will give humanity the 'certitude rationnelle' it craves and, with it, the power to control its own evolution:

> Dès que le code génétique serait entièrement déchiffré (et ce n'était plus qu'une question de mois), l'humanité serait en mesure de contrôler sa propre évolution biologique; la sexualité apparaîtrait alors clairement comme ce qu'elle est: une fonction inutile, dangereuse et régressive.[51]

50　*Les Particules élémentaires*, p. 271.
51　*Les Particules élémentaires*, p. 268.

The key word in Michel's condemnation of sexuality is 'régressive'. There is to be no going back. Movement can only be in one direction, forwards and away from the past. Science is not about restoring the past or repairing the present. It must look to the future. The thinking on evolution must be considered one of the 'acquis' of human thought and should be the basis of our explanations of life. Like the aristocracy, which thought to perpetuate and improve itself through the control of breeding, so modern-day humanity should seek to harness evolution to its own benefit. The unlocking of the DNA code, the fundamentals of our humanity, will, Michel believes, give us the sort of control over our evolutionary future that the aristocracy to which the Duchesse de Guermantes sought to achieve. Humanity will have the power to design its future, to give itself the sense purpose that evolution lacks. Thus through science, humanity seeks to make nature obey its will. In this respect, science is not unlike the kind of religious thought that seeks through prayer and sacrifice to compel the deity to grant petitions. Both seek to bind the universe to the will of humankind.

Yet it is legitimate to wonder if the unlocking to the genetic code will give the sort of control that will be beneficial. The aristocratic attempt to created a purer being did not work as shown be the disappearance of the Duchesse's class, superseded by Bruno and Ben. Indeed Michel's advances benefit humanity's successors and turn out to be to the disadvantage of humanity itself – a theme illustrated even more graphically in *La Possibilité d'une île*.

It is a breakthrough that is long in coming. Michel's starting point is that reproduction is itself the problem:

> À mon avis, l'erreur est de vouloir travailler uniquement à partir de l'ADN naturel. L'ADN est une molécule complexe, qui a évolué un peu au hasard: il y a des redondances injustifiées, de longues séquences non codantes, enfin il y a un peu n'importe quoi. Si l'on veut vraiment tester les conditions de mutation en général, il faut partir de molécules autoreproductrices plus simples, avec au maximum quelques centaines de liaisons.[52]

---

52   *Les Particules élémentaires*, pp. 272–273.

Certainly, the lives of the characters evolve during the course of the novel 'un peu au hasard'. The disorderly conduct that is associated with sexual reproduction (particularly as Houellebecq depicts it) mirrors an inherent disorderliness in the system itself. There is so much redundancy in our DNA that it is impossible to predict how things will develop, what direction they will take. There is no smooth and ineluctable unfolding. Nor is there any goal towards which evolution is tending. New and unpredictable combinations will always be possible as redundant elements acquire relevance in new permutations. The successful ones will survive – in accordance with evolutionary theory.

Lack of stability is the weakness of the evolutionary process. Its dependence on the random as a means of creating new traits, filtering out the unsuccessful one – the survival of the fittest – is harsh. This harshness finds expression in the prevalence of cancers and degenerative diseases as the major causes of death in the novel. Such illnesses are not attacks from without as in the cases of pathogens such as bacteria and viruses. The contrast with Camus' *La Peste* is quite instructive in this respect. The major threat to humanity in that novel is from without, attack by the plague bacillus. It is a pathogen from without that enters the bloodstream, poisoning the victim. The doctors search for a serum, which may or may not work, to counteract the poison and in the meantime seek to prevent further contamination by putting in place quarantine procedures.

In Houellebecq's world, quarantine is not possible. We are open to what lies outside us and it is open to us. The Polish genes are passing through Michel and will be passed on should he ever have children. Similarly, cancer is a disease of cell mutation – another form of Michel calls 'configurations mutables'.[53] The changes wrought can be harmful, causing structural changes that are ultimately fatal. The body's coherence, its structure, breaks down and we die. As the graveyard scene suggests, this grim disaggregation of the human body continues after death so that even the most favoured human beings can be gathered into a plastic bag.

---

53 *Les Particules élémentaires*, p. 273.

Michel's struggle then is with his own nature as a human being which embodies the very instability that he seeks to subdue. He sees that the problem might be solved by looking elsewhere – a tour into the territory of physics:

> Ce sera certainement très long, [...] à priori rien ne distingue les configurations mutables. Mais il doit y avoir des conditions de stabilité structurelle au niveau subatomique. Si on arrive à calculer une configuration stable, même sur quelques centaines d'atomes, ce ne sera plus qu'une question de puissance de traitement ... Enfin, je m'avance peut-être un peu.[54]

The value of bringing the insights of physics to biochemistry was advocated early in the novel. Now, it is being done. Michel is looking beyond the atom to the sub-atomic world of quantum physics and trying to work out how the structures to be found there can help in stabilising the structures in the world in which we live.

Thus stability is the goal and flux is the obstacle to be overcome. In order to do this, dynamic structures need to be mapped and Michel achieves this, publishing the results in 2004:

> *Trois conjectures de topologie dans les espaces de Hilbert*, parue en 2004, devait surprendre. On a pu l'analyser comme une réaction contre la dynamique du continu, comme une tentative – aux résonances étrangement platoniciennes – de redéfinition d'une algèbre des formes.[55]

Les Particules élémentaires was published in 1998 and so the 'parue en 2004' is a dynamic plotting of a point in relative time. What we have is an account of an event whose location can be plotted from a number of different perspectives – rather in the way that we can plot the relative position of Snoop Dogg, Bill Gates and the Duchesse de Guermantes. Bruno's conjectures help us locate them with some degree of certainty relative to each other – even if we are not able to locate them is a natural, fixed and unchanging hierarchy. What counts is that there is a functioning model. This is precisely

54   *Les Particules élémentaires*, p. 273.
55   *Les Particules élémentaires*, p. 297.

what Michel is now able to do. He grasps that the sub-atomic world can be mapped, structures can be identified even though those structures are inherently mobile – 'la dynamique du continu'. He has learned to do in science what his brother could do in the realm of popular culture.

What Michel does is not just something which affects science but also the way living beings think about the world. In seeking to understand the inner dynamics of the sub-atomic world, he reveals the complexity that underpins the structures of the world in which we live. His re-envisaging of the way the world functions allows him to make the calculations needed to identify and control the future directions humanity might take. His aim is no longer to modify the conditions of existence as applied to individual objects but to look instead at the states. His scientific investigations lead him to a new way of theorising existence:

> ... le remplacement d'une ontologie d'objets par une ontologie d'états. Seule une ontologie d'états, en effet, était en mesure de restaurer la possibilité pratique des relations humaines. Dans une ontologie d'états les particules étaient indiscernables, et on devait se limiter à les qualifier par le biais d'un observable *nombre*. Les seules entités susceptibles d'être réidentifiées et nommées dans une telle ontologie étaient les fonctions d'onde, et par leur intermédiaires les vecteurs d'état – d'où la possibilité analogique de redonner un sens à la fraternité, la sympathie et l'amour.[56]

In reading passages like these, we should be mindful of Wesemael's warning that it is difficult to disentangle the sincere from the provocative. Houellebecq, through Michel, is building a structure that is coherent – not necessarily true. It is an analysis that is intended to appear to be plausible – fictional science.

He employs the style of science metaphorically so that the novel illustrates the principles that Michel sets out. This not only makes the science convincing, it also enriches the narrative. Michel reasons in a logical manner but links the abstract back to experience just as religion links the divine with the human. Individual entities no longer register except as traces that they leave when they move. Entities are understood not as stable things or beings but as wave-forms or movement. Their ever-changing position (for even at rest we are moving relative to something else) can be plotted by means of vectors. This is something that the novel illustrates for us. The movement of Bruno along the Boulevard Saint-Michel and then down the Rue de la Harpe can be plotted by means of very simple vectors. Furthermore, the way forces operate on Bruno's body is an illustration of how 'fraternité ... sympathie ... amour' might function in this new theory of knowledge. The action at a distance to which Bruno is subjected operates on the basis of a bond of brotherliness that creates the conditions for sympathetic action – Bruno is operating in sympathy with the mind of his brother. Understanding the dynamics of the universe in this way is the necessary precondition for controlling them. Now Michel hopes to be able to direct that movement. His insights allow him to tap into the fundamental dynamic structures that operate at all levels of the universe.

However, if the brothers are closely linked, then we need perhaps to remember what is happening to Bruno during this delving into the deeper structures of the universe. The most significant element at this point is the mental eclipse of his brother. At their final meeting, the funeral of their mother, Bruno is on release from the sanatorium where he is undergoing treatment for his severe depression. Bruno is on strong antidepressants which numb his willpower and drain him of sexual potency. He is no longer a will functioning in the world and when we see him on the eve of the millennium – the last time that we do see him – he is dancing mechanically, his sadness alleviated by drugs.

Despite his shortcomings, the Bruno we encounter for most of the novel is a creative individual, a writer who impresses more than a few and an interpreter of literature, indeed of the world around him. We do not have to agree with his judgements. The point is that he does make them. He sees a meaning in Ben's gestures when he hears the passage on the Duchesse de Guermantes. One of Bruno's major characteristics is that he responds to the world as a rich tapestry of interrelated meanings.

This is what Michel comes to understand as he pursues his researches. It is as though the power of Bruno's mind is now able to meld with that of Michel, allowing the latter to appreciate the deeper structures of reality. If

Desplechin regretted that the research teams could not think outside their narrow specialisms, missing the implications of developments in physics, then what happens to Bruno puts at Michel's disposal (subconsciously, of course) a faculty of insight that nourishes and enriches his research. New ways of thinking have been created by the work of scientists like Planck and Bohr but it is the combination of the literary and scientific in Michel that completes the work that they embarked upon.

It is his response to the *Book of Kells* that proves decisive for Michel's development of his thought, according to his chief disciple and biographer:

> Hubczejak n'hésite pas à affirmer que la rencontre avec ce manuscrit enluminé, d'une complexité inouï, probablement l'œuvre de moines irlandais du VIIᵉ siècle de notre ère, devait constituer un moment décisif de l'évolution de sa pensée, et que c'est probablement la contemplation prolongée de cet ouvrage qui allait lui permettre par le biais d'une série d'intuitions qui rétrospectivement nous paraissent miraculeuses, de surmonter les complexités des calculs de stabilité énergétique au sein de macromolécules rencontrées en biologie.[57]

There are a number of points here – some almost incidental and yet at the same time illustrative of deeper issues. As in the illuminations contained in the *Book of Kells*, the incidentals turn out to be the main point of interest. Firstly, there is the contrast with the research teams that were content to stay in the same rut, reading the same newspaper that did not disturb their way of thinking about events in the world but confirmed their prejudices. In this case, Michel is faced with something completely novel – an illuminated collection of the gospels. Seeing them represents 'un moment décisif' – it is a life-changing event. Furthermore, the reading of the manuscripts is different from normal, linear reading. It is a 'contemplation prolongée'. This is way of reading that allows, indeed obliges, whoever is reading it to read differently. Different aspects of the text are brought into play. It is no longer a line of words conveying information but is rather a site that the eye can decipher spatially, rather like a map of the Quartier Latin on which the

---

57 *Les Particules élémentaires*, p. 300.

movements of Bruno can be traced as he goes in search of food. Indeed, the eye can travel back and forward, making links and seeing connections. The textual space succeeds in depicting images in a way that suggests multiple dimensions. They hint that there is a realm beyond what we can see – or that our world is part of a richer, more complex whole. Pictures and letters intertwine and the decorative is as much a part of what the *Book of Kells* has to communicate as the words themselves. As for the words themselves, these are not in themselves new but preserve, through copying, what was previously written. Unlike the newspaper, or indeed this novel, what is written is not composed specially. It is not novel – nor is it disposable. It is meant to be true for all time and so is both in time and beyond. It has a message that goes beyond the transient and at the same time celebrates the unchanging message of the gospel.

Secondly, the fact that this is a religious text needs to be taken with Desplechin's view that religions needed to take into account the insights of science if they were to be meaningful in the contemporary world. Here, science and religious art are on common ground. Scientific thinking springs from the insights of the Irish monks who, in their illustrations of the gospel message, depicted their vision of the world in structures that are dynamic, a new algebra of forms. What is also clear is that the reading process, the understanding that comes from deciphering, requires something differ- ent from mere linearity. Desplechin criticised his colleagues for a purely mechanical approach to information: 'On décrypte on décrypte'. This he dismissed as 'Du bricolage, de la plaisanterie'. Rather what is required is the sort of reading that the *Book of Kells* seems to invite. The intricacies of its illuminated text, when he contemplates the work spread out before him in the library of Trinity College, allows Michel to grasp the geography of existence in a way that he has not done heretofore.

He is not lost in the work nor seduced by its intricacies. Rather his appreciation of the vision of the *Book of Kells* comes when he allows himself to follow the reading practices of the more literary Bruno. Thus he does not work out his solutions in a methodical fashion but, as would the mem- bers of a research team. Rather, he proceeds by 'une série d'intuitions qui rétrospectivement nous paraissent miraculeuses'. The miraculous nature of Michel's progress echoes the subject matter of the text he is contemplating in that the gospels are accounts of miracles. At the same time the adverb 'rétrospectivement' shows that breakthroughs can only be understood backwards – and indeed can only be recognised as progressive when we can use hindsight and are able to see from where we are coming. This is the profound paradox of progress. Breakthroughs are made not be looking forwards and identifying gaps to be filled – that is the 'bricolage' of the journeyman researcher. It is only when Michel follows intuition that he is able to appreciate fully the reality of the structures that govern the way the world works.

The *Book of Kells* is not the answer to a question. It is not offering a solution. Rather it is offering a map of reality, a picture made of text and drawings where it is sometimes hard to define which is which. One thing leads to another. Michel's experience is not unique. The novel then quotes a commentator from the late twelfth century, Giraldus Cambrensis, on the *Book of Kells*:

> *Ici on verra l'aigle, là le taureau, ici le visage d'un homme, là celui d'un lion, et d'autres dessins presque innombrables. En les regardant négligemment, en passant, on pourrait penser que ce ne sont que barbouillages, plutôt que compositions soignées. On n'y verra rien de subtil, alors que tout y est subtil. Mais si l'on prend la peine de les considérer très attentivement, de pénétrer du regard les secrets de l'art, on découvrira de telles complexités, si délicates et si subtiles, si étroitement serrées, entrelacées et nouées ensemble, et de couleurs si fraîches et si lumineuses, que l'on déclarera sans ambages que toutes ces choses doivent résulter non de l'œuvre des hommes mais de celle des anges.* [58]

Thus at the very moment when we might expect to find an explanation of the science behind Djerzinski's revolution, we find something that is a piece of art appreciation – one that could, with little trouble, be applied to *Les Particules élémentaires*. Anyone reading this novel sensitively will also find '*de telles complexités, si délicates et si subtiles, si étroitement serrées, entrelacées et nouées ensemble*'. The mixture of styles and registers is far from a hodgepodge.

---

58   *Les Particules élémentaires*, pp. 300–301.

Contemplation of the work reveals that it is more complex than it might appear – there is no redundancy. Thus, the characterisation of Ben by using animal imagery takes on a new significance – an additional one, for the original, racist one, is not lost – when we read the above paragraph which juxtaposes the animals, including a human animal, which represent the four evangelists. The contiguity of the human and the bestial is part of the structure of the universe. We have the eagle soaring skywards alongside the domesticated bull and the lion that lives in the wild. Both texts reach not just different parts of the animal kingdom but also different realms of physical space. The division between man and beast and also between the human and the divine is not clear cut. The calligraphy and illuminations in the *Book of Kells* encourages a melding of message and image. This copy of the gospels is a communication from the divine to the human but is also a hymn of praise from the human to the divine. The secrets that can be discovered by exploring what lies within the surface patterns of the manuscript (themselves recalling the patterns that Bruno created on Christiane's back) are a testimony to the way meaningful communication is possible between the fundamental order of the universe and human consciousness.

Indeed, the text becomes the common ground that creates a bond between human beings who might otherwise be isolated by geography, time or circumstances (a theme elaborated in Houellebecq's *La Possibilité d'une île*). Giraldus and Michel have a similar reaction to the book and this allows the twelfth-century commentator and the twentieth-century scientist to connect despite the gap between them. Indeed the link between them is one that spans the chasm of death since Giraldus is a presence in a way the remains of Michel's grandmother held up in a plastic bag are not.

The message that Michel draws from this is that space is not a site of separation, an emptiness that terrorises us by reflecting back our nullity. It is rather a place where our imaginations can trace out the links that will connect us and thereby save us. Thus Michel writes in his *Méditation sur l'entrelacement*:

> *Dans cet espace dont ils ont peur, écrit encore Djerzinski, les êtres humains apprennent à vivre et à mourir; au milieu de leur espace mental se créent la séparation, l'éloignement et la souffrance. À cela, il y a très peu de commentaires: l'amant entend*

l'appel de son aimée, par-delà les océans et les montagnes; par-delà les montagnes et les océans, la mère entend l'appel de son enfant. L'amour lie, et il lie à jamais. La pratique du bien est une liaison, la pratique du mal une déliaison. La séparation est l'autre nom du mal; c'est également, l'autre nom du mensonge. Il n'existe en effet qu'un entrelacement magnifique, immense et réciproque.[59]

This opens with an evocation of existentialist angst, of humanity's fear in the face of the vast emptiness of space, both the emptiness of the universe and the spiritual emptiness of the human soul. However, across the gaps, links are made by means of love. This leads to the conclusion that doing good means connecting with someone or something outside one's self. Doing evil is to weaken the connections. It is separation. Thus the breakdown of the human body in the grave is the ultimate triumph of evil. Similarly the uncoordinated reproduction of cells is also harmful – as in the case of Annabelle's cancer – because it is disorderly. The *Book of Kells*, like Michel's *Méditation*, celebrates the power of the links that structure the world. The universe is an '*entrelacement*'. The phrase in which it occurs – '*un entrelacement magnifique, immense et réciproque*' – is evidently positive in its associations. The way everything is linked together so that nothing is left out seems to make everything significant. There is thus a value to be had in finding a place in this network.

However, we cannot take this seriously. The science is tosh – even if it is plausible tosh. The vision may be eminently seductive but as Rabosseau has pointed out, Houellebecq's conceives his novels 'comme une provocation utile et salutaire, comme un texte programmé pour susciter une réception troublée, comme une arme de combat et de résistance'.[60] We need to see Michel's argument not as advocacy but as a stimulus. If we can distance ourselves from Bruno's racist views, then we should perhaps hesitate before being swayed by the apparently more benign eugenics of his brother. Michel's insight leads not just to a reform of the conditions in which we live but also the nature of the life lived and the people who live it. Humanity is not so much transformed as left behind as Michel's researches

---

59   *Les Particules élémentaires*, p. 302.
60   Rabosseau, p. 45.

create the successor race: 'l'humanité devait disparaître; l'humanité devait donner naissance à une nouvelle espèce, asexuée et immortelle, ayant dépassé l'individualité, la séparation et le devenir'.[61]

Walter Wagner calls this: 'une réponse post-moderne au vouloir-vivre postulé par Schopenhauer'.[62] In one respect this is true. The sexual desire and attendant frustrations (manifestations of the 'vouloir-vivre') that tormented Bruno have no place in the lives of this new race. However, the solution is also a provocation. It is an answer that perhaps in true post-modern style raises a further question. If the ending of the sufferings of humanity is to remove what is also the source of joy (and indeed the relationship with Christiane brings Bruno much happiness) then is it worth it? Furthermore, the human beings who are born human beings do not directly benefit. On the contrary they are the losers. As the novel concludes, we find that the new improved humans have inherited the earth (not the meek, as the gospels of the *Book of Kells* would have it) and humans survive in pockets in disadvantaged conditions. In short, what happens is that a new elite of immortals is created and they elbow out the rest of us in order to dominate what was once ours. None of the characters, not even Michel, benefit. Frédéric Sayer aptly comments that this in 'un programme eugéniste qui ne manque pas de faire froid dans le dos'.[63] In a curious and perturbing way, Bruno's racism thrives in this brave new world.

Indeed the fate of Bruno, left drugged and incapable in a mental institution, should perhaps give us cause for thought. There is a price to be paid for Michel's advanced mental agility – and it is Bruno who pays. His passivity increases as Michel's power to penetrate the inner secrets of the universe increases. He voluntarily submits to the regime of the asylum but, if he is not strictly speaking a prisoner, then it is hard to see exactly what degree of freedom he does in fact have. Indeed, the word '*entrelacement*' also suggests that things are tied to together in such a way that freedom

61   *Les Particules élémentaires*, p. 308.
62   Walter Wagner, 'Une lecture schopenhauerienne de Houellebecq', in Wesemael and Clément, pp. 109–122, p. 116.
63   Frédéric Sayer, 'Transformations de symboles: Michel Houellebecq et Bret Easton Ellis', in Wesemael and Clément, pp. 145–155, p. 150.

of movement is restricted. Like Bruno's dance steps, there is a set pattern that one cannot break free from without provoking the sort of chaos that terrorises humanity. Giraldus Cambrensis uses the phrase '*entrelacées et nouées ensemble*' which highlights the ambiguity. The decorative patterns he sees before him also recall ropes that restrain.

Thus Michel's breakthrough is less positive than might be supposed. The ending of the novel is a happy ending for the successor race. However, it is also an elegy for humanity:

> Au moment où ses derniers représentants vont s'éteindre, nous estimons légitime de rendre à l'humanité ce dernier hommage; hommage qui lui aussi finira par s'effacer et se perdre dans les sables du temps; il est cependant nécessaire que cet hommage au moins une fois, ait été accompli. Ce livre est dédié à l'homme.[64]

The placing of the dedication, which should normally come before the main story, conveys something badly wrong. In a novel where space is so important, where movement and place are key factors, to put the dedication of the book at the end has considerable impact. It is a shock ending.

However, there is a sense in which the dedication is in the right place – at least for the neo-humans. The story of humanity turns out not to be the real story but the prelude to it – from the perspective of the neo-humans, of course. We are the warm-up act – just as comedian Daniel1 will be the precursor of a race of clones. Even more humiliating for humanity, the tribute that will be paid will in turn be erased. The dedication will crumble into nothingness and our successors will continue to live on, no longer mindful of us. The forces that dissolved the body of Michel's grandmother into a few disconnected remnants will presumably be the forces that will turn even our elegy into grains of dust to be lost among the sands of time. It will be the ultimate defeat of humanity by the forces of '*déliaison*'.

Yet '*déliaison*' was an important part of our humanity. It refusal to follow order and routine was what gave freedom. If Michel's exaltation of '*liaison*' to the dominant position of guiding spirit of the new humanity is what creates the new race of humans, then it casts aside something important. It is important to bear in mind that this new race has been predetermined by the powerful calculations that Michel was able to make on the computers in Ireland. Their destiny is pre-determined – they dance the dance that Michel has calculated they need to dance. They are prisoners of their genetic programming, of Michel's view of how they should be genetically related to the rest of the universe. The '*entrelacement*' that is the ground of this race's existence is indeed an imprisoning in a future laid down by a vanished member of a vanishing race. The neo-humans are '*noués*'. They may have been protected from the negative effects of '*déliaison*' but they are unable to untie the genetic knots that are holding them. It was human beings who had the ability to glimpse the complexities and work them out for themselves. The new humans are followers of doctrine not creators. Indeed the new race seems from this vantage point to be more like the team of jobbing researchers with their conventional correct views. They are not going to create new knowledge, new ways of looking at the world.

This is the paradox then. Michel does something that his creations cannot do. He innovates. He is able to do so because he has first been able to free his mind from its preconceptions or limited views. His work depends on the power of '*déliaison*' as much as on that of '*liaison*'. He sees the patterns in the *Book of Kells* and understands how he can harness the mode of thought they exemplify – but he is not bound by them.

Thus what appears to threaten us with extinction is what may yet save us. The ending of the novel shows a future unrolling ineluctably, with everything going according to plan. However, we know that in reality none of this can be true. We as readers are already living in part of that future and it is different – for example, there was no *Trois conjectures de topologie dans les espaces de Hilbert* published in 2004. What is a prescribed future has not happened. We are free. Human beings, we realize, are not necessarily doomed. Our besetting problems have not been solved either but something in the novel has moved us away from the straight path laid down by Michel. We are no longer on the Boulevard Saint-Michel.

CHAPTER 3

Lanzarote: A Detour?

If *Les Particules élémentaires* is about the creation of a purer race, the neo-humans, *Lanzarote* investigates the impure. Wesemael rightly remarks that the story 'n'a certes rien d'édifiant' and that is 'une vision du monde par le bas.'[1] Where the *Les Particules élémentaires* strips out the degenerative, *Lanzarote*'s main characters are deviants – and remain so. *Les Particules élémentaires* leads us towards the triumph of the bland while *Lanzarote* dwells on the monstrous – before turning aside from it. Its key structure, then, is the 'déviation'. The narrator's life is not, as we might expect, where the main interest of the story is found. Our interest is drawn to what lies off that narrative track. While the cavorting of the narrator with two German lesbians may have a certain appeal, there is a much more tragic story unfolding elsewhere. We catch incidental glimpses of this story only when its protagonist, Rudi, impinges upon the narrator's awareness. Only when Rudi disappears from the hotel leaving a letter for the narrator do we find out how the glimpses form part of a bigger picture. It is another life, one visited by the narrator – it is worth a detour, 'vaut le détour', as the Michelin guide might put it. The narrator discovers his companion's life in the same way that he gets to know the island. It is a place he can visit but which he can also leave behind, as the ending of the novella shows. Rudi's life is no longer worth visiting.

At first, the focus is on the narrator. A sudden realisation reveals a crisis in his life. Furthermore there is a pattern of failure. This time, however, he wants to start a new story about himself:

---

1   Wesemael, p. 153.

Le 14 décembre 1999, en milieu d'après-midi, j'ai pris conscience que mon réveillon serait probablement raté – comme d'habitude. J'ai tourné à droite dans l'avenue Félix-Faure et je suis rentré dans la première agence de voyages. La fille était occupée avec un client. C'était une brune avec une blouse ethnique, un piercing à la narine gauche; ses cheveux étaient teints au henné. Feignant la décontraction, j'ai commencé à ramasser des prospectus sur les présentoirs.[2]

From the outset, the theme of deviation appears – though it is done obliquely. The narrator is merely making a detour – the first of many such 'détournements'. His use of 'raté' suggests not just an event that is ruined but one that is missed. Missing out on the party is a pattern in his life: the action is always elsewhere. It is an indication of his own feeling of marginality, something that he will have in common with Rudi. He is never in the right place at the right time. This marginality could perhaps be seen as the source of his individuality, his refusal to be part of the pack. It is what allows him to understand Rudi whereas the mob hounds him.

The reference to Félix Faure is a sly comment that mixes the absurd and the tragic. Félix Faure is one of those politicians who are remembered not so much for their accomplishments in life as for the manner of their dying. Not that there was anything particularly noble or uplifting about his final moments. On the contrary his death of a seizure while having sex with a prostitute is more likely to bring about a fit of sniggering than anything else. The lack of dignity and the fatality of the act rob both death and sexuality of any grandeur or nobility.

When the narrator enters the travel agency, the girl behind the counter is dealing with another client. Deprived of attention, he feels uneasy and so collects the brochures in order to give the impression of not needing that attention. The gaze he directs over the brochures and towards the woman is analytical. She is presented not as a whole person but in three visible parts – the narrator only gives us what can be seen above the counter. It is as though his gaze dismantles her into three pieces – the blouse, the earring and her dyed hair. She is presented as decoration, a subtle indication

2   Michel Houellebecq, *Lanzarote et autres textes* (Paris, Librio, 2002), p. 9. All subsequent references are to this edition.

of the narrator's misogyny and his tendency to view women not so much as equal human beings but as being there to serve his needs.

If the narrator is someone not at ease in his mind, she seems not to be at ease with her body – hence her decision to make changes. Both she and the narrator consider themselves as being in someway deficient – as failures, 'raté' in French. The travel agent needs to improve upon her body with a ring though one of her nostrils and by dying her hair.

On the other hand, her disconcerting appearance could be read as an attempt on her part to be different from the crowd. She does not dress conventionally. Yet her very attempts at being different from the expected image of a business suit or other form of conservative dress have led her into adopting a style that is in its own way conventional. This is a trap that awaits Rudi whose unconventional sexual appetites place him within a group of like-minded people and whose appearance increasingly conforms to expected images of the paedophile. In this case, what the travel agent is wearing is in its way suitable for an industry that epitomises globalization. The style of dress is non-specifically ethnic and together with the body markings and dyed hair suggest a simultaneity of identities, none of which is allowed to predominate. The travel agent is a consumer of meanings, purloined from round the world. She is a monstrous composite, rather than a coherent individual presence. The contrast with the image of the Duchesse de Guermantes as presented in *Les Particules élémentaires* is most striking.

Significantly, the dialogue opens with words that are presented as heard rather than spoken. The conversation between the two of them seems to consist of two streams that exist in quite different timescapes. The dialogue is a sequence of misses:

'Je peux vous aider?' ai-je entendu au bout d'une minute.

Non, elle ne pouvait pas m'aider; personne ne pouvait m'aider. Tout ce que je voulais, c'était rentrer chez moi pour me gratter les couilles en feuilletant des catalogues d'hôtels-clubs; mais elle avait engagé le dialogue, je ne voyais pas comment m'y soustraire.

'J'aimerais partir en janvier ...' fis-je avec un sourire que j'imaginais désarmant.

'Vous voulez allez au soleil?', elle embrayait à cent à l'heure.
'Mes moyens sont limités' repris-je avec modestie.[3]

The real-time dialogue is expanded by a detour through the thoughts of the narrator. Houellebecq's prose is a complex construct of emotional incident with conscience acting as an instrument of self-torture. The passage traces the workings of a mind that is, beneath a veneer of ironic self-awareness, lacerating itself. There is a split in the self, between the part that is in the travel agency and the part that wishes he were at home – something which foreshadows the ending with the narrator in Indonesia wondering about events in Brussels. The human psyche is a composite and complex thing and it is here dismembered by the narrator's self-reflective gaze just as he had earlier separated out the different elements that made up the travel agent's appearance.

The exchange ends with a self-deprecating phrase, 'avec modestie', reflecting the narrator's self-effacement and contrasting with the travel agent's more flamboyant style. Yet it is ironic given the narrator's lack of another kind of modesty elsewhere in the novel – his three-in-a-bed romp with the two lesbians. Although the narrator proclaims himself a man of limited means, limitations are something that the story makes a point of exceeding. Indeed, there is a marked lack of modesty in the novel's treatment of important themes such as paedophilia, which takes the story into quite outrageous territory, particularly in its account of the paedophiles' explanations for and defence of their behaviour. Limits on their behaviour is are what Rudi, the paedophile, and in a different way the Raëlians in general do not accept.

But the narrator's 'modestie' also has a more immediate relevance and is part of a tactic in the exchange between the travel agent and the narrator. If the travel agent's opening question is posited on a lack that she is to remedy, the narrator's final response is to point to another lack that will determine the parameters within which he can take action. Indeed, the fulfilling of a perceived need or lack is what underpins every commercial

3   *Lanzarote*, p. 9.

transaction but not quite to the same comic extent as here. A simple request leads to an expression of existential angst, a feeling of utter hopelessness and despair based on a deep-seated sense of personal inadequacy.

Yet the very disproportion of the response is comical and if there is any doubt, the bathos of the narrator's desire to be at home scratching his balls, leaves us in no doubt. The gesture, reprised from Bruno's observation of his student, Ben, is an indicator of a mind not filled with philosophical yearnings but with more animalistic ones. He is not just a mind but he also, like the travel agent has a body and that body is just as much an aspect of the self.

The comedy is further heightened by the deconstructing of what is presumed to be client-provider relationship. The travel agent adopts a stance of subservience but one based on power. She is not unlike many of Houellebecq's pairings where the seemingly dominant partner turns out to be weaker. The powerful Jean-Yves in *Plateforme* is married to woman who prefers to dominate men in sado-masochistic role-plays. The Thai prostitutes in that novel are economically weak but are not without some power over those who exploit them. Here, the verb 'aider' nicely indicates the fact that it is the travel agent who has the power to do something.

The tempo of the exchange speeds up. There is less lingering on the inner thoughts of the narrator. The travel agent then rattles out a further question. The phrase 'à cent à l'heure' is comically inappropriate since tourism is supposed to be about taking the time to enjoy the experience. Furthermore, the speed of delivery suggests that this is not so much a spontaneous response as a learned one. Much of the time, we speak by using routines – the 'comme d'habitude' of the opening sentence. Indeed, it is not just the two party-goers in *Extension du domaine de la lutte* who converse by 'aligner les platitudes'. Indeed, those of us who have been on the receiving end of cold calling are often bemused, for want of a better word, by the machine-gun rattle of a pitch that is being made for the umpteenth time.

What Houellebecq gives us next is a detour on an even bigger scale. Tone and register change suddenly, something made all the more obvious by the break in the text. It is as though we have started to read a different kind of book, told by a different kind of narrator:

> Le dialogue du touriste et du voyagiste – c'est du moins l'idée que j'ai pu m'en faire, sur la base de différentes revues professionnelles – tend normalement à outrepasser le cadre de la relation commerciale – à moins plus secrètement, qu'il ne révèle, à l'occasion d'une transaction sur le matériau porteur de rêves qu'est le 'voyage', le véritable enjeu – mystérieux, profondément humain et presque mystique – de toute relation commerciale.[4]

The text is still dealing with the subject of holidays but it is now adopting a very different approach and one is perhaps tempted to wonder what sort of person reads trade magazines. This is another detour but it is an excursion that allows us to explore the complexity of the first-person narrator's personality, discovering new and contradictory aspects of him that would otherwise remain unknown. As well as being a crude vulgarian, he is an informed amateur with a penchant for intellectualising experience and appreciating its complexities. He is fascinated by the thought that the atypical example may turn out to be more revelatory of the dynamics of the transaction than cases that fit the paradigm more easily. This is because the atypical disrupts and thereby opens up the workings of the commercial transaction to our scrutiny. It reveals the secret workings beyond easily grasped structures and so stands revealed not as unusual but rather as central.

The narrator is putting forward a hermetic vision of society's structures – hence the use of 'secrètement', reinforced by 'mystérieux' and 'mystique'. It is perhaps amusing here but Houellebecq is preparing the ground for later developments in his story by showing that the seeds of cultism are present in many areas of society even though they may not fully flower in them all. Indeed it is a feature of Houellebecq's fiction that characters act in the belief that there is more to reality than meets the eye. Indeed, the way Bruno's will seems to meld with that of his brother in *Les Particules élémentaires* and the exploration of the way the deepest structures of the atom have implications for the way the world functions indicates a world that is more mysteriously complex than we can know.

The belief that there are hidden truths that are perhaps being withheld from us is a necessary ground for the establishment of a cult. Members of

4   *Lanzarote*, p. 9.

a cult will believe that they have been given special access to the secrets of life, secrets known only to themselves or to their leaders. This encourages the acceptance of the authority of elites whose role is to lead. This is not to argue that the narrator here is one of the elite or would like to be. What he does have is a predisposition (a fascination with hidden structures in some ways similar to Michel's interest in the structure of the atom in *Les Particules élémentaires*) that makes him susceptible to cults even if ultimately his scepticism prevents him from joining the Raëlians. Houellebecq allows us to understand how such a thing can come about but he does not advocate it nor does he defend it. To understand course of action is not to promote it.

The mixture of the intellectual, emotional and physical foibles of the character of the narrator create a feeling of intimacy. We feel that we are getting to know him. The contradictory nature the character, his refusal to be pinned down to any simple formula or consistency is perhaps typical of the way we know people in life. They can suddenly surprise us or reveal hidden depths. Indeed, knowing someone is not so much a state as a process. It is a voyage of discovery (echoing the theme of travel in the novella).

We can view the role of the travel agent similarly. It is to explore – and exploit – the psyche of the client, a role that also will obtain in regular commercial operations:

> De son côté, il s'agit – loin de l'application stéréotypée d'une formule de vacances 'standard', et quelle que soit la brièveté de la rencontre – de cerner au mieux vos attentes, vos désirs, voire vos espérances secrètes.[5]

This is something that looks forwards to the methodology of the Thai prostitutes in *Plateforme*. Houellebecq's society is one where the commercial transaction is based on desire that springs from an unmet basic need. This is a modern hunger. It is a very powerful force and it gives the provider considerable power. The characters do not buy food but dreams. The interesting thing is that even though the narrator is aware that this is what is happening, he allows himself to be sold a holiday. The commercial

---

5   *Lanzarote*, p. 10.

transaction, like any conversation, involves a degree of complicity. The client is willing, indeed anxious to have his or her needs met. The transaction is powered by an impulsion, an internal driver that can be strengthened from without. One is pulled in the direction that one wants to go.

Yet impulsions are also dangerous and may with repetition and reinforcement become compulsions. Rudi's paedophilia is a dark and dangerous compulsion. We first meet him having a curious encounter with camels:

> Je me retournai et aperçus Rudi près du troupeau, composé d'une vingtaine de bêtes. Inconscient du danger, les mains croisées derrière le dos comme un enfant curieux, il s'approchait des monstres qui tendaient vers lui leurs cous longs et flexibles, serpentins, terminés par de petites têtes cruelles. Je marchai rapidement à son secours. De tous les animaux de la création, le chameau est sans conteste un des plus agressifs et hargneux. Il est peu de mammifères supérieurs – à l'exception de certains singes – qui donnent une impression de méchanceté aussi frappante. Fréquemment au Maroc, les touristes tentant de caresser le museau de l'animal se font arracher plusieurs doigts. 'J'avais dit à la dame faire attention ... se lamente alors hypocritement le chamelier. Chameau pas gentil ...'; il n'empêche que les doigts sont bel et bien *dévorés*.[6]

This is in certain respects a variation on the opening of the novel and is an illustration of Houellebecq's subtle patterning of his narrative. As before, the narrator has a realisation that something is amiss and moves in order to do something about it. The difference is that this time it is not he who is in a bad situation but his companion who occupies that place by being unaware of what is going on. As he explains a few lines later on: 'je voulais juste regarder', a phase that echoes the mutual scrutinising gazes of narrator and travel agent in the earlier episode.[7] In this instance, the narrator is observing Rudi observing the camels. However, the latter does not see the danger that the narrator is aware of.

Rudi's curiosity is specular. He is fascinated by the strange Other that is the camel just as the narrator's attention is drawn to the strange style of

6   *Lanzarote*, p. 20.
7   *Lanzarote*, p. 20

the travel agent. That is, he is looking at the camels and the monstrosity returns his gaze. The scene is revelatory. The danger that is staring back at Rudi is not just the danger to him also the danger he represents to others. The monstrosity gazing back at Rudi is his reflection. It is an opportunity for him to read himself – just as the travel agent does with the narrator and just as the Raëlians do with prospective cult members through their use of the questionnaire.

The description of the camels as monsters suggests a hydra, a multi-headed danger. The long and flexible necks with the cruel heads are likened to serpents, reputed to fix their prey with their stare so that aware of the danger the latter cannot flee. The description of the troupe of camels may be the narrator's own but one might well wonder if Rudi does not share this vision of horror. Whatever the case, the fact is that Rudi is drawn towards this danger. There is no indication as to why he might want to approach them. The vagueness of the impulse ('only looking') is perhaps part of its power, and also part of the horror. It raises the possibility that Rudi may subconsciously be aware that he is in danger but such is the power the source of that danger exercises over him that he is unable to escape. However, just as a mirror reverses what it presents, so the description of Rudi as a curious child and the camels as dangerous monsters is a reverse image. It is Rudi who turns out to be a threat to children.

For the moment it is Rudi whom we see drawn towards a destructive force. Even though he is an educated man and, like the narrator, knows the difference between a camel and a dromedary, he is ignorant of the danger he faces. It is hidden from him – but not from the narrator who is able to grasp what is going on (the 'véritable enjeu' as he put it earlier). However, the difference between the narrator and Rudi is less than it might appear. Rudi, in peering at the camels is trying to find out more but is doing so in a way that puts him at risk. Physically he is an adult, and yet at that moment he is 'un enfant curieux'. The difference between him and the narrator is only one of degree: both are driven to fill gaps in their experience.

Our curiosity can also be our undoing. The need to know can be reckless. The child has no awareness of what the dangers are because he or she lacks the experience that would protect them. Thus satisfying our thirst for knowledge is a double-edged power that can give us the experience to avoid danger while also impelling us towards danger. At this moment, Rudi is a child, an innocent abroad, despite his knowledge of the biological classification of the camel.

Characterisation of Rudi as a curious child also has more serious implications in terms of how we view future revelations about him when he is drawn into a cult, many of whose members are found to be abusing children. Describing him as 'un enfant curieux', as is done here, complicates and unsettles the conventional picture of the paedophile as an adult exercising power over and preying upon children. Rudi at this moment is a child menaced by a monster whereas later he is depicted in the press as the monster menacing children. However, Rudi is an adult – and this is never denied. The description of him as an 'enfant curieux' is a detail, a piece of information, which we may wish we did not have – a truth about him that we would prefer to ignore. This is because it makes us less able to be comfortable with our judgement. The description of Rudi marks him out as someone who has not fully grown up, who has not fully accepted his role as an adult.

Yet even if we appreciate the complexity of the situation in which Rudi's criminal behaviour is set, this does not make his actions acceptable and it most certainly does not excuse them. The complicity that Rudi seems to see in his victims is nothing of the sort: '"Elle me disait que j'étais gentil, de fois c'est elle qui me demandait de faire minette …" avait-il déclaré aux enquêteurs, sans cesser de sangloter'.[8] This is another example of the lack of responsibility of the older generation for the younger. Rudi seems to think that it is only natural for the younger generation to want to take care of the needs and desires of its elders. It is a horrible travesty of the care and affection Bruno and Michel in *Les Particules élémentaires* have for their grandmothers. The reference to 'enquêteurs' is one more reminder of the importance of investigation in Houellebecq's world even though that does not mean that one will be able to find a satisfactory answer.

Nor is it enough to accept Rudi's protestations and his tears. Aïcha's words should be compared to the way the narrator acts in the travel agency

8   *Lanzarote*, p. 58.

at the opening of the novel. On some respects there are similarities between the two – and also with Rudi looking at the camel. The narrator faced a woman whom he describes as a monstrous composite, just as Rudi is facing the monstrous group of camels and Aïcha will face the moral monster that Rudi will become. The narrator's sense of his own weakness, one that the travel agent could discern, gave the latter power over him. Hence the feeling of fear and hence that smile that he hoped would be 'désarmant'. Unable to do anything about the fear (even though it is within him or perhaps because it is within him), he sought to disarm his interlocutor. Something similar can be seen in the words of Aïcha. The victim, faced with this powerful man, has no alternative. She is not speaking out of desire but out of fear. The only thing that she desires is that the abusive adult will be sufficiently pleased not to hurt her. Here remarks are, like Michel's, meant to be 'désarmant'. The use of 'gentil' is significant too because it is an explicit verbal echo – this time of the scene with the camels. Rudi may think that his victim sees him as 'gentil' but like the camel he is in fact 'pas gentil'. Houellebecq's treatment of the theme shows the brutal reality. Rudi's excuses are not to be taken as exculpation. The reader should see the remarks within a complicated structural framework that shows them for the delusional comforting that they are.

This mingling of pathos and brutality, the tears of a now powerless Rudi in the face of investigators who are now in charge of his destiny, is not comfortable. Indeed, Rudi has again changed status and is back to being a child – this time a naughty child, tearfully facing authority figures. The reader may (or may not) feel some tug of sympathy for the plight of Rudi, but, like Tisserand, we should resist being dragged along by the force of that impulse. In Houellebecq there may be a sense of right and wrong but there is no comforting sense that we know exactly where the border between them can be drawn. It is easy to stray. The wrong can have powerful arguments. Worse still the bad can perform good actions and the good can be bad at times. Indeed, with hindsight, one might well wish that the camel had attacked Rudi. Aïcha might have been spared. The narrator's act of kindness cannot be definitively classified as good. Its value varies.

Indeed our perspective on the narrator is ever shifting. The scene with camels starts by painting him in an apparently positive light. He is concerned for a fellow tourist, though even in that case we might later have cause to wonder about the unintended consequences of this rescue. In fact there is an even more immediate darkening of this positive presentation, an addition of complexity. When the narrator depicts what he imagines the likely reaction of the camel-driver will be, the use of the term 'hypocritement' seems objectively to be unwarranted. There is nothing in the text to confirm that the driver may not have warned the unfortunate customer. Similarly, the italicisation of '*dévorés*' seems to verge on the hysterical. It seems to imply that the narrator thinks that camel-driver is not fully appreciative of the damage done. What we have is an attribution of malice to local workers. Added to this we may note the broken syntax which suggests somehow that the lack of mastery of the incomers' language is somehow a fault, a comical fault – rather than the problem lying with the failure of the visitors to learn the language of the locality.

In short, the attitudes underlying the concluding lines can be viewed as being imbued with the narrator's conscious and unconscious racism. If we allow this, we can see what the text is hinting at: the tourist has been attacked and had her fingers bitten off because she did not adapt to local conditions but behaved as she would with animals in her own country. Oblivious to the possible consequences of her own action or to the idea that her actions, even if well-intentioned, might not be well-received the tourist exemplifies attitudes not far removed from those prevailing in colonial times.

The notion that the locals are somehow inferior and economically dependent on giving service to the incomers is also there. Consequently, when the camel, itself the victim of stereotyping in the way it is described, bites back it is as though it acts on behalf of a suppressed local population which cannot directly oppose the wealthy patrons for fear of the consequences. This is one explanation of the use of 'hypocritement' – the camel driver is letting the camel act as a mouthpiece for his own hatred of the wealthy visitors whose economic strength allow them to lord it over the locals. It is not impossible that the narrator is aware at some level that the expression of regret is in fact covering up a vengeful pleasure that has been fed by resentment.

Any feeling that the narrator might have of being superior to the locals is not justified in any way. At one point he asks Barbara, one of the German lesbians he has befriended: '*You look a good girl. May I lick your pussy?*'[9] His fascination with the two women borders on the predatory though they do not seem to mind. However, the later example of Aïcha should perhaps make us wonder if they were able to be sincere. Whatever the truth of the matter, the important thing to note is that the English that the narrator uses is not accurate. One of the indicators of the supposed inferiority of the camel driver was the broken French used. Consequently, if the imperfect mastery of a foreign language one is obliged to speak (for whatever reason) is a mark of inferior status, what does that say about the narrator? Significantly, Barbara's assent is given in German. She does not need to submit to a language other than her own.

There is another interesting parallel with Rudi. The latter put himself in danger by putting his face close to the camel, which was less docile than it appeared. The use of the word 'pussy' in English indicates, in other contexts, docility and harmlessness. However, given the story's preoccupation with risky and dangerous sex – as exemplified by Félix Faure's death, Rudi's paedophilia and the sado-masochistic swingers' clubs – then there is perhaps reasons to believe that the docility – like the camel – may conceal a threat. The woman's sexual power is both attractive and a threat to the power of men. Michel, as his use of language to 'disarm' the travel agent shows, does indeed feel that women are a threat. Misogyny is never far from the surface. Michel's living out his pornographic fantasies with the two lesbians is an indication of his inability to treat women as equals. It is yet another side to his personal inadequacy.

The scene with the camels darkly foreshadows what is to come. It is prophetic. Prophecy and prophets have important roles in cults, certainly those depicted by Houellebecq. They relate the present to a mythical past

9   *Lanzarote*, p. 42.

and connect it to a future that fulfils a promise. In this they are not unlike the narratives produced by both science and religion, seeking to overcome the flux of evolution by imagining and plotting a straight, undeviating line towards an improved future. Houellebecq's cults succeed by combining the narratives of both science and religion, as the following account of the Raëlians shows:

> J'avais déjà entendu parler de cette secte: elle était dirigée par un certain Claude Vorilhon, ancien chroniqueur sportif dans un journal local – 'La Montagne' de Clermont-Ferrand, je crois. En 1973, il avait rencontré des extraterrestres lors d'une excursion dans le cratère du puy de Lassolas. Ceux-ci se faisaient appeler les Elohim; ils avaient créé l'humanité en laboratoire, bien des millions d'année auparavant, et suivaient de loin l'évolution de leurs créatures. Naturellement ils avaient délivré un message à Claude Vorihon, celui-ci avait abandonné son métier de chroniqueur sportif, s'était rebaptisé Raël et avait créé le mouvement raélien dans la foulée. Une des missions qui lui avaient été confiées était de bâtir l'ambassade qui servirait à accueillir les Elohim lors de leur prochain passage terrestre. Mes informations s'arrêtaient là; je savais que la secte était classée comme plutôt dangereuse, à surveiller.[10]

The above account is an abbreviated but accurate account of the basis of the actual Raëlian cult. Houellebecq is incorporating, not for the first nor last time, a reference to a current phenomenon. Claude Vorilhon is a real person who claims not only to have been given a message but to have been taken to the Raëlian home world. However, the deadpan style which appears to be scrupulous in its attempt to be neutral allows two damaging blows to be landed, blows which are all the more effective for being few. Firstly, the use of 'naturellement' is sly. Used in a conversation it indicates that what follows is organically the outgrowth of what has just gone before. However, when used as part of an account, as here, it indicates that the link is one forged by convention. In other words this is what happens because it is what always happens in these kinds of stories. If Claude Vorilhon's account follows the conventions, then it starts to look like fiction. The Raëlian cult is telling a story in order to obtain donations. The building

10   *Lanzarote*, p. 34.

of the embassy starts to look like not so much an expression of respect as a way of getting adherents to part with money. In short, we are back with the commercial transaction with which the novel opened.

Secondly, there is no change in the cool tone when we get to the last sentence, where we are informed by the narrator that the sect is dangerous and is being kept under surveillance. The word 'surveiller' evokes an important aspect of the gaze – as a means of controlling. Keeping someone under observation is a way of assessing risk and ensuring that norms are not breached.

Vorilhon is a false messiah pretending to be a true witness and in so doing he exemplifies the 'véritable enjeu' of the phenomenon of the cult. His story is accepted by his followers because it taps into their hidden desires. This is a prophet who calls on us to believe because his story is the answer to what we have been seeking. Like the travel agent Raëlianism must let us know that it can provide for our needs. The cult succeeds by establishing in advance what our desires are. It then frames the questions in its prospectus in such a way that it suggests that these desires are normal and, moreover, that the cult will provide a framework permitting us satisfy them:

> Le prospectus que m'avait remis le type, en tout cas, était parfaitement anodin. Baptisé 'ÉVALUEZ VOTRE QUOTIENT SENSUEL', il se composait de questions du genre: 'Vous masturbez-vous souvent?' ou 'Avez-vous déjà pratiqué l'amour en groupe?'; on aurait pu trouver ça dans n'importe quelle numéro de *Elle*.[11]

The text like the cult is 'à surveiller'. It is to be read carefully, its meanings investigated. What many people would consider abnormal or excessive in some way is passed off as 'anodin'. Truth for the Raëlians, as indeed for the narrator, is whatever is acceptable.

The reference to *Elle* reinforces the notion that this questionnaire is about fantasy-fulfilment and indeed marketing. It is like the ones in the magazine, those which inevitably feature on the front cover. They are in reality come-ons and make no attempt to disguise the fact that they are

11   *Lanzarote*, p. 34.

seeking to entice the public. They suggest that sexual fulfilment is something not just that we desire but that we should desire. Indeed the 'déjà' hints that threesomes are something that can almost be taken for granted. It hints that those who have not experienced it are in some ways missing out. In this way what might by some be considered taboo (group sex) or undesirable (masturbation) is normalised – they are made 'anodin'. The magazine and the cult are seeking to shift consensus for their own ends – in the case of the magazine for commercial ends, something which confirms suspicions about the motivation of the cult. The normalising of desire, when applied to group sex and masturbation, serves to re-define what is acceptable, thereby allowing people to indulge themselves.

However, Rudi's version of the acceptable desire is rejected by the rest of society. It is highly unlikely to find such tastes catered for 'dans n'importe quel numéro d'*Elle*'. Yet all he wants is to be accepted. He wants to be at the party – like the narrator in the opening paragraph of the story. An additional way of reading Rudi's looking at the camel as though at a mirror is to take it as an indication of his hunger for knowledge not just about who he is but about where he fits in. He is a man who is tortured by his inability to be accepted. The letter he leaves behind in his hotel for the narrator expresses gratitude because the latter has treated him like a normal human being:

> Je tiens d'abord à vous remercier de m'avoir, pendant ces quelques jours, traité comme un être humain. Ceci peut vous paraître évident; pour moi ça ne l'est pas.[12]

This changes the view that we might have formed about Rudi. He appeared to be a man who kept himself apart, who seemed unwilling to join in the activities of his friends. His disappearance from the hotel comes as a surprise to both us and to the narrator. This is because we have been viewing him from the outside. His is a consciousness to which we do not have access, unlike the narrator's.

---

12   *Lanzarote*, p. 49.

The letter is a way of allowing us to enter Rudi's inner world. It is darker and more troubled than we could have expected. It is as dark and alien as the landscape of Lanzarote itself. As a policeman and as a Belgian, he has problems being accepted. He locates the source of these problems in the problem of identity. As a Belgian, he sees himself as part of a country that lacks cohesion. It is 'raté'. It is a monstrosity, a combination of two ethnicities that cannot co-exist. They stare at each other across an ethnic divide – like Rudi at the camel – each seeing in the other something dangerous. The two fundamental parts that make up Belgium are not compatible. The sympathy that should link them is absent.

Rudi seeks relief from the tensions he experiences by visiting sex-clubs with his wife:

> Ma femme et moi, lors des deux dernières années de notre mariage, fréquentions assidûment ce qu'il est convenu d'appeler les boîtes pour couples 'non-conformistes'. Elle y prenait du plaisir, et moi aussi. Pourtant, au fil des années – et je ne sais pas exactement pourquoi – les choses ont commencé à mal tourner. Ce qui était au départ une fête joyeuse et sans tabous s'est peu à peu transformé en un exercice de dépravation sans joie, avec quelque chose de froid et de profondément narcissique.[13]

Already the later predicament of Rudi the paedophile is foreshadowed. His sexual tastes depart from what society expects. Furthermore, they are not stable. They change in nature and in ability to satisfy his needs – or distract him from them. Like a cancerous cells, Rudi's tastes mutate. As Michel Djerzinski would put it, they are 'configurations mutables'.

In a curious way, non-conformism and conformity are not so much contradictory states as a spectrum. The non-conformist activities in the clubs have their own rules and norms. Once these are established, they cease to satisfy those whose desire is inherently transgressive. Thus Rudi's initial act of breaking with accepted norms finds itself enclosed within a newly formed 'boîte', structured by a set of rules that set their own limits and lay down their own acceptable criteria. Thus the act that was initially

13   *Lanzarote*, p. 50.

so appealing to Rudi becomes a matter of routine and loses its power to excite.

The thrill of danger may be gone but the danger itself remains – as indicated by the use of the adjective 'narcissique'. More perhaps even than that, 'froid' indicates a deadening of feeling. Rudi's narcissism (a feature that can also be seen in the episode with the camels) points to the danger of self-absorption by reminding us of Narcissus who perished through paying too much attention to himself. His fascination with himself draws him into the darker reaches of the pool wherein his image is reflected. It is as though he is drawn to the more dangerous aspects of himself and so he perishes when he crosses the boundary separating the human world from that of the pool. Sexuality is a powerful force and has considerable power, disrupting the settled order. Rudi is a man of order but who is fascinated by the possibility of breaking that order. In becoming a policeman, he is perhaps expressing his desire to share the more settled values of the majority. He has a need for strong boundaries, to live within them, accepted by others. He wants norms of behaviour that he can enforce. At the same time, he is tempted towards the non-conforming practices of the sex-clubs. In short he is Belgian in more ways than one in that his personality is fractured. His torment is as much internal as anything else.

Thus the same acts which once appeared to set Rudi and his wife free from the constraints of convention begin to pall. Stronger and stronger stimuli are required to maintain excitement. They seem not to exalt the spirit but rather to degrade it. The acts themselves have not changed, just the way they are experienced. What seems to be happening is that they allow Rudi and his wife to venture away from conventional expressions of desire into parts of their personality that turn out to be dangerous to their existence as a couple. This is a voyage of discovery that reveals that dreams are really nightmares. What is a first strange and exciting becomes strange and frightening.

Their voyage of discovery is not a journey to a destination but a detour – a 'dépravation'. The fantasist has to return to reality at the end. This is what happens to Rudi and his wife. They cannot turn aside from the reality of their bodies. Indeed, it seems that reality starts to invade and destroy the quality of their fantasy:

Nous n'avions pas su nous arrêter à temps. Nous en sommes venus à des situations humiliantes où nous nous contentions d'assister en spectateurs passifs aux exhibitions de monstres sexuels parfaits, dont nous ne pouvions plus faire partie, vu notre âge. C'est probablement même cela qui a précipité ma femme – c'était quelqu'un d'intelligent, de sensible, de profondément cultivé – vers les solutions monstrueuses et rétrogrades de l'islam. Je ne sais pas si cet échec était inéluctable; mais en y repensant – et cela fait deux années que j'y repense – je ne vois toujours pas comment j'aurais pu l'éviter.[14]

The use of 'su' instead of 'pu' conveys something important in French: Rudi and his wife made an unwise choice. It was lack of willpower that was their undoing. As a result they outstay their welcome. It is their choice that makes their failure inevitable. They who had sought fulfilment outside the norms of conventional society are no longer able to remain full members of their new coterie. The result is humiliation – a denial of worth. Rudi and his wife are reduced in status, no longer doers but passive observers. They can only watch what others choose to place before them. In a sense they are in bondage to the displays of the others whose more active status is stressed by the use of 'exhibitions'.

However, the most striking terms in the passage are 'monstres' and 'monstrueuses', particularly because Houellebecq uses them in contrasting contexts. Both words come from the Latin verb meaning 'to show' and are thus linked into the specular theme of the passage. Monsters are things which inspire awe or fright in the beholder. They make their impact by the way they look. This is not the first time the novella exploits the theme of monstrosity. Earlier, Rudi was looking at the camels as though at a monster. If the camels show what lies ahead of Rudi, the sexual athletes are a vision of what he and his wife have lost. Thus he and his wife are looking at what they once were.However, 'monstres' and 'monstrueuses' are contrasted – the first applies to the other swingers and the second to Islam. Yet it also suggests that links between the two ways of life might be greater than either might like. The other adjective coupled with 'monstrueuses' and used to qualify Islam, 'rétrograde', also conveys narcissism of a kind since it suggests

14 *Lanzarote*, p. 50.

a retracing of, and absorption with, one's past. It is not unlike the staring of Rudi at the camels. Nevertheless, this is not the primary meaning of 'rétrograde' in this context. Rudi uses it to explain why Islam is monstrous in his eyes: it is going backwards and is fighting against the libido.

Furthermore, Islam is submission not just to God but also to the community of believers. However, the 'non-conformistes' are similarly a community and Rudi's contravention of communal norms takes place within a community of rule-breakers. Furthermore, this community humiliates and marginalises Rudi and his wife when they transgress a rule that is inviolable: they must be young and attractive. If Islam is submission to the will of a deity, then belonging to the community of swingers also represents submission.

This is the price we pay in order to connect to others. We cannot live alone – a theme explored in *La Possibilité d'une île*. Islam, like the sex-clubs, fulfils a human need to belong. At its most noble, it is a suppression of the selfish demands of the ego so as to create a harmonious polity. It seeks in this way to avoid the kinds of tensions that are tearing Belgium apart and which are wracking Rudi, the rule-breaking policeman. This explains the strong appeal of Islam for Rudi's wife. She returns to the fold. He, however, cannot conform. His sex-drive is too strong.

Ironically in trying to avoid what he considers to be the monstrosity of repression, he indulges in monstrosity of another sort, a sexuality that goes beyond even the wider boundaries to be found in the sex clubs. Yet his need to belong remains. In joining the Raëlians, he can find acceptance. Sexual freedom and acceptance of his proclivities are not, however, what Rudi sees as the primary reason for joining. He himself attributes it to a desire for immortality. It is important to note that both here and in the later *La Possibilité d'une île*, it is not the physical body that is given immortality but rather thoughts. The physical body is too monstrous because it is subject to gross appetites. Although Raël indulges the body, in reality the aim is to suppress it. It is the mind that will achieve immortality not the body. It is a subtle and curious form of repression of an essential part of us. In effect, what Raël is doing is to suppress by neglect. He allows his followers to indulge the body but he has no care for its preservation. Thus

Raëlianism is in the long run just as inimical as Islam to the desires of the flesh. The immortality offered to Rudi also liberates him from the hunger that ravages the physical body with its insatiable needs.

Raëlianism is innovative because it harmonises religion and science, instead of making them antagonists:

> Allant plus loin, Raël propose l'immortalité des pensées et des souvenirs – par transfert du contenu mémoriel sur un support intermédiaire, avant réinjection dans le cerveau du nouveau clone. Cette proposition, il est vrai, relève davantage de la science-fiction, dans la mesure où on n'a pour l'instant aucune idée des bases techniques de sa mise en œuvre. Quoiqu'il en soit, il paraît étrange de qualifier de 'secte' une organisation qui apporte des réponses aussi novatrices et techniciennes à un ensemble de problèmes traités par les religions conventionnelles de manière beaucoup plus irrationnelle et métaphorique.[15]

As the previous chapter demonstrated, Houellebecq's science is not escapist fantasy. He raises the issue of science fiction only to forestall objections. He seeks to maintain a scientific discourse that focuses on problems and which outlines the shape a solution might take. Thus Rudi's argument is plausible because although it is impractical at the moment, he is analysing the situation in a way that appears to make scientific sense and which appears to sketch out a possible solution. The problems and their solutions are the sorts of things that Michel in *Les Particules élémentaires* might consider and they are issues raised in more detail in *La Possibilité d'une île*.

Rudi's account focuses on the difficulty of transferring consciousness. His analysis reveals a certain conception of the human being, based on the way computers operate. The body is little more than the carrier and consciousness is the software that can be uploaded to another carrier as needed. Indeed, the conception of humans as modelled on the computer would not surprise us if it were articulated by the Michel of *Extension du domaine de la lutte*. As a software systems expert, the computer as processor of knowledge would provide him with a ready analogy. Such a conception downgrades the body to being little more than a vehicle, like the car

15   *Lanzarote*, p. 51.

that Bruno had such difficulty in controlling. As such, the body can be maltreated or even discarded in the interests of consciousness – hence the indulgence and indifference to the body that is a feature of the cult.

However, while Raël may believe this and encourage his followers into a sect where such a notion underpins their aspiration, the novella, like the other fictional works of Houellebecq, also confirms the importance of the physical body. It is an integral part of what it is that makes us human and Rudi's account of Raëlianism seems to disavow the very physicality that makes him who he is. His indulgence in sex and indeed in paedophilia (a vice that has to be hidden from prying eyes) is a covert acknowledgement of the power of his physical appetites. Raëlianism is haunted by the physicality which it indulges in order to repress.

This is where we see the danger of the sect. It is possible that Rudi is not primarily a paedophile. He is first and foremost someone who feels the tremendous power of sex. Sex is a transgressive force, a disruptor of boundaries and conventions. Raëlianism seeks instead not to inhibit the force of sex but rather to let it be. It adopts an attitude of neglect, by legitimising everything. This is the point of the questionnaires. They simply accept our sexual desires, the primal urges that flow through us like an irresistible energy. However, these desires do not differentiate between objects. Something of this can be seen in the activities of the narrator and the two lesbians. The latter are not, as he points out, exclusive. The power of sex is such that it does not allow boundaries to be drawn. Any person can be the object of desire.

This is in effect what happens:

> Il apparut bientôt que l'ensemble des raéliens, mariés ou non, avaient des rapports sexuels très libres, et que des orgies réunissant jusqu'à une centaine de personnes étaient régulièrement organisées au siège de l'association, à Bruxelles. Les enfants des adeptes n'étaient pas tenus à l'écart de ces scènes; ils étaient parfois simples spectateurs, parfois participants. Aucun témoignage de violence, ni de contrainte à l'égard de enfants, ne put être relevé; mais on avait clairement affaire à un cas d'incitation de mineurs à la débauche.[16]

16   *Lanzarote*, p. 57.

This is another detour, 'détournement de mineurs'. Something wrong is happening, something is taking place where it should not. The second half of the above quotation might appear exculpatory, an ironic comment on the way newspaper reports jump to conclusion without evidence. There clearly no indication that the children were threatened or constrained. Is the text inviting us to be more permissive? I think not. The comparable case of Aïcha shows that the children may have complied out of unarticulated need to placate. We should also remember that the narrator himself was quick to condemn the neglectful non-intervention of the camel-drivers when tourists were under threat from the animals. Letting things run their course is not acceptable in either case. It is sufficient to recall the scene in *Les Particules élémentaires* where the infant Michel is found slipping around on his own faeces, to realize that it is not enough to refrain from coercing children. Something more is required in the way we treat children. The narrator's comment, which places compulsion against incitement to evil, leaves a moral gap which the reader is invited to fill.

Indeed our discomfort increases when we read: '"Quand des amis de papa restaient dormir à la maison, je montais leur faire une pipe", rapportait Aurélie douze ans'.[17] Underlying Aurélie's remarks is the expectation that it is the role of the child to take care of the adult and to minister to his or her needs. This is a reversal of the normal order. The newspaper reports of the abuse are so bathetic, in their mixture of the comic and the appalling, that they are bound to make readers feel very uncomfortable. It would be easier if the reports could be dismissed as purely a satire on the tabloid sensationalist style. The content is shocking but the style is even more so. In fact it is monstrous. It is the amalgamation of elements that our culture has declared should be kept apart. The power of sex to break down barriers is clearly exemplified, nowhere more so than in the effect on the reader who finds that his or her capacity to maintain a sense of proportion has been undermined. There is the incongruity of the imagery. The tiny girl trying to minister to much larger men evokes a topos of humour that cannot be denied but which we are reluctant to admit. This is a subject

17   *Lanzarote*, p. 57.

that we do not want to laugh at. The name, 'Aurélie', suggests that the girl comes from a reasonably well-off, well-educated milieu and so the horror is located in a place where we are reluctant to see it. The use of 'papa' in its familiarity shocks with its betrayal of trust. Finally, the use of 'pipes' shows a knowingness that one would hope was not the case. The girl has forbidden knowledge. It is the corruption of innocence. This is a child who has had her curiosity satisfied – without her consent. In this respect, the description of Aurélie is clearly linked to the description of Rudi as 'un enfant curieux' – a linkage that only serves to increase our sense of the complexity of the personal tragedies unfolding.

Transgression is thus not a positive force but a troubling one. It has the same power to disrupt that comedy has. Hierarchies and roles are destabilised. But the upheaval is not necessarily beneficial. The disruptive enlightenment of the narrator when he realizes that he has missed out on the New Year celebrations is quite different in effect from the enlightenment of Aurélie about sexual activities. In the first case the narrator has knowledge of what he lacks while Aurélie has knowledge that she should lack.

The sect is supposedly dedicated to enlightenment – as evinced by the message to Vorilhon and the alliance with respectable science – but it is actually something very dangerous. Nevertheless, Houellebecq is certainly not advocating that we should foster ignorance – though the way characters in the other novels use 'stupéfiants' indicates his acknowledgement that this is a powerful attraction – but rather that we should be aware of what a dangerous force we are playing with. The urge to satisfy our curiosity by acquiring knowledge is a powerful force but one that is morally neutral. At its most harmless, it is used in the travel industry as the basis on which choices can be encouraged. The travel agent assesses a customer's needs and works out how to cater to them but really does not care what the reason for any particular choice is. There is no moral stance. This is also the point about organisational structures in general, not just the ones that manage information. Like Desplechin's gatherers of facts, they never question the worth of what they are doing and are driven more by economic values than by a sense of inherent value. This is exploited to comic effect in *Plateforme* where the mechanisms of quality assurance and enhancement are applied to prostitution – and the result is improved profits and the prospect of greater expansion. The only values that count are monetary.

The Raëlians operate using the same kind of mechanism – and their aim is also to gather money. Their questionnaire is a formal device that could be used in many different situations. In this respect it is indeed 'anodin' and fairly mainstream. That is its point. The aim is not to collect information about future members but to allow members to acknowledge what it is that they desire. Its aim is to tease out those desires and hence acceptable. Raëlianism is about the acknowledgement and indeed privileging of one's hidden desires. It allows Rudi and people like him to feel that what they are doing is acceptable. It makes the monstrous tolerable in the eyes of those who are monstrous:

> Ce qui frappait le plus les commentateurs, c'était l'attitude des prévenus. En principe le pédophile est un être honteux, prostré, parfaitement vaincu. Lui-même révulsé par ses propres actes, il est terrorisé par le caractère incontrôlable qu'il découvre en lui. Soit il se réfugie dans une abnégation farouche, soit il se précipite vers le châtiment, se vautre dans la culpabilité et le remords, exige d'être soigné, consent avec reconnaissance à la castration chimique. On ne retrouvait rien de tel chez les raéliens: non seulement ils n'éprouvaient aucun remords, mais ils se considéraient en quelque sorte à la pointe de l'évolution des mœurs, et affirmaient que la société irait mieux si tout le monde avait l'honnêteté de se comporter comme eux. 'Nous avons donné du plaisir à nos enfants. Nous leur avons appris dès le plus jeune âge à éprouver du plaisir, et à donner du plaisir aux autres. Nous avons pleinement rempli notre rôle de parents', telle était à peu près leur position commune.[18]

As was the case with the earlier comment from Aurélie, this quotation plays with our moral expectations. The paedophiles protest that they were merely carrying out their social and parental duty. The popular image is cast aside in favour of a chilling self-justification. This is how it may appear to the reader but it is possible that the Raëlians believe what they say. As members of a group of like-minded people, tending only to have contact with other like-minded people, they will not have been challenged or forced to

---

18 *Lanzarote*, pp. 57–58.

question such statements. Rather, they will have tended to confirm each other in their beliefs.

However, we must also consider the context. The narrator is not giving us the thoughts of the Raëlians but their words, words that were reported in the press. Thus, the comments are not necessarily a reflection of the intentions of the parents at the time but rather could be an attempt to give an account of their actions that will resonate with people. By claiming to be acting in the interests of the children, they seek to mitigate their crime by making it appear that they had good intentions and, more significantly, that in this respect they were acting no differently from the majority of people. They are trying to put an acceptable gloss on their actions. It does not matter that most people will not believe them: this is their story and they will repeat it because it depicts them as good people who are misunderstood. The Raëlians are masters of presentation. The purpose of the questionnaires in the resort is to find out how they can influence people. Indeed, the whole Raëlian project is a clever story well presented.

The parents are doing the same here. They speak not out of conviction but for effect. They seek control of the terminology, giving it an interpretation that will include them. What they did, they claim, was what any good parent would have done and, far from being ashamed or contrite, they feel that they are ahead of the rest of society in terms of childcare. If characters like Jane in *Les Particules élémentaires* and Daniel1 in *La Possibilité d'une île* are deficient parents because of their lack of care for their offspring, then the paedophile parents raise troubling moral questions. By claiming to care for their children and to be doing the best for them, they are bringing a moral argument that few would accept but which is difficult to refute in the terms in which it is framed. If it is a positive moral value to take care of children and bring them pleasure while encouraging them to bring pleasure to others, then the Raëlians have a point. Why, then, does the argument not hold? Why does it not have the effect intended?

One reason is that they did not really expect to win the argument in the first place. The intended audience is not so much the general public as themselves. These words are to keep up morale. Like, Michel in the Thai massage parlour in *Plateforme*, they want to be able to think of themselves as doing good. However, the general consensus is not with them. As was evident in the case of Aurélie, the innocence of the child was corrupted. This is precisely what is wrong here. The children are not being respected as children but are treated as instruments of pleasure. Indeed, to a certain extent the parents also see themselves as instruments of pleasure. To see children in this way is to fail to recognise their worth. They are degraded. Indeed, the swingers' clubs frequented by Rudi and his wife are places where adults are similarly degraded. They are commodified and treated as consumable objects of pleasure. When Rudi and his wife are too old, too worn out, they are dumped on the sidelines like refuse. Houellebecq does not comment directly on the moral issues raised in his novels but the mosaic of incidents is laid out in such a way as to encourage the reader to examine the issues in depth.

The humour is truly what some would consider 'edgy'. This is because the novel is positing fractures in the social consensus by pointing to their possibility in an area where there would appear to be unanimity. Virtually no-one would defend paedophilia. Yet the argument of the parents shows that there is room for disagreement over what constitutes proper care of children. They show that in fact there is no fixed, immutable standard by which we can judge the rightness or wrongness of actions. Such matters are a matter of social agreement. Thus there is a moral consensus over how children should normally be treated. Marc Djerzinski is acting in accordance with that consensus when he takes the infant Michel from his mother. The reader does not condemn this as a kidnapping – which in a sense it is. Rather, it is seen as a fit and proper response.

However, this moral consensus is still a matter of agreement – no matter how strongly people might feel about it. Those who fail to be guided by that consensus face sanctions – in a way that is no different to what happened to Rudi and his wife in the swingers' club. What is right is enforced by power. Morality, lacking a foundation, can only exist by agreement but that agreement needs instruments of enforcement. Our actions need to be policed – and, as Rudi shows, the police also need to be policed. This need for enforcement, whether it be by expulsion from the community or other means, shows that in the community there is always real or possible dissidence. A community is not as homogenous as it might at first seem but is full of tension, as is Belgium. Morality is inherently unstable because its dependence on enforcement within a community makes it subject to change. It evolves not smoothly but as a result of tensions between different points of view that struggle to establish hegemony – an 'extension du domaine de la lutte'. Thus we have 'l'évolution des mœurs'.

Houellebecq exposes the mechanism by which such change is brought about in society. The Raëlians are a group whose numbers are sufficiently large to be noticeable and who contest the norms of society. This gives them an advantage over an individual, who is powerless, no matter how good the argument, because a single person can be ostracised and demonised. He or she can be treated in such a way that they come to accept how wrong they are and how right the rest of us are. There are shades of *1984*, in the phrase 'avec reconnaissance' from the above extract. Just as Winston Smith comes to a realisation that he loves Big Brother, so the individual paedophile may come to be grateful for having the libido, the power of sexuality, removed from him even if it is by castration.

A group on the other hand is a different matter. A group does not just provide mutual support. It can also set itself up as being an alternative to or an extension of the prevailing moral conformity. It seeks to enlarge the concept of the acceptable not render the categories of the acceptable and unacceptable redundant. This is perhaps its crucial function. We see this here. The Raëlian parents articulate a notion of proper parenting that seeks not to abolish the category but to extend the range of actions that may be included in it. In order to succeed, all that is necessary is for the group to articulate a coherent or rational case around which followers can rally and round which they can rally others who will accept if not share their beliefs. It is not necessary for the case they make to be true, but for it to appear a reasonable extension of prevailing beliefs. If they succeed in mobilising a critical mass of the like-minded or indulgent, they will acquire not just tolerance but the ability to enforce their newly-accepted beliefs.

Knowledge operates in the same way. Science is a matter of consensus. The 'enquêteurs' are not seeking absolute truth – something which is apparent from the way science is treated in *Les Particules élémentaires*. Paradigms or frameworks of belief can be overthrown. Science operates on the basis of what scientists accept to be true and that can change. It is not the disinterested seeking after truth, a godlike vision that Houellebecq's novels eschew.

Rather it consists of accepted ideas and candidates for acceptance – those dissident or heretical ideas that aspire to achieving acceptance.

Thus what matters is not the truth but sharing enough to establish consensus. Thus it is not a surprise to find that Vorilhon has joined forces with the scientist Richard Seed to pursue their interest in cloning. The point is that they are united by common interest though not by total agreement: 'Seed se proclamait toujours, pour sa part, chrétien et méthodiste'.[19] Houellebecq's isolates are so unhappy because they are alone. Even the Michel of *Les Particules élémentaires* is a singular figure. Houellebecq's insight is that it is not Michel who changes humanity but his followers, those who latch on to his insights and are able to extend their reach. The ideas of Michel are only successful when there is a group of believers ready to advance the cause. Vorilhon and Seed are more powerful as allies that they are as individuals and Vorilhon's value to Seed is that he can deliver the backing of a group who also believe in cloning.

Thus the advancement of science progresses rather in ways that resemble the cults that appear to be its very antithesis. That the grouping which results is most likely a heteroclite grouping is not important. What matters is that it works – and the group will work as long as the members make common cause. However the limits of this are exposed when the accused paedophiles cast themselves in the roles of caring and responsible parents. In so doing they go too far in re-defining what good parenthood entails. They claim that they acted as they did because they sought to do what they believed was for the best for their children. This is too much to accept and the cult members are arrested and put on trial for the way in which they act. The tension between their definition of responsible parenting and that of the rest of society is not unlike the tension that Rudi identifies as being inherent in the two communities that comprise Belgium.

Houellebecq is not putting the case for paedophilia so much as revealing how it fails to integrate itself. He also shows how it might have succeeded in integrating itself. However, it fails to do so and the pro-paedophile

19   *Lanzarote*, p. 55.

arguments prove to be another detour. Soon the classic image re-asserts itself:

> Rudi lui-même avait l'air serein et presque heureux. Je remarquai sur les photos qu'il portait maintenant de grosses lunettes carrées à montures noires; ce n'était pas très judicieux. Avec son ventre, sa moustache et ses grosses lunettes, c'était lui qui évoquait le plus nettement l'image classique du pervers pédophile. L'opinion publique était très remontée contre les accusés, de manifestations avaient lieu presque chaque jour devant le Palais de justice. Des voix s'élevèrent, comme à chaque fois, pour demander le rétablissement de la peine de mort.[20]

Houellebecq captures the moral panic that can grip a society. In so doing, he reminds us that 'évolution des mœurs' does not have to be in a progressive direction. Bringing back the death penalty is 'rétrograde'.

It is somewhat disconcerting if plausible that Rudi and the group are being judged on the basis of the appearance of one man not on principles. The image of Aurélie may make us favour a guilty verdict but on the other, the sight of the mob baying for blood is not one that can have our backing. Mob justice is not an enticing prospect but our disquiet does not sit easily with our knowledge that Rudi and his friends are unrepentantly guilty. The dynamics of the community, the uncomfortable alliances evoked earlier, are just as much at work here. We can find ourselves sharing a common purpose with those whom we might otherwise have little truck. Furthermore, the call for the death penalty shows how priorities can be usurped. On the back of this hard case, a retrograde step will be taken. The death penalty is not a fitting punishment for child-abuse but the latter can used to whip up emotions in order to re-instate it.

Moral certainty is not something that Houellebecq's fiction provides. What it does is show the mechanisms by which we understand the issues and the factors that can influence our judgements. Reason is not an impartial search for truth. It is an instrument that can be used to make a case and attract support. Throughout the novel, Houellebecq has sought to lay bare the ways in which the society of persuasion works, the ways in which we

20   *Lanzarote*, p. 60.

collude with those who seek to influence us, to take us away from where we are going. Such a society works because we are ready to let ourselves be taken away. The ending of the novel, with its oblique reference to the verdict that takes place when Michel is on holiday is far from being anomalous. It is a fitting end to a novel which is about people being taken for a ride.

CHAPTER 4

Plateforme: Writing about Sex-tourism

Tourism is a combination of two elements: travel and hospitality. The travel element is an example of Delorme's '*voyage circulaire*' since tourism involves visiting places before returning to the point of origin (home) so that there is a lack of full engagement with a locality and its people. The level of engagement is further skewed by economic advantage since the tourist purchases hospitality. A visitor who comes from abroad may engage on terms whereby everything that is specific to the locality is accepted totally or, more likely, there may be a refusal to accept anything considered too foreign so that the local has to re-create at least some of the elements with which the incomer is familiar – as when restaurants in Turkey, for example, advertise a full English breakfast. The tourist has an economic advantage which the local provider must acknowledge.

Sex-tourism exploits that economic advantage. It allows the visitor to exercise power not just over services but over bodies. It exploits the welcome at its most intimate and caring. It devalues the exchange between people of different cultures and makes of it a commercial transaction. Heidrun Friese's describes the ideal of hospitality in the following terms:

> Hospitality enacts the deferment of definite belongings and evolves in a space that neither demands sacrifice nor the 'pure gift', nor calculates greedy use or predatory exploitation.[1]

One can trace point by point the ways in which the sex-tourists in *Plateforme* violate the principles of hospitality outlined by Friese. Indeed one of the characteristics of Rudi in *Lanzarote* is his inability to defer gratifica-

---

[1]   Heidrun Friese, 'The Limits of Hospitality', *Paragraph*, Vol. 32, No. 1 (2009), pp. 51–68, p. 64.

tion. Rather he gives in to his impulses, encouraged by the cult. However, the fact that Rudi's offenses are multiple and repeated suggests that giving in to impulse is not a way of satisfying desire. Desire continues and the person who gives in to it is locked in another '*voyage circulaire*', returning to an urge that cannot be assuaged. Deferment implies a placing of value in the future as a repository of desire. In general, Houellebecq's characters are more concerned with present exploitation that with exercising responsibility towards the people who come after them. Their more immediate needs are primary.

Sex-tourists act similarly, behaving as though they had greater rights in the locality than the indigenous population. They act both as though they belonged there and as though the place belonged to them. The local people are abused in the very places where they live and have to sacrifice their integrity in the faceof the wealthy foreigner's need for satisfaction. It is a feature of Thai prostitution that it functions on the basis of gift-giving. However, gifts are in reality the payment for services rendered. They are certainly not pure gifts in Friese's sense. It is this abuse of hospitality that arouses indignation among those opposed to it. Sex-tourism is a predatory practice exercised on the relatively weak by the relatively strong. It takes unfair advantage of the host.

Until Houellebecq made his remarks on Islam, published in the literary review Lire in September 2001, it was his treatment of sex-tourism that exercised many critics of the novel *Plateforme*. As late as 1 September 2002 its English translation was reviewed in the *Sunday Times* under the heading: 'Adventures in the sex trade'. The reviewer, Peter Parker, was not well-disposed to the novel – 'A book that could have been drole turns out to be merely dull' was his conclusion. A year earlier, when the novel appeared in France, *Le Monde* of 27 August 2001 (just before the furore caused by his remarks on Islam) had a dossier of articles on the theme. It claimed on page 8 that 'La parution, Vendredi 24 août, du nouveau roman de Michel Houellebecq, *Plateforme*, a relancé le débat sur le tourisme sexuelle. Depuis le premier congrès mondial contre l'exploitation sexuelle des enfants, à Stockholm, en 1996, la France a adopté des lois facilitant les poursuites'. On page 11 of the same issue, *Le Monde* argued that we should not try to hide from the seriousness of problem: 'On n'est pas dans l'exotisme léger, mais dans le sordide et la misère, l'exploitation et la violence, bref, dans une des formes modernes de l'esclavage'.

Houellebecq is touching on a subject that arouses strong feelings among liberals just as his views on Islam do among believers. As *Le Monde* shows, the subject engages and scandalises. It raises issues of law, justice and retribution. Yet when retribution is visited on the sex-tourists at the end of the novel, there is no sense of rightness, only of an even greater wrong. One violation of hospitality has been met with another. The novel is not a polemic but, as *Le Monde* might put it, a debate, disturbing our preconceptions and not seeking any comfortable consensus or sense of fairness. It takes the reader on a tour of a world that is unfair.

Nonetheless, attempts to achieve fairness are hard to resist. If Houellebecq's detractors feel that they have been maligned, then the supporters of Houellebecq are no less forthcoming in their complaints. Dominique Noguez, a friend of Houellebecq, claims *Le Monde*'s approach was:

> Réduction de la littérature à la sociologie (glissement d'une fiction où il est question entre autres, de tourisme et de sexualité à la réalité du tourisme sexuel), réduction d'un phénomène à ses dérives criminelles, réduction de ces dérives à ce qu'ils appellent improprement la pédophilie: ce genre de journalisme réduit tout à sa taille (petite) et à ses obsessions (grandes).[2]

It is not, Noguez maintains, a fair argument. He points out that sex-tourism is not the same as paedophilia and castigates the newspaper for using rhetoric to confuse the two. Noguez is aware that language is not about truth but about effect. Just as the paedophile parents nay be using the press to create a certain image even if it is primarily for their own consumption, so *Le Monde* is doing the same with the phrase: 'la France a adopté des lois facilitant les poursuites'. It seems to be addressing readers with an established point of view, confirming and comforting them in their rightness. *Le Monde* is not so much speaking out as reinforcing conformity of thought and reinforcing a cosy feeling of self-righteousness. The narrator of *Plateforme*, another Michel, notes a similar phenomenon. At one point, he explains how he

---

2   Noguez, p. 176.

admires the skill of Julien Lepers on *Questions pour un champion* because of the way that he seems to establish a connection with the guests on his show, making them feel that he is genuinely interested in them and in the role that they play in their families and the wider community. Julien Lepers makes the contestants feel that they are an important part of a larger whole: France. The upshot is: 'On retire en général de l'émission l'impression que les gens sont heureux, et soi-même on se sent heureux et meilleur'.[3] It is important to note the 'meilleur' at the end. People want to be thought of as being good. Indeed being thought well of is one of the driving motivators of characters in the novel.

Le Monde is doing the same in that it is helping people to think well of themselves. But to do so, these right-minded people need to have someone against whom they can compare themselves. In this instance it is Michel Houellebecq but more generally it is the sexual predators who are the scapegoats. Thus readers of *Le Monde* feel good at the expense of others. Again, Houellebecq himself recognises the way the outsider is pushed to the margins in order to make way for what people feel is more acceptable. Michel falls asleep and wakes up to in the small hours to find that the television is broadcasting a programme abut silurids, a kind of catfish. Michel remarks:

> La suspicion populaire qui entourait les silures semblait en quelque sorte se communiquer à ceux qui se consacraient à leur pêche; la petite confrérie des pêcheurs de silures était mal acceptée au sein de la famille plus large des pêcheurs.[4]

Normal fishermen reject those who fish for silurids and thereby enhance a sense of community. In a similar way, normal parents define themselves against paedophile parents by excluding the latter. The danger in *Lanzarote* lies in the fact that in their statements in the media, the paedophiles stake a claim to being included. They seek to define good parenting in a way that will include rather than exclude them. In the case of the fishermen, the issue

---

3   Michel Houellebecq, *Plateforme* (Paris, J'ai lu, 2001), p. 13. All references are to this
     edition.
4   *Plateforme*, p. 15.

is more subtly articulated. Those who fish for silurids are not excluded so much as marginalised. The programme is broadcast at a time when few might see it but it is still broadcast. The message that this seeks to convey is that the concept of France is sufficiently large to encompass even such as these. It is an inclusive vision that is being propagated.

Noguez makes a simple enough case – and the use of 'dérives' suggests how the evolution of the argument or line of thought is distorted. But he too is seeking to make the best possible case. However, one of the principal characters does indulge in paedophile activity (as defined by the law) when he has a sexual relationship with his children's babysitter back in Paris. Consequently, despite Noguez's protestations, the novel does depict paedophilia – though not in the way that *Le Monde* might imply.

While Noguez is correct to point out the false trail of reason that in *Le Monde* links *Plateforme* with the sexual exploitation of minors, where he is on less sure ground is in his condemnation of the link between the novel and sociology. It is easy to see why he takes the line that he does: he is trying to defend Houellebecq against claims that his book is promoting practices many would condemn. In fact there is a very strong link between sociology and literature, particularly in *Plateforme*. The novel clearly is interested in how society constitutes itself. It is not just that this novel is fulfilling the traditional function of holding a mirror up to society, it looks at issues that might be expected to interest a sociologist: sexual habits and practices, religion, reading habits, criminality, violence, culture, economic organisation and so forth. Indeed, the novel includes a presentation by a sociologist on trends in tourism – just as *Les Particules élémentaires* gives a brief account of Max Planck's contribution to science. If sex-tourism derives from the combination of sexual activity and tourism, *Plateforme* is the outcome of a meeting of novelistic form with elements taken from the discourse of sociology.

However, we need also to take Noguez seriously when he stresses that Houellebecq is writing a work of fiction about sexuality and tourism. It is not a work of pure sociology. More generally, *Plateforme* explores the borderline between modes, incorporating other fictional and non-fictional discourses. This is what gives it its power. An illustration of this effect occurs early in the novel:

De retour dans le salon, j'allumai le téléviseur, un Sony 16/9e à écran de 82 cm, son surround et lecteur de DVD intégré. Sur TF1 il y avait un épisode de Xena la Guerrière, un de mes feuilletons préférés; deux femmes très musclées vêtues de brassières métalliques et de minijupes en peau se défiaient de leurs sabres. 'Ton règne n'a que trop duré, Tagrathâ! s'exclama la blonde; je suis Xena, la guerrière des plaines de l'Ouest!' On frappa à la porte; je baissai le son.[5]

The narrator does not just tell us that the television was switched on but gives us make, model and features as well. Rather than give a description based on shape, material and colour such as might be found in a nineteenth-century novel, he uses a style that belongs to the twenty-first century. This is how objects are presented in a consumer society – in a showroom or a brochure or in the speech of a salesperson. We relate to domestic goods in terms of their features which are presented as desirable ones. We purchase the object precisely because we have been persuaded to desire it. This link between desire and possession is also the dynamic of the sex-trade.

Indeed, the images that are shown on the television when Michel switches it on show that Xena and Tagrathâ are objects of sexual desire. What we desire, we seek to possess. This can be manipulated by inculcating in us knowledge of what is desirable. There are approved objects of desire and that approval is bound up with issues of authority. Thus the television, a desirable model in itself, becomes the vehicle of further models of desire, making known further objects which we are permitted to desire. Xena and Tagrathâ are presented for the delectation of the spectator, in this particular instance the male gaze.

Furthermore, since these are women who are about to fight, Houellebecq associates violence with desire. Both violence and desire have the power to excite. Significantly, the two women are strong and dominant and this part of their fantasy appeal. Nevertheless, they are mastered by the masculine gaze. At the same time there is a circulation of desire between them, a hint of lesbianism (confirmed by a reference on the next page) but one that is the stuff of male pornography – though since the television channel Michel is watching is the equivalent of BBC1, this is very much soft-core lesbianism, the sort that can be tolerated by if not approved of by the authorities – on the spectrum of behaviour it can be tolerated in a way that Rudi's cannot. Thus desire is authorised. And it is precisely that which is at issue in the fight. Xena is seeking to overthow Tagrathâ, to end her reign, her authority. It is fitting that the knock on the door, which necessitates the muting of the desires emanating from the television, indicates the arrival of Aïcha, the lover of Michel's father – a man killed because Aïcha's brother did not approve of that desire and used physical force to end it.

What the above extract also shows is the way the discourses circulating in the world shape our thoughts. Michel's description of the television is not in his own words but in language that derives from advertising or the language of salespersons. Our thought processes are not sealed off but feed on the thoughts of others. Thinking is a hybrid process, a combining of ideas that may well originate outside us. Just as the main characters in *Les Particules élémentaires* are ethnically mixed, the result of outsiders mingling their genes with the native population, so are our thoughts and desires a mixture of what is ours and what comes from others. Michel frequently mentions what he and others eat. Our minds are also fed thoughts. What our minds take in is important to way we experience life.

The description of the television may be little more than regurgitation. However, our thinking is derived from the way we process what is fed into our heads. At the beginning of the second chapter, Michel is visited by the investigating officer. Michel gives his opinion of police-work:

> La gendarmerie, trop accaparée par les tâches administratives, souffrait de ne pas avoir suffisamment de temps à consacrer à sa véritable mission: l'enquête; c'est ce que j'avais pu déduire de différents magazines télévisés.[6]

The policeman agrees that this is true. Michel's opinion is based on television which purveys both fiction and documentaries and in the process, breaking down the barriers between the two – 'magazines télévisés'. The real and the fictional are permeable. Crucially, Michel's thoughts exemplify

---

6   *Plateforme*, p. 17.

the way that we navigate our way through life. We interpret phenomena through knowledge acquired.

This is why Noguez is so upset by the way *Le Monde* has dealt with the publication of his friend's novel. The way in which the paper portrays the issues risks prejudicing the reception of the book. What we take in shapes what we think. But he also knows that counter arguments can be put into the reader's mind – hence his protest. It is as though Xena and Tagrathâ continue to challenge each other in the columns of *Le Monde* but with pens not swords.

Noguez's intention is to force us to take sides by showing that there are sides. Without such a challenge readers will accept the authoritative opinion of the writer just as Michel accepts what television reveals about police procedure. This is in effect a surrender or submission by the mind – a significant act given the importance of Islam as a theme in the novel. Islam means 'submission'. Our thought processes, therefore, oscillate between acceptance and rejection of ideas.

Given that it is a time when we relax, tourism is an activity where the temptation to let ourselves be guided is inherent. We accept being told what to do, what to see. We are content to follow an established text. Andrea Loselle argues that in extreme cases the text supplants the object:

> An extreme example is the battlefield marker. Try as hard as one might to find it, there is no referent, because the battlefield is just a field, not the event that took place on it. When we visit battlefields we are motivated by the language in a brochure or guidebook, by the language inscribed on the marker itself, or by a history book.[7]

Thus, in the novel the tourists take guided tours where not only do they not have to take any decisions as to itinerary or other activities but they are told what it is they are looking at.

---

7   Andrea Loselle, *History's Double: Cultural Tourism in Twentieth-Century French Writing* (New York, St Martin's Press, 1997), p. 4.

On the trip to Thailand, Michel's reading material contains guide-books – information that shapes his experience of the places visited. In his case, however, he does not accept what he is told but is inclined to contest it:

> S'il se proposait dans son principe de préparer au voyage en Thaïlande, le *Guide du Routard*, émettait en pratique les plus vives réserves, et se sentait obligé dès sa préface de dénoncer le tourisme sexuel, cet *esclavage odieux*. En somme ces routards étaient des *grincheux*, dont l'unique objectif était de gâcher jusqu'à la dernière petite joie des touristes, qu'ils haïssaient. Ils n'aimaient d'ailleurs rien tant qu'eux-mêmes, à en juger par les petites phrases sarcastiques qui parsemaient l'ouvrage, du genre: 'Ah ma bonne dame, si vous aviez connu ça au temps des z'hippies!...'[8]

What is noticeable in the above is the absence of a Thai perspective. There is a clash of two points of view, that of the narrator and that of the authors of the *Guide du Routard*. They have diametrically opposing views on Thailand and sex-tourism. Casey Blanton speaks of 'the tendency of all travellers until recently to carry with them the unexamined values and norms of their own culture and to judge foreign cultures in light of those habits of belief, thus establishing a kind of control over them.'[9] The reduction of a whole civilisation to 'ça' devalues it and the quotation attributed to the authors of the guide assumes a proprietorial air. It is as though they resent sharing with the newcomers. The Thais have no say in the matter. Their silence shows their disempowerment.

But it is not just the Thais that are disempowered. Houellebecq's words are a subtle and trenchant critique of a particular form of travel writing which is really an attempt to exert power over tourists, to keep them dependent and docile. The latter are guided to particular places and then told that it is their presence in such numbers that is ruining what they have come to admire. The guide, however, lays claim to a purer and thus superior form of knowledge that by its nature is denied to tourists. At the same time, it

8 *Plateforme*, p. 54
9 Casey Blanton, *Travel Writing: The Self and the World* (London, Routledge, 2002), pp. 7–8.

discourages the independence that would enable tourists to go off on their own and author their own experiences. The irony is that the hippies were just as much an excrescence, an interpretation of life and an accompanying lifestyle that has little to do with Thailand.

Tourism is an experience of dominance and submission – a theme picked up elsewhere in the novel in the exploration of the S and M scene in Paris. We have already seen in the discussion of Friese's remarks quoted above that the tourists in *Plateforme* exemplify an exploitative form of tourism, one that subjugates the local environment to the wants of the tourists. The latter are not free either. The tour guide Sôn keeps her little flock on a tight rein as they follow their prescribed trajectory through Thailand. At the beginning of the seventh chapter, the tourists are taken to a border region where they encounter refugee Karen from Burma: 'Karens bien, estima Sôn, courageux, enfants travaillent bien à l'école, pas de problème. Rien à voir avec certaines tribus du Nord, que nous n'aurions pas l'occasion de rencontrer au cours de notre périple; et, d'après elle, nous ne perdions pas grand-chose'.[10] These are what Michel refers to on page 70 as '*Karens ordinaires*' as opposed to '*rebelles karens*' – ordinary, decent Karen as opposed to rebel Karen. Although refugees – an ironic twist on the theme of tourism since they have also travelled but not for pleasure and the hospitality they receive is not commercially purchased nor, most likely, willingly granted – the Karen '*ordinaires*' are given approval because they fit in or have perhaps been forced to fit in with the norms of the dominant society, hence Sôn's singling out the performance of the children at school.

Against these tamed Karen are set not only the rebels seeking independence but also the Akkha people. Once again Sôn pronounces:

> 'Akkhas mauvais, souligna Sôn, avec énergie: à part culture pavot et cueillette fruits, savent rien faire; enfants travaillent pas à l'école. Argent beaucoup dépensé pour eux, résultat aucun. Ils sont complètement nuls', conclut-elle avec un bel esprit de synthèse.[11]

10   *Plateforme*, p. 69.
11   *Plateforme*, p. 69.

However, this judgement is questionable because of the way in which it is said. The clash in register between the formal 'un bel esprit de synthèse', which would evoke for French people the school and higher education, and what Sôn actually said (the highly informal 'Ils sont complètement nuls') ironises her judgements. Sôn's rather fractured French invites the reader to wonder if she worked hard at school. If she had, she would not be speaking so ungrammatically. Sôn appears not to care about her level of French. Michel suggests that one of the reasons she does not eat with the tourists is that 'les longues discussions en français semblait lui peser un peu'.[12] She is not taking advantage of native French speakers to improve her skills – interestingly, acquiring knowledge of language structures is associated with eating. There is about her something of the self-satisfaction that irritated Michel in the *Guide du Routard*. She is comfortable in the rightness of her knowledge. The Akkha are outsiders and so are not valued.

Sôn, however, is not an outsider. In fact she is the mouthpiece for the values of the society in which she lives. Indeed, what seems to fit Sôn for her job is not so much her skill in language but that she is quite content to pass on received opinions that she has learned. She accepts the ideas that have been fed to her. This is why she can be given this role despite her language skills. She is ideologically sound, having acquired from her education what is in fact truly essential for success. Accepting the consensus is what counts. A skilled communicator expressing controversial opinions would soon be in trouble – a fact borne out by the controversy that follows Houellebecq around.

With Sôn, we can grasp the silliness and prejudice of her received ideas. Her language draws attention to itself and her unwillingness to improve her grasp of French ensures that this state of affairs will continue. On the other hand, where the surface of the language is smooth, the mind is led more easily. Noguez is aware of this. He describes the language as slipping ('glissement') from one idea to another even though logic does not justify it. His protest lays bare the rhetorical strategies that are being used to have

12   *Plateforme*, pp. 72–73.

the reader think in an approved fashion – just as Sôn attempts to have her tourists think in the approved fashion.

Noguez may protest about the way *Plateforme* has been treated but what is significant is that it has aroused this much passion. Houellebecq for good or ill deals with subjects about which people have strong opinions – even if those opinions are but well-rehearsed platitudes imbibed from sometimes dubious sources. Other subjects will arouse less feeling. Thus, while there may be controversy over sex-tourism, there is no fuss about the way local people are depicted for the benefit of tour groups or about the economic and structural structures that underpin the industry. Yet perhaps we should be perturbed. The fact that the tourists in *Plateforme* are offered French cuisine may not register with the reader as being more than a humorous detail showing that tourists only want what *Le Monde* might well call 'light exoticism' – 'l'exotisme léger' – rather than a full engagement with the locality. However, it does have serious implications as Yvon Pruche argues:

> Et que penser des troupeaux de touristes qui peuplent les Club Med, Fram et autres Eldorados? Ils dorment mangent visitent et dépensent entre eux, au seul bénéfice des tours opérators étrangers ou de la nomenclature des pays d'accueil. Sans contact réel avec la population, instruits comme il faut par des guides stéréotypés, ils sont pourtant les premiers à juger – fort de pouvoir dire: j'ai fait tel ou tel pays.
>   Et le *Guide du routard* qui incite les paumés à se rassembler dans des établissments des petits copains expatriés, ou entre eux dans quelque coin isolé ... Est-ce stupidité ou amoralisme? Accepter de dépenser de l'argent à la hauteur de notre niveau de vie, chez eux, pour eux, c'est entre autre leur offrir une alternative à la prostitution.[13]

This is the same kind problem that *Plateforme* deals with. The tourists do not patronise sufficiently the local but expect that something of their

---

13   Yvon Pruche, *Amours siamoises: la prostitution en Thaïlande* (Aire-sur-l'Adour, Atura, 2001), pp. 40–41.

home country will greet them on arrival. So, food and drink may have to be imported which denies benefit to local workers.

The rest of Pruche's remarks are also pertinent to Houellebecq's perspective, notably his references to the facile judgements based on controlled information and the self-satisfied, onanistic complacency of the authors and followers of the *Guide du Routard*. What is clear is that sociological perspectives enrich and inform *Plateforme*. It adds considerably of our appreciation of Houellebecq's novel and helps explain his work's popularity and relevance if we grasp this. His work is not reduced, as Noguez fears, but rather shown to be important – and insightful. If there is slippage from talking about sex and tourism to sex-tourism, from fiction to reality then it is encouraged by Houellebecq's own narrative practice and by the way sex-tourism itself draws on the telling of stories in order to function.

Sex-tourism is imbued with the devices of fiction and sociological studies of the phenomenon not only draw on accounts given by the women and their clients but reveal the importance of story-telling within the trade. People on both sides of the transaction tell stories about themselves. Seabrook remarks:

> Men come to Thailand with money, and this gives them a feeling of great power and strength. It is strange how many are transformed in their own imagination, into victims: they, the conquerors, the invincible, wind up feeling they have been cheated, their 'innocence' taken advantage of, their good-heartedness exploited. It is a strange reversal of reality.[14]

What is important to men is not just what they experience but what they tell themselves about that experience and about themselves as participants in it. Their complaint is that they have not been treated fairly, something they can only believe if they edit out the privileged position they enjoyed with respect to the women in the first place.

The women too tell themselves stories about what it is they are doing:

---

14 Jeremy Seabrook, *Travels in the Skin Trade: Tourism and the Sex Industry* (London and Chicago, Pluto Press, 1996), p. 35.

The women in the sex-industry often regard themselves as small entrepreneurs. They believe that prostitution offers them a chance for upward mobility, the opportunity to meet a farang, to be kept by or marry a rich man, which will raise their status. Although this can happen, it is rather rare.[15]

A farang is a foreigner. Cohen supports this:

> They generally see themselves as 'working with foreigners' (tham ngan kap farang) and at least pretend to be insulted if treated as prostitutes. While it may be argued that this is simply a device to preserve their self respect, it also draws a line of social distinction between themselves and the girls working in brothels.[16]

Fictions are part of the way both parties relate to each other and to themselves. Sometimes awareness breaks through. Greg, a client from from New Zealand says in an interview with Seabrook: 'The bars, it's theatre, it's showbusiness. They're good actresses, that's one of the qualifications for the job.'[17] Greg's comments on the theatrical elements in Thai sex-tourism are of interest because they take us back to *Plateforme*. Desire operates through spectacle and role-playing – something foreshadowed in the references Houellebecq makes to the television and the Xena serial.

The theatricality of the sex-trade is quite specific. Indeed the thin line between fiction and reality is explored in the proposed scenario Michel proposes for a porn film. The story involves Bob, a young American student, and Sirien, a young Thai woman from the north of the country. They meet when Bob accidently ends up in a brothel, having been led there by drunken friends:

> Bob ne l'avait pas touchée, il s'était contentée de la regarder de ses beaux yeux bleu clair et de lui parler de son pays – la Caroline du Nord, ou quelque chose d'approchant. Ils se voyaient ensuite plusieurs fois en dehors du travail de Sirien,

---

15   Seabrook, p. 80.
16   Erik Cohen, *Thai Tourism: Hill Tribes, Islands and Open-ended Prostitution: Collected Papers*, Studies in Contemporary Thailand, 4 (Bangkok, White Lotus Press, 1996) p. 256.
17   Seabrook, p. 22.

mais malheureusement, Bob devait partir pour achever sa dernière année d'études à l'université de Yale.[18]

This drips saccharine sentimentality and could come straight out of a romantic novel or screenplay but for the odd discordant note – the reference to North Carolina and to Sirien's work. The scenario is another mixing of modes of writing, combining discourses that are normally kept strictly separate. Things get even more absurd with the description of Sirien waiting for Bob:

> Sirien attendait avec espoir tout en satisfaisant aux exigences de ses nombreux clients. Quoique pure dans son cœur, elle branlait et suçait avec ardeur des Français bedonnants et moustachus (second rôle pour Gérard Jugnot), des Allemands adipeux et chauves (second rôle pour un acteur allemand).[19]

The juxtaposition of elements creates a clash of registers as mighty as that between Xena and Tagrathâ. One finds it hard to believe in the purity of a woman who has so many clients and who goes about her job with such enthusiasm. Perhaps she enjoys it? Or perhaps she does not place too much faith in Bob's return. In any event the scenario is plausibly ridiculous right down to the realisation that an American will have to have a starring role in such a film and the French will only get a supporting role as will the Germans – though Michel can think of no German actors.

The story proceeds with the return of Bob, the intervention of the Americans including a role for Jane Fonda, as an American woman in charge of a humanitarian charity against the sex-trade. There is a battle with the forces of evil – the Chinese mafia and some Thai generals – ending with a battle on the streets of Bangkok before the end. The assigning of a role to Jane Fonda is an example of Houellebecq's mischievousness – but one that will only work if you appreciate the actress' stance at the time of the Vietnam War and the importance of American soldiers on leave from Vietnam in fuelling the sex-trade. Her role as Barbarella in her husband, Roger Vadim's

18 *Plateforme*, p. 109.
19 *Plateforme*, p. 109.

film of the same name is a further point to be considered. Gérard Jugnot is very highly-paid screen actor who is an officer of the Légion d'honneur. The idea that he might have a bit-part in a porn movie is so incongruous as to be hilarious but it remains an uneasy mixture of the real and the unreal – not to mention the surreal. English readers may well call to mind the later film career of Olivier, particularly his role in *The Betsy*.

The overall effect of Michel's fantasy is to heighten the reader's awareness of a sordid reality that illusion may veil but can never get rid of. That reality surfaces in the description of the rather unlovely clients of Sirien. Seabrook's study illustrates the complex psychological play that story-telling gives rise to in Thai prostitution and shows how the ugliness of the client is an essential ingredient:

> 'There is no man living,' says Seri vehemently, 'who is so old, so ugly, so disagreeable, whose flesh hangs in repulsive folds, whose breath smells worse than the fumes on Rama IV, who does not somewhere, somewhere in his mind, believe that he is lovable.' This is the Thai woman's secret. This is why she will pick the most unattractive feature, the baldness, the paunch, the drooping kueh and make it the object of her particular attention; as though the most ugly aspect of him were what she most admires. It is irresistible.[20]

This is why the Thai women so successfully target the features of the men that western society and women deem unattractive and by that judgement deny them love. The men believe that failure to give them the love they feel they deserve is fundamentally unfair. The Thai women are able to redress the balance and restore a sense of justice. The men now feel that they are being treated as they deserve. Therein lies the women's power and what Cohen calls 'the often despondent dependence of apparently powerful, well-to-do *farangs* upon the apparently weak and submissive Thai women'.[21] Thus the economically disadvantaged seek out and exploit the weaknesses of those who are more powerful than them – a strategy that reaps immediate benefits while failing to address the structural inequalities that subordinates Thai women (and others) in the first place.

20   Seabrook, p. 118.
21   Seabrook, p. 321.

In this respect then, the novel and sociology give similar accounts of the phenomenon. The Thai women in *Plateforme* behave in ways that are documented by researchers such as Cohen and Seabrook. The same goes for the clients and their motivations. Towards the end of the novel, Michel describes some elderly German sex-tourists:

> Plus que tout autre peuple ils connaissent le souci et la honte, ils éprouvent le besoin de chairs tendres, d'une peau douce indéfiniment rafraîchissante. [...] Il est rare également qu'ils fassent de la gymnastique, qu'ils entretiennent leur propre corps. En général ils mangent trop, boivent trop de bière, font de la mauvaise graisse; la plupart mourront sous peu.[22]

These are the unlovely specimens that Thai women will be able to play to. They are unlovely but need love. Cohen talks of how the clients often try to maintain a relationship at a distance through letters. He describes the 'dismal personal predicament and sexual distress of the girls' *farang* correspondents, the roots of which have to be sought in their life-situations'.[23] In short, what drives the sex-tourism phenomenon is the existence of a pool of Western men deprived of satisfying relationships – a lack which Thailand with its well-developed home prostitution service is in a position to remedy.

As Cohen points out above, the Thai women do not consider themselves to be prostitutes. They do not sell their bodies. Rather they extract sums of money in the form of presents. In other cases, they will spin a story about having to support dependent relatives. Beth, a charity worker, comments:

> There is often a whole family depending on them and that may include brothers as well as parents, younger sisters and brothers. I'm always surprised how many say they have adult brothers who do nothing and expect to be kept by them. Quite a lot also have children.[24]

22   *Plateforme*, p. 350.
23   Cohen, p. 321.
24   Seabrook, p. 87.

Consequently, fiction is an essential element in the way sex-tourism functions. Its commercial aspects are articulated around story-telling. The Thai women project to the male clients a story of their power, desirability and loveliness and tell them a story that portrays the women themselves as abject and in need of their caring. The purpose of this is to arouse sympathy and gain economic advantage.

Houellebecq's account of the phenomenon matches this. After sex with Michel, the masseuse Sin tells her story. The first-person narrative shows how Michel responds – it is a story for him:

> J'appris qu'elle avait trente-deux ans. Elle n'aimait pas son travail, mais son mari était parti, la laissant avec deux enfants. 'Bad man, dit-elle: Thaï men, bad men.'[25]

The story concludes:

> Dans quelques années elle pourrait arrêter, et retourner vivre dans son village; ses parents étaient âgés maintenant, ils avaient besoin d'aide.
> Au moment de partir, je lui donnai un pourboire de deux mille bahts; c'était ridicule, c'était beaucoup trop. Elle prit les billets avec incrédulité, me salua plusieurs fois, les mains jointes à la hauteur de la poitrine. 'You good man' dit-elle. Elle enfila sa mini-jupe et ses bas; il lui restait deux heures à faire avant la fermeture.[26]

Sin fits the typology identified by Beth. Houellebecq's character could appear in the books by Seabrook and Cohen, telling her story. She does not ask for money directly. Instead she works by implication and manipulation. She tells Michel that unlike the other girls she does not spend her money foolishly but rather saves it up so that she can retire to look after her parents. She implies that as soon as she has enough, she will go back home. Consequently, any gift will help towards getting her out of the sex-trade and will also help the aging parents.

Michel's reaction is interesting because instead of positive feelings, he has very negative ones. He has given more than he should. It is a ridiculous

25   *Plateforme*, p. 117.
26   *Plateforme*, pp. 117–118.

action. It is as though his impulse is always to blame himself rather than to credit himself for doing a good action. It is this lack of belief in himself that is the source of Sin's power, a lack of belief that finds an echo in her 'incrédulité'. Is Sin's disbelief genuine or feigned? Is it an act, designed to make Michel feel good – the flattery that Thai women were especially good at? If he is convinced of his own inadequacy, her act aims to convince him that she at least believes in his goodness – even though she had never expected to encounter such generosity. The value of Michel's gesture is somewhat undercut by the final line. It indicates that Michel is aware that the basic conditions under which she must live have not been changed. Sin needs to move on to her next clients – clearly the money he gave is not the solution to her problems. Her advantage is only that of the supplicant and the economic conditions that trap her in her way of life remain.

In this novel Houellebecq attributes the demand for sex-tourism to the failure of the Westerners to form mutually satisfying relationships at home, something that Cohen also points to when he speaks of the clients' 'dismal personal predicament and sexual distress'. Thus they seek validation from the Thai women. Houellebecq sees this existential dimension as being more general:

> C'est dans le rapport à autrui qu'on prend conscience de soi; c'est bien ce qui rend le rapport à autrui insupportable.[27]

This is a bleak realisation, at once a comment on relationships with others and about the self. Houellebecq's characters think a lot but they do not think about the self. It is as though they do not have a self to ponder. They muse on the world and think about other people but at heart they are empty shells. There is no essence to which they can be true. We are only our actions in the world and our relationship to other people. Human beings are bodies that are sited in relation to other bodies. It is from this that we derive the meaning that we give our lives. How other people treat us determines our vision of ourselves. Whereas the tourists who frequent sex-workers will by

---

the nature of the transaction have their psychological and physical needs taken care of, Houellebecq's characters cannot be so sure that interacting with others will necessarily be a positive experience. The second part of the quotation is pessimistic since it assumes that what will be reflected back to us will be a knowledge that we cannot bear. Michel's constant drinking and consumption of sleeping pills show him to be some-one who seeks oblivion. His father used physical activity for the same purpose:

> S'il avait fait tant de sport, m'avait-il expliqué une fois, c'était pour s'abrutir, pour s'empêcher de penser. Il avait réussi: j'étais persuadé qu'il avait réussi à traverser la vie sans jamais ressentir de réelle interrogation sur la condition humaine.[28]

Michel and his father are all too aware of the human condition. We have no values or certainties within ourselves and attempts to form relationships with others will not bring the feelings of worth that we crave. Thus pursuing love becomes not a meaningful goal but a source of further problems: 'Séduire une femme qu'on ne connaît pas, baiser avec elle, c'est surtout devenu une source de vexations et de problèmes'.[29] Indeed, there seems to be little place for love. Sexual relationships are reduced to anonymous seduction without any meaningful connection. Consequently men prefer to go to prostitutes in order to get sexual relief but not to Western prostitutes whom Michel calls 'de vrais débris humains'.[30]

However, Michel believes that this phenomenon increasingly affects wealthy western women. As they become more and more involved in their careers, they will adopt masculine habits: 'elles trouveront plus simples elles aussi, de payer pour baiser; et elles se tourneront vers le tourisme sexuel'.[31] The problem, then, is one that concerns both sexes in Western countries even if for the moment it is primarily the concern of men unwilling or unable to cope with the evolving status of women in society. Women's roles are changing and they are no longer the home-makers who sought to keep their husbands happy. Thai women are prepared to meet this need.

28 *Plateforme*, p. 67.
29 *Plateforme*, p. 142.
30 *Plateforme*, p. 142.
31 *Plateforme*, p. 143.

There are, then, two aspects of the problem. On the one hand there is the unhappiness of people who cannot form meaningful and mutually sustaining relationships in advanced Western societies and on the other there is the unhappiness of reactionary men who cannot conceive that women are equal human beings and who would prefer to dominate the opposite sex, proclaiming their belief that this is what women really want. Michel quotes the views of a Mr Sawanasee, a marriage broker interviewed in the *Phuket Weekly*:

> There seems to be, ..., a near perfect match between the Western men, who are unappreciated and get no respect in their own countries, and the Thaï women who would be happy to find someone who simply does his job and hopes to come home to a pleasant family life after work. Most Western women do no want such a boring husband.[32]

He goes on to contrast what Western women want when they advertise in the personal ads with what Thai women want. The Westerners want the sort of attractive personal and social skills that none of the men in the novel, with one notable exception, exhibit. The Thais want domesticity and security. He concludes, as Michel points out, by cheekily suggesting that he is really helping Western women by catering to the old-fashioned desires of men. There is something Swiftian in the line of argument. It starts from the reasonable propositions that Western women want something more than to be domestic chattels while Thai women would find that the security of Western marriage a big improvement on their lot in Thailand. However, Mr Sawanasee ends up arguing that brokering marriages between Western men and Thai women is ultimately serving the best interests of Western women. It is the sort of 'glissement' that Noguez protested about, the railroading of the reader's thoughts by a cunning use of rhetoric. The difference is that Houellebecq does not intend us to accept meekly such a caricature of domestic bliss. Indeed the extent to which Michel accepts it is also debatable. When Seabrook and Cohen quote, they efface themselves and when they put their own point of view, it is with sincerity. As we have

32   *Plateforme*, p. 124.

seen, viewpoints and arguments in *Plateforme* are treated ironically. Michel reframes Mr Sewanasee's arguments by using the phrase 'non sans culot'.

Yet he has quoted the article to Valérie to explain why Western men prefer Thai women. So is he agreeing or disagreeing with the article? It is impossible to say. Certainty is impossible in a Houellebecq novel. Indeed, the sex-tourists we encounter – Robert, Lionel and Michel himself – seem unlikely to be providers of domestic security and a happy family life, though this not impossible, at least in the case of Lionel. Consequently, the image of Western men that Mr Sawanasee presents needs to be treated as something of a fantasy.

Among the male characters, the exception would appear to be Jean-Yves, Valérie's boss. He is attractive, dynamic, fit (he takes care of his body) and has a successful career that gives him a good income. However, his desirability functions as a commercial commodity. In a sense he is the male equivalent of the Thai sex-workers. He is pursued, however, not by another woman but by another company. A secret rendezvous and a wooing leads to a divorce from one employer and an enhanced relationship with a new one. He uses desire to acquire money and material reward and to enhance his status within the economically dominant group to which he belongs. Yet his personal relationships are not good and reach a particularly low point when he seduces the baby-sitter even though she is underage.

What Houellebecq's novel shows is that it is the emotional deficiencies of the European and the economic difficulties of the developing world there that fuel sex-tourism. He is aware of the misery that lies behind the sex-trade but equally he recognizes that there is something too deep for it to be eradicated easily. Steven Daniell comments that:

> Michel Houellebecq's third novel, *Plateforme*, looks at a society that is becoming devoid of meaning. As the story unfolds, it becomes apparent that this emptiness threatens not only materialistic Westerners but also the anticapitalist forces desperately trying to forestall globalization, especially in the name of religious or political ideology.[33]

33　Steven Daniell, '*Plateforme*', *World Literature Review*, 76 (3–4) (Summer–Fall, 2002), p. 110.

One way in which this emptiness shows itself is that those who voice opposition to this trade are shown to be as superficial as those who indulge.
Houellebecq poses the ethical question but does so in a way that shows the
extent of the problem. Hence, as we have already seen, his criticism of the
Guide du Routard shows a self-satisfied complacency and he dismisses
the writers as 'connards humanitaires protestants'.[34]

During the tour of Thailand, a discussion of sex-tourism arises. Josiane
objects to what she sees as economic exploitation of the poor. Michel
points out that he paid a reasonable price, what he could have expected to
pay in Paris, and Robert opines that he may have paid too much. In this
scene, reasonable points are made but in a way that robs them of efficacy.
As with the arguments of the paedophile parents in *Lanzarote*, there is a
lack of concern for the other person that points to the absence of a moral
dimension. The Thais are treated as commodities and denied their just
status. Yet those who see the moral dimension are not treated sympathetically. Josiane shouts and does not listen to others and at one point appears
ready to hit Robert, himself a rather unpleasant character who seems to
enjoy the discomfiture of others. Typical of the exchange is:

> Josiane tremblait de tous ses membres, elle commençait à m'inquiéter un peu.
> 'Eh bien! glapit-elle d'une voix suraiguë, moi ça me fait vomir qu'un gros porc
> puisse payer pour fourrer sa bite dans une gosse!
> – Rien ne vous oblige à m'accompagner, chère madame ...' répondit-il calme-
> ment.[35]

Josiane may occupy the moral high ground in the eyes of many, if not most
readers but her unreasonable delivery robs her argument of force. The words
are delivered as though by a raving lunatic. More seriously, she commits the
mistake of over-stating her case. Her use of 'gosse' is not warranted. We are
not dealing with paedophilia. The prostitutes that the characters encounter
are young but they are certainly not children. As Noguez points out, sex-
tourism is often portrayed as though that were its mainstay. Paedophilia

---

34   *Plateforme*, p. 55.
35   *Plateforme*, p. 75.

does take place in the novel but, tellingly, back in Paris. Consequently, Josiane is wrong on this point and this weakens her stance.

Robert replies with a witticism. It hits home because it implies that Josiane is acting in a totalitarian way seeking to impose her own moral vision on others. He seeks to establish his own moral superiority by claiming that he is not forcing her to adopt his values. Robert is arguing that there should be a tolerance. His wit is an attractive characteristic that complicates and enriches the way he is portrayed. Nevertheless, it would be hard to argue that Houellebecq is on Robert's side. The latter is presented as a rather sleazy, predatory individual. He is a racist who is also probably impotent. Thus his plea for tolerance is fine but in this particular instance it is hard to justify. Does the reader really think that Robert should be left to his own devices? His witticism that seeks to establish him as an upholder of liberty and freedom of choice ignores what the novel has already shown us of the poverty that forces women into prostitution. Yet Josiane is depicted as a shrill, interfering busybody. The moral and ethical position is complex.

The difficulty of establishing an ethical consensus is demonstrated on a later occasion when another one of the group, Sylvie, explains that she would not go to Burma because that would be to give economic help to an odious regime. However, actions based on an ethical stance can be challenged by someone whose ethics support a different viewpoint – just as Xena challenges Tagrathâ. Robert comments:

> 'Personnellement, j'ai cessé d'aller en Espagne après la mort de Franco', intervint Robert en s'asseyant à notre table. Je ne l'avais pas vu arriver, celui-là. Il avait l'air en pleine forme, toutes ses capacités de nuisance reconstituées.[36]

This is once again a witty sally but as the extract suggests, Robert is speaking not to voice his convictions but to stir up trouble – though he is the sort of person who would be likely to boycott Spain. Whether we like it or not, supporting fascism is an ethical stance. Not everyone will agree – and that is the point. There is no pre-given value system and those that we attempt to build are flawed in that they lack consensus. Thus they enter into com-

36 *Plateforme*, p. 80.

petition with each other and become places of contestation rather than concerted action. Robert's assertion is absurd – and that is the point – but it also points up the fact that Sylvie's position is just as shaky.

The debate between Robert and the others is not just about values. One reason for it being so difficult to identify sympathetically with the position of one or other character is that none of them have any real substance. Robert speaks as he does not because of a profound conviction that reflects who he really is but because it is a stance in relation to other people. He does what he does for effect. He is an exhibitionist. In this he is like other characters in Houellebecq – particularly Daniel1, the hollow man who is a professional mimic. In a sense, Daniel1 is prefigured by the people in *Plateforme* who think by re-circulating the thoughts of others rather than by coming up with new and original ideas. Indeed it may be impossible to do so. As we have seen, Michel in *Les Particules élémentaires* succeeds in overcoming the existing scientific paradigm not by a fresh thought but by synthesising thoughts from other areas of knowledge. Human beings are derivative creatures, using and re-using what is to hand.

Yet we long to know that what we are doing is right and to have it acknowledged as fair, just as Michel in the massage parlour longs to be seen as a 'good man' when he gives Sin a large tip. Yet it is perhaps the need to be seen to be acting ethically that is the more important of the two. The tourism debate resurfaces back in Paris when Jean-Yves takes over responsibility for a chain of tourist resorts with the aim of re-launching them. A sociologist, Lindsay Lagarrigue, has been hired to compile and present a report on what the public wants in a package holiday. He is supposed to propose solutions to the current crisis. However, what he presents is far short of that:

> Il commença par leur distribuer un dossier très mince, surtout composé de graphiques avec des flèches et des cercles; sa serviette ne contenait rien d'autre. La première page était constituée par la photocopie d'un article du *Nouvel Observateur*, plus précisément de l'éditorial du supplément vacances, intitulé: 'Partir autrement.'
> 'En l'an 2000, commença Lagarrigue en lisant l'article à haute voix, le tourisme de masse a fait son temps. On rêve de voyage comme d'un accomplissement individuel, mais dans un souci éthique.' Ce passage, qui ouvrait l'éditorial, lui

paraissant symptomatique des mutations en cours. Il bavarda quelques minutes sur ce thème, puis invita l'assistance à concentrer son attention sur les phrases suivantes: 'En l'an 2000, on s'interroge sur un tourisme respectueux de l'autre. On aimerait bien aussi, nous les nantis, ne pas partir seulement pour un plaisir égoïste; mais pour témoigner d'une certaine forme de solidarité.'[37]

These arguments are the same as those made by Sylvie and Robert. Both want to show solidarity but the fact that this solidarity is based on opposing ethical viewpoints undermines the very value of solidarity. Lagarrigue's views are without foundation and completely undermined by Houellebecq's manipulation of style and presentation. This is supposed to be a scientific exposé of current trends and how they might be applied. Instead, the sociologist reads from the travel supplement of a mass-market magazine. He has clearly not done any serious research and is relying on improvisation and the ignorance of his audience to make an impact. Michel recognises that Lagarrigue is a master of verbiage: 'Le sociologue des comportements avait du métier, il aurait pu continuer pendant des heures.'[38] This is a back-handed compliment, a judgement that hovers between praise and condemnation. Jean-Yves is not impressed and dismisses the man.

The sociological investigation of people's holiday habits returns later on. A further study in the more specialist *Tourisme Hebdo* stresses that people want something that is more authentic than the conventional beach-holidays. However, despite the Eldorador resorts providing what they wanted and despite clients expressing satisfaction, business continues to decline. Jean-Yves is forced to conclude:

> Je crois simplement que les gens mentent, dit Jean-Yves après avoir relu, pour la deuxième fois, le rapport de synthèse sur les questions de satisfaction. Ils se déclarent satisfaits, ils cochent à chaque fois les cases 'Bien', mais en réalité ils se sont emmerdés pendant toutes leurs vacances, et ils se sentent trop coupables pour l'avouer.[39]

37   *Plateforme*, p. 163.
38   *Plateforme*, p. 164.
39   *Plateforme*, p. 197.

The gap between what people say and what they do stems from their lack of knowledge of an inner, authentic self. They speak as they do not because they are reflecting on their experiences but because they are talking to an interviewer, someone with whom they have relationship no matter how fleeting and superficial. If the only knowledge that we can have of ourselves that which arise when we relate to others, then the will speak for effect. It is not so much that they are seeking to impress an interviewer but rather that they are seeking to find value in themselves. They are like the paedophile parents who present themselves to the public as misunderstood and well-meaning, not so much because they seek to persuade the rest of society that this is so but rather because this is what they themselves want to think about their actions.

The stories that people tell themselves and others about their holidays are important because they are related to the creation of an acceptable self-image and to a sense of its fragility. People are unwilling to admit to something not being right for them, to not having needs that are not being fulfilled. It is this sense of a lack that is the motor of sex-tourism, as we have seen above. The flattery of the Thai woman is based on an awareness of the *farang*'s sense of dissatisfaction. In a sense they show more insight into the real needs of the tourists than do the sociological surveys.

This provides the impetus for the novel's most outrageous plot twist. Michel accompanies Jean-Yves and Valérie on a trip to Cuba to observe how the tourists behave and to try to identify ways of improving the business. It is Michel who observes that the tourists are at their happiest not when making use of the facilities and activities laid on but rather when they are flirting with the staff. Indeed, he discovers that the certain members of staff are prepared to provide extra services for a tip – all against the rules, of course. However, such is the desperate economic situation in Cuba that they are prepared to take the risk:

> Apparemment, dans ce pays, personne n'arrivait à vivre de son salaire. Rien ne marchait vraiment: l'essence manquait pour les moteurs, les pièces détachées pour les machines. D'où ce côté utopie agraire, qu'on ressentait en traversant les campagnes: les paysans qui labouraient avec des bœufs, qui se déplaçait en calèche ...

Mais il ne s'agissait pas d'une utopie, ni d'une reconstitution écologique: c'était la réalité d'un pays qui n'arrivait pas à se maintenir dans l'âge industriel.[40]

What looks like a paradise is in effect a result of failure. It is a devastating critique of the tourist's search for the authentic, the picturesque. Accepting the local is to accept its poverty and to reinforce the conditions that permit the wealthy tourist to remain superior in economic terms. It demolishes the Rousseau-esque notion that the primitive is better than the more sophisticated and developed ways of the Western world. The contrast with the simplistic sentimentalities and the pious platitudes of the *Guide du routard* is evident. Only the 'nantis' will find this picture inviting. Ecological concerns are far from being the main concern of the Cubans. Finding oneself and being close to nature are luxuries for the rich. The poor are concerned with survival but it is the rich who have time to worry and be bored. This is a country where people have difficulty making a living. It is not the way forward but is a falling back. The apparent utopia is a dystopia.

However, while western tourists may have material advantages that the poor envy, they are no more living utopian existences than the poor of the developing world. As Michel's analysis shows westerners lack emotional and physical intimacy. Thus, on the one hand we have the poor of the developing world who are desperate to survive and on the other we have the tourist who is dissatisfied with his or her way of life. At the moment, tourists are having relationships with the indigenous population but it is not acknowledged. Michel's proposal is to act on that truth. He makes his proposal by discounting what people say for effect and instead acts on the basis of what people do:

> Propose un club où les gens puissent baiser. C'est ça, avant tout, qui leur manque. S'ils n'ont pas leur petite aventure de vacances, ils repartent insatisfaits. Ils n'osent pas l'avouer, peut-être est-ce qu'ils n'en prennent pas conscience; mais, la fois suivante, ils changent de prestataire.[41]

---

40 *Plateforme*, p. 216.
41 *Plateforme*, p. 232.

This appears to be sensible. Until now, sex-tourism was an adjunct to the trip but one that had a determining influence on how people felt. What is innovatory is that this allows the sex-tourism to be acknowledged. Jean-Yves points out that at present, tourists have every opportunity to have sex in the resorts. By this he means that the tourists can have relationships with each other. However, Michel points out, in line with his earlier analysis, that the problem is that Westerners are reluctant to have sex with each other. Yet the need for sexual gratification, he goes on, does not grow any less intense.

This provides a unique business opportunity that unites sex and tourism on a scale never before imagined:

> 'Donc, poursuivis-je, d'un côté tu as plusieurs centaines de millions d'Occidentaux qui ont tout ce qu'ils veulent, sauf qu'ils n'arrivent plus à trouver de satisfaction sexuelle: ils cherchent, ils cherchent sans arrêt, mais ils ne trouvent rien, et ils en sont malheureux jusqu'à l'os. De l'autre côté tu as plusieurs milliards d'individus qui n'ont rien, qui crèvent de faim, qui meurent jeunes, qui vivent dans des conditions insalubres, et qui n'ont plus rien à vendre que leurs corps, et leur sexualité intacte. C'est simple, vraiment simple à comprendre: c'est une situation d'échange idéale. Le fric qu'on peut ramasser là-dedans est presque inimaginable: c'est plus que l'informatique, plus que les biotechnologies, plus que les industries des médias; il n'y a aucun secteur économique qui puisse y être comparé.'[42]

Presentation is all. It allows the participants to tell themselves that they are really doing good. Like the Raëlians on trial for child abuse, the tourists will be able to tell the world and more crucially themselves that they were only trying to remedy dire poverty in a way that gave pleasure to all. Calling what happens a 'petite aventure', as in the earlier quotation, allows the exploitative nature of the activity to remain hidden. Similarly, 'une situation d'échange idéale' strives to give the impression of a free market that miraculously manages to find a solution to the worst kinds of poverty that afflict the developing world. This is a savage irony that is Swiftian in the application of the adjective 'idéale' to a situation comprising the har-

42 *Plateforme*, p. 234.

rowing list of the poor's misfortunes. What Michel proposes is not fair trade but the exercise of dominance by a visitor who assumes rights which are granted only by virtue of greater economic power. There is a failure to acknowledge the wrong done to the host country or the economic inequalities that underpin it. Michel's grand scheme depends on what is left unsaid: that sex-tourism is based on structural economic imbalances between rich and poor. As a result, it is an inherently exploitative abuse of the hospitality that the wealthy exact from those they visit.

Michel's remedy, far from providing a solution, as he pretends, depends on the maintenance of the very inequalities it appears to deplore. Its remedies, like the drugs taken by the characters in various Houellebecq novels to alleviate mental distress, are merely palliative and at best render tolerable what should be in tolerable Indeed, it is a way of managing ills that prevents them from getting out of control and becoming such a threat that they have to be addressed. Michel's proposal will allow the economic problems to the developing world to persist.

Furthermore, the role of Michel, Jean-Yves and Valérie exposes another aspect disturbing aspect of the situation. The use of 'fric' signals a change of register when Michel moves from standard French to a more intimate register. It is as though he first uses an official, public register to justify and persuade but when it comes to detailing advantages to his companions, he can use a more private and intimate form of address. This is the bit that they need not speak of in public but only among themselves. It is the core motivation of the three. Michel may speak of helping the deprived, both rich and poor, but in reality what is attractive is that this proposed exchange will not be direct but rather facilitated by the clubs he and the others run. This will allow them to take part of the money, a significant part no doubt, for themselves. Michel, Jean-Yves and Valérie are not producers of goods and services but rather administrators who leech off what others produce. They are not unlike the bureaucrats in the Ministry of Agriculture (described in *Extension du domaine de la lutte*) who do not farm but administer farming. Similarly, Michel is not an artist but some-one who is an accountant in an arts organisation. Indeed, most of Houellebecq's characters are employed in the tertiary sector. They are not creators but people who depend on what others produce. This is reflected in Michel's list of profitable activities. With the possible exception of biotechnology, these industries are in the tertiary sector. Just as Valérie's father could not make a living as a farmer but becomes rich when he sells his farm to a leisure consortium, so the most profitable parts of the economy are those which concentrate not on making things or growing things but on parting people from their money.

Michel is drunk while he is proposing this. Being intoxicated is nothing new for him and so we may assume that his thoughts are not to be discounted (and indeed he later confirms that, though he was drunk, he meant what he said). Furthermore, the extracts quoted above show no signs of impaired reasoning and indeed the logic as laid out is ineluctable. It seems to follow the example of Swift who, like Houellebecq lived in Ireland, and who came up with the ideal solution for the relief of the poor of Ireland. Swift's impeccably argued solution was cannibalism. The hapless reader who accepted his premises was lead to accept his hideous conclusions – even though they were madness. Similarly here, the fact that Michel is drunk is an indication that his solution is to be read with a similar awareness of the complexity of the text. Reason is not an infallible guide to right action. It is used not to uncover the truth but for effect. It has a momentum of its own that can lead us to absurdities.

Thus, Michel's proposal develops and the details are worked out. Room facilities and market positioning are discussed and measures taken to harmonise charges:

> Tout s'enchaînait naturellement sans hésitation et sans doute; il faudrait voir avec les chefs de village pour normaliser les tarifs de la prostitution locale.[43]

Prostitution is being subjected to the techniques of business. It is being discussed as though this were a normal planning meeting to develop a product or a service and to ensure consistency and quality across the range. It is absurd but funny. However, anther kind of absurdity is evoked when Houellebecq inserts the following sentence:

---

43   *Plateforme*, pp. 246–247.

Au même moment, à moins d'un kilomètre, deux adolescents de la cité de Courtilières éclataient la tête d'une sexagénaire à coups de battes de baseball.[44]

Violence haunts the novel. It opens with the murder of Michel's father
and there are sporadic incidents throughout, the most horrific of which is
the attack on the holiday resort in Thailand. However, the violence may
be gratuitous but its function in the narrative is not. Here, Houellebecq
juxtaposes, as he frequently does, two apparently unrelated circumstances,
prostitution and violence. Is he implying that prostitution is form of male
aggression against women? Or does the actual violence of the suburbs signal
the implied violence that underlies prostitution even when it adheres to the
quality criteria that seek to normalise it? Is the fact that the delinquents
use baseball bats a signal that the spread of the resorts is akin to American
imperialistic expansion at the expense of the disadvantaged? In addition, the
phrase 'cité de Courtilières' would have the same resonance as 'inner-city'
would have for English readers. It may point towards racial strife without
articulating it clearly. There are a host of interpretative possibilities. Is 'une
sexagénaire' used instead of 'une femme d'une soixantaine d'années' used
because the word 'sexagénaire' provides an echo (the syllable 'sex') back
to prostitution. The uncertainties are deliberate, but no more so than the
motive for the attack. This is presented as an attack that has no motive.
It is absurd. This, however, is a different kind of absurdity from Michel's
proposal. The latter is humorously absurd while beating up an old lady is
not. However, this is not the main difference. We might suppose that the
beating was a mugging, violence in order to obtain money. There is no
evidence for this, whereas the stated aim of Michel and his companions is
to get money from their scheme. It is, as we have seen, its sole justification.
Both the scheme and the attack are ethically vacuous.

Nevertheless, it is amusing to watch how Michel and the others dress
their plans in the language of quality control. In seeking to regulate tariffs
and provide security for all parties, they appear to be striving for fairness.
However, this is sham fairness because, as pointed out, it does not address
fundamental inequalities – to do so would be to prevent the primary aim
of the scheme, the accumulation of even more wealth by the proposers.

44 *Plateforme*, p. 247.

When Houellebecq applies business principles to prostitution, he demonstrates their emptiness quite clearly. Transparency, fair pricing, value for money, looking after employees and caring for customers are all held up as good business practice. But these values have no intrinsic worth and can be applied to anything. Indeed at one point Jean-Yves looks out a copy of the mission statement of the Aurora group, the company employing him to rescue its chain of failing resorts:

> Il prit subitement conscience que ce baratin nauséeux pourrait très bien s'appliquer une chaîne de bordels bien organisée.[45]

There is thus a sick joke at the heart of the novel: attempts to ensure that things are done properly do not necessarily mean that those things are right. Business ethics lack a foundation.

Furthermore, there is a kind of perversity when Jean-Yves realizes that there is more profit to be had since gone will be the need for activity coaches and child facilities:

> Après une première simulation, Jean-Yves se rendit compte avec incrédulité que, tous amortissements inclus, le prix de revient annuel des clubs allait baisser de 25%. Il refit trois fois ses calculs, obtint à chaque fois les mêmes résultats. C'était d'autant plus frappant qu'il comptait, pour les frais de séjour, proposer des tarifs catalogue supérieurs de 25% à la norme de la catégorie – c'est-à-dire qu'il comptait en gros sur la norme médiane des Club Med. Le taux de profitabilité faisait un bond en avant de 50%.[46]

This seems inevitable once you start down the road imagined by Michel. It is hard to fault the logic. The principles of management are applied just as we would expect. Houellebecq confronts us with the consequences of a belief that the application of sound business practice will lead to the greatest good. This confrontation leaves us free to ask if we do indeed want a world where the rich nations exploit the poor for sexual gratification or individual development but do so in accordance with the rules of sound business practice.

---

45 *Plateforme*, p. 254.
46 *Plateforme*, p. 258.

When prostitution no longer lurks in the shadows but emerges in to the visible economy where it can be regulated in an effort to promote quality, this causes it not to wither away but rather to be an even more attractive prospect. Houellebecq shows what will happen if sex-tourism is fully integrated into the fabric of the tourism industry. It will become highly profitable, regulated according to best practice in health and safety – Valérie insists on condoms in every room.

However, Houellebecq's narrative strategy is risky. As was clear from the reception the novel was accorded on publication, the subject matter arouses strong reactions in readers. Even a sensitive and sympathetic critic like Clément is perturbed by Houellebecq's treatment of his subject:

> Le lecteur averti, éduqué, au courant des genres littéraires en rit. Il y voit une parodie, des clins d'oeil. Il s'amuse: c'est du second degré. Je pense que ce lecteur a tort. Pas de s'amuser. Non, bien au contraire. Mais de ne pas prendre cette littérature au sérieux et de la lire au premier degré, justement.[47]

Clément sees the novel as depicting dangerous tendencies in our societies and claims that there is a risk that the danger that they pose will be dismissed because we are able to laugh at them. She warns us that in politics dangerous men with dangerous views are often discounted and treated as figures of fun – until it is too late. She cites as examples Jean-Marie Le Pen and Pim Fortuyn. In embarking on such an argument, Clément demonstrates that she sees the writer as a person with a social role, one who should warn and admonish. She would see Houellebecq as someone who encourages the reader (and her quotation above places responsibility firmly on the reader) to treat lightly what is a potential menace.

Yet this is a dangerous line of argument to take for when a writer engages with the real world, as Clément suggests, he or she risks getting it badly wrong – as Clément does. Le Pen was trounced by Chirac in the presidential elections of 2002 and remains marginal – though of course I could be wrong. As for Pim Fortuyn, he is definitely not a threat. The point of the novel is that it welds together the comic and tragic sides of

---

47   Murielle Lucie Clément, *Houellebecq, Sperme et Sang*, Collection Approches Littéraires (Paris, L'Harmattan, 2003) p. 190.

an absurdist vision. This is not to deny the unpleasantness of the world or the nastiness that may issue from our actions.

Ní Loingsigh takes Houellebecq to task for not doing enough to counteract what he portrays:

> Notably and disconcertingly for critics of the text, the portrayal of Michel and his fellow tourists seems almost entirely devoid of irony, a fact that further adds to the discomfort felt when reading the text. This suggest that unlike the strategy adopted by certain 'marginalised' writers to challenge stereotypical portrayals of them, Houellebecq does not appear to use Michel, or clichéd discourse, as counter-stereotypes to disarm the reader and neutralise negative, clichéd images of tourists and tourism.[48]

Ní Loingsigh's comments are accurate only if you share the belief that the portrayal of Michel and the tourists is 'almost entirely devoid of irony'. But as we have seen, Houellebecq's characters do not think what they think out of conviction. They recycle thoughts and ideas with the intention not of expressing what they sincerely hold to be true but in order to produce an effect. Houellebecq's irony does not lie in the gap between what characters say and what they really believe but rather in the acknowledgement that beyond the words uttered or the thoughts held there is no truth by which to judge them. Houellebecq's discourse is less straightforward than Ní Loingsigh would have us believe. His counterpointing of comment and incident encourages readers to reflect ironically on what they are reading. If the criticism of sex-tourism is less overt than Ní Loingsigh and others would prefer, it is perhaps because Houellebecq is more concerned with revealing the conditions that permit and encourage sex-tourism. He uncovers the systemic problems that underlie the phenomenon and reveals the stories we tell ourselves (and allow ourselves to be told) in order to avoid doing anything about it. He is perhaps aware that it is useless criticising Michel and the other actors who portray stereotypes that should be out-

---

48   Aedín Ní Loingsigh, 'Tourist Traps: Confounding Expectations in Michel Houellebecq's *Plateforme*', French Cultural Studies, Vol. 16, No. 1 (February 2005), pp. 73–90 (p. 82).

dated if the underlying conditions that permit those same stereotypes to exist are not unmasked.

Ryan and Hall have quite clear views:

> It is the argument of the authors that prostitution needs to be legalised so that the conditions under which the sex worker operates and the sex industry is run are as transparent as possible to external evaluation. The illicit marginal spaces need to be brought out of the shadows if they are to be adequately controlled. [...] This short-term measure would hopefully improve the health and economic conditions of prostitutes at a minimum.[49]

This proposal would concentrate on alleviating the situation of prostitutes. It does not question the exploitation of women by tourists nor does it address the factors that create the bad conditions in the first place. Ryan and Hall would probably justify their stance that they are proposing solutions that are feasible rather than ideal. Yet their argument has echoes of Jean-Yves plans. The terms 'transparent' and 'external evaluation' reveal the authors' belief that the application of sound business practice to prostitution will lead to a moral and ethical improvement in that the sex-workers will enjoy better rights and better health. It seems a plausible argument and the outcome is so desirable that who could oppose it? Houellebecq does not make any such recommendation. Rather, he shows us what would happen if we were to take sex-tourism out of the shadows and subject it to the kind of institutional controls that are being advocated. The implementation of Michel's idea is, as Jean-Yves might put it, a 'simulation'. The results are not as we are lead to believe by Ryan and Hall. That they are just as plausible if not more so, is perhaps shown by the reaction of critics such as Clément and Ní Longsigh. Showing that the phenomenon will expand under the kind of conditions recommended by Ryan and Hall is not the same as approving of that expansion. If it is true that regulation of sex-tourism is but the necessary condition of its expansion under the control of multi-national corporations, then that should compel us to consider more carefully what action to take.

---

49   Chris Ryan and C. Michael Hall, *Sex Tourism: Marginal People and Liminalities* (London and New York, Routledge, 2001), p. 147.

Furthermore, it is clear that these resorts – 'club' in the original French – share something of the exclusivity of clubs for the privileged. Only the well-off will have access. More seriously though, they will exist as colonies in the host countries, little enclaves where the rules and regulations are set in corporate headquarters not by local inhabitants, another abuse of hospitality as defined by Heisse. It represents the expansion –well-intentioned – of Western rules and values. The Christian do-gooders who worked hand in glove with the imperialists of the nineteenth century are replaced by the regulatory do-gooders in league with global corporations.

It is in the light of this that the attack on the Thai resort should be seen. A group of Muslim fundamentalists destroy the resort after an earlier warning (the killing of a tourist and a prostitute) had been ignored. It is indeed a tragedy and one that destroys Michel's chance of happiness. It brings to the surface the violence that underlies exploitative sexual practices such as prostitution, turning that violence back upon the exploiter. It takes us full circle, back to the murder of Michel's father at the start of the novel. His relationship with Aïcha is not unlike what his son proposes – and the outcome foreshadows the bloody slaughter of the end of the novel.

The attack on the resort can also be seen as a response by people who do not want to be coerced into an acceptance in their midst of something that is defended by the arguments, beliefs, values and economic powers of the West. Arguing will not win their case especially in the light of Valérie's claim to Michel that 'le capitalisme était dans son principe un état de guerre permanente, une lutte perpétuelle qui ne peut jamais avoir de fin'.[50] Capitalism and commerce are the continuation of warfare by other means. Violence is implicit in its structures. This is not to excuse the violent attack on the resort but it does cause us to reflect on the complications of the situation. This in the end is what makes *Plateforme* far more than a mere sociological depiction. It is an imaginative work that engages us in a reflection on its subject and on the human condition in general. If tourism as exemplified by Sôn and the *Guide du routard* is a mere travelling through pre-packaged itineraries, evoking stock responses, Houellebecq's journey is one of exploration.

50 *Plateforme*, p. 274.

CHAPTER 5

La Possibilité d'une île: Life is Real

Writing in the Saturday edition of the *Guardian* on 29 October 2005, Michael Worton was less than impressed by the English translation of *La Possibilité d'une île*:

> The real flaw at the centre of this novel is that Houellebecq can't think or talk interestingly about love, the novel's main concern. We are treated to a series of Scrooge-ish maxims, such as 'Living together alone is hell between consenting adults'. Dogs are 'machines for loving', but the novel articulates a stunted and confused view of love, where love between a man and a woman is equated with love for a pet.

He added:

> The best way to read Possibility is quickly, without pondering its cod philosophy and portentous metaphysical pronouncements, which take the anatomisation of banality to a paroxysm of the baroque. There is little point in thinking about what Houellebecq says or following up his references, since their irrelevance is the point.

Tim Adams writing in the *Observer* on 30 October was only slightly less dismissive:

> There could be some pathos and reach in this scenario and in the ways it plays itself out, but Houellebecq's range, which always veers quickly and self-consciously from disgust to sentimentality, does not want to allow for simple humanity; it would be too damaging to his vision. In its absence, you are left with a repetitive, clever shell of a world, a calculated atmosphere of pornography, gratuitous and starkly lit, which, though it is perhaps what the author is striving for, never feels quite enough.

Both these critics make points that are hard to dismiss. However, I do not think that they pursue their observations far enough. As we shall see, love between a man and a woman proves fraught and love for a pet should be set in such a context. When no other love is successful, the love of a pet acquires a significance it might not otherwise have. Furthermore, given Houellebecq's attitude to machinery in earlier novels – as exemplified in his examination of suicide in *Les Particules élémentaires* – to call dogs 'machines for loving' is not the same as equating them with a human lover. Humans are not machines and dogs are not humans.

Adams' remarks also fail to go far enough. He is correct to see the world Houellebecq depicts as 'a repetitive, clever shell of a world' but seems to see that as an aesthetic or creative failure on the author's part. In fact, as we shall see, the notion of the shell and the yoke it contains is very much germane to the main plotline of the novel: cloning. Adams is correct to say that the world or worlds Houellebecq depicts never feel 'quite enough'. That is actually the point. At the heart of Houellebecq's vision of existence, as purveyed by Daniel1, is the emptiness that we have seen in earlier novels. His depiction of that emptiness is truly horrific. The concluding pages of Daniel1's narrative are indeed, in Worton's words, 'a paroxysm of the baroque'.

Maud Granger Remy draws our attention to the similarities between the content of *La Possibilité d'une île* and that of Houellebecq's other novels:

> Les clones mis en place par la secte élohimite de *La Possibilité d'une île* ne sont pas seulement les successeurs de ceux inventés par Djerzinski dans *Les Particules élémentaires*, ils sont également les dignes descendants des touristes décrits dans *Plateforme*. La filiation est manifeste. Les néo humains [*sic*] vivent, comme les touristes, isolés dans des retraites sécurisées, sur un territoire qui leur reste étranger.[1]

---

[1]   Maud Granger Remy, 'Le tourisme est un posthumanisme: Autour de *Plateforme*', in Clément et Wesemael, pp. 277–286, p. 286.

This is a novel about clones. It is in part narrated by clones. The original, human narrator is called Daniel and, as the first of his line, is known as Daniel1. His distant successors are Daniel24 and Daniel25 who also supply part of the narrative, largely, though not exclusively, by commenting on Daniel1's account. The novel could also be described as being a clone. This revisiting of past works may permit the development of earlier themes but principally it draws attention to the fact that this novel (like its predecessors) is a story constructed out of, and thus generated by, other stories, just as the clones' bodies and lives are constructed on the basis of those of their predecessors. Indeed, there are many other similarities than those Granger Remy points out. There is the island of Lanzarote and the preoccupation with cults. The foundation myth of the 'Elohim' told in *Lanzarote* re-appears though now the putative founders are the 'Élohim'. There is a violent murder as in *Plateforme* and, as in *Les Particules élémentaires*, the novel depicts a future where human beings have been superseded by their successors.

However, it is equally important to note the differences. *Les Particules élémentaires* describes how humanity is succeeded by a new and improved version thanks to the efforts of Michel and while in *La Possibilité d'une île*, the same theme reappears – the replacement of humanity by the 'néo-humains' – this time the story is different: the neo-humans are the creation of a scientist financed by a cult. Thus things have changed. The new story contains remnants of the old but exists within its own narrative landscape.

This reflects what happens in the storyline of *La Possibilité d'une île* itself. The novel ends with one of the central characters, Daniel25, exploring the futuristic, post-apocalyptic world beyond the protective cocoon in which he has passed his life. He is traversing a landscape that one of his predecessors knew very well indeed. He mentions locations, such as streets in Madrid and Barajas airport. The unfamiliar terrain is not completely unfamiliar – but it is not familiar either. It is not completely futuristic but represents continuity with the past while being quite distinct from it. It is the same landscape but now it has different features. The airport has disappeared from Barajas but has left behind the tarmac runways. Lanzarote is still there but is now a peninsula.

Thus the reader is always very much aware that the present moment is always derived from what has preceded it. Time moves on and brings change but a link to the past always remains. Daniel₁ is always connected to the seventeen-year old boy who invents a sketch telling of a revolt among the inmates of a holiday resort. Indeed, the lifestyle of the clones is in some respects based on that of the resort where all one's needs are taken care of and Daniel₂₅'s leaving the compound where he lives is an act of revolt not unrelated to the uprising imagined by his predecessor. Events form an interconnecting web that stretches backwards. Even objects have a history. Thus the reader is conscious of time not just as a movement forwards but also as itself an interconnecting web since the interleaving of two timelines shows the extent to which what is for us the future (but for the clones is the present) is in fact a derivation of the past (for Daniel₁, the present). In addition, the interweaving timelines can be visualised as a double helix, reproducing the structure of DNA. The movement of time is an essential part of the narrative of creation.

This should be contrasted with the ending of *Les Particules élémentaires* which seems to suggest that time does not move as far as the neo-humans are concerned. They are immune to change since their form has been stabilised – unlike the remaining humans who will be faced with extinction. Thus *Les Particules élémentaires* implies an impasse, a cul-de-sac in which the neo-humans are trapped in all their blandness. Evolution has been halted. *La Possibilité d'une île* does not reject such a view but takes that idea and shows what it means. Swift's Struldbruggs were cursed with immortality but continued to suffer the degenerating effects of the passage of time. The clones are modern Struldbruggs but, although the problem of degeneration of the body has been solved, the novel shows the immortals are still accursed. Thus the web of time becomes a net that holds them prisoner, preventing them from moving forwards, from renewing themselves.

The new process for achieving immortality separates the physical from the mental parts of the self. The body is renewed by growing a replacement which will house the memories of the original. Memory is the key element in ensuring the success of the cloning process since it preserves the continuity of the human consciousness. It perpetuates the self that death threatens.

However, memory is ironically the very thing that reveals change. It allows us to compare what is with what was. Thus the reader, if not the clone, will be aware that Daniel25's journey over a changed landscape is an indication that time cannot be stopped. Subjectively, Daniel25, like Daniel24, may be a re-run of his predecessor, but time continues in the world outside their consciousness. Thus memory both preserves and shows us how far things have changed. However, when characters discuss memory, it is its role as a preserver that they deal with. They ignore its important second role.

The way memory is tied to personality is described by three rules set out by a theoretician named Pierce:

> La première loi de Pierce identifie la personnalité à la mémoire. Rien n'existe, dans la personnalité, que ce qui est mémorisable (que cette mémoire soit cognitive, procédurale ou affective); c'est grâce à la mémoire, par exemple, que le sommeil ne dissout nullement la sensation d'identité.
> Selon la seconde loi de Pierce, la mémoire cognitive a pour support adéquat le langage.
> La troisième loi de Pierce définit les conditions d'un langage non biaisé.[2]

This is Daniel24's explanation of the laws of Pierce, situating memory at the core of our sense of self. The person who wakes up in the morning is the same as the person who went to sleep. The account is plausible. The confident mastery of the prose imitates scientific discourse and we need to remember – and the verb is significant – that Daniel1, the progenitor of the Daniel clones, is a mimic. Cloning is, in a sense, his profession – that is who he professes to be. Thus language has an important part in the way we are defined – we are who we say we are. Daniel1's earliest show business success was in his own one-man-show where he played all the parts. Using language is one of the ways in which he convinces his audience that he inhabits these different personae. He is someone who exploits his knowledge that language is a device, an instrument that creates what he calls an

2 Michel Houellebecq, *La Possibilité d'une île* (Paris, Fayard, 2005), p. 27. All subsequent references are to this edition.

'*effet de réel*'.[3] In the above quotation, Daniel24 sets out the Laws of Pierce in a quasi-scientific way. His prose is a clone, a mimicking of what scientific discourse is like and thus conveying what Daniel1 calls an '*effet de réel*'.

However, Daniel1 also recognises that language is a shared phenomenon and this makes his personality public property, not just in the sense that he can be known by the public but that they too can create an '*effet de réel*' by fabricating their own version of what he is like:

> Mon humanisme supposé reposait en réalité sur des bases bien minces: une vague saillie sur les buralistes, une allusion aux cadavres des clandestins nègres rejetés sur les côtes espagnoles avaient suffi à me valoir une réputation d'*homme de gauche* et de *défenseur des droits de l'homme*. Homme de gauche, moi? J'avais occasionnellement pu introduire dans mes sketches quelques altermondialistes, vaguement jeunes, sans leur donner de rôle immédiatement antipathique; j'avais occasionnellement pu céder à une certaine démagogie: j'étais, je le répète, un bon professionnel.[4]

Daniel1 exemplifies the double nature of the personality, its duplicity. On the one hand our personality is our idea of how we identify ourselves to ourselves. On the other hand, it is how others identify us. It is what they expect us to do consonant with what they know about us. As the passage quoted above demonstrates, the image that others have of us need not be the same as the one we have of ourselves. Images can be manipulated – but not just by the owner of the original.

The label 'un bon professionnel' is one of the most important things that Daniel1 tells us. In all of the above quotation the only thing that gets us close to the real is that phrase. Even 'en réalité' is used to highlight Daniel1's lack of authenticity. The real person, his values and drives, are withheld, hidden behind a mask. Like the first actors in Greek theatre who wore masks, Daniel1 hides himself. He never reveals who he is. He lacks authenticity.

---

3   *La Possibilité d'une île*, p. 22.
4   *La Possibilité d'une île*, p. 23.

At the start of his narration, he introduces himself as having a 'vocation de bouffon'.[5] He is situated by language in the role. Daniel1 has a calling not to some noble endeavour whose aim is to better humanity (hence his bemusement at his reputation for 'humanisme') but rather to entertain and, perhaps more significantly, to be admired and applauded. He is called to present a face that will please. He wants not to win but to have winning ways. His first foray into entertainment is a dramatisation based not on something that happened to him but on an incident he observed. Like the clones who will follow him, he is a commentator on the world not an explorer of his inner self – hence his refusal to see himself as a major artist. He is disconnected from who he really is.

Given this, it becomes legitimate to ask if there is a real Daniel1, an authentic self. If it is hidden behind a façade, there is no way of verifying its existence. Daniel1 may in fact be the façade, no more than an '*effet de réel*'. The 'je' who is speaking may be an empty shell – or a cell with the nucleus removed. The method that scientists use to create cloned animals, such as Dolly the sheep, consists of removing the nucleus from a cell and replacing it with a donor nucleus. From this the new animal is created. The 'je' of Daniel1 is like a cell that has no nucleus. His lack of authenticity creates a space that can be filled. There is no essential Daniel1. The same is true of Daniel24 and Daniel25. They too are shells. However, this emptiness is never filled – hence the dissatisfaction of Daniel25 and those clones who leave their compounds. In a similar way, Daniel1 is a very needy person. There is an emptiness within that is not filled. Thus he seeks to fill that sense of emptiness through clinging to others, particularly Esther1. Indeed, this sense of emptiness can be found at the heart of most of Houellebecq's major characters. In the case of Bruno, in *Les Particules élémentaires*, that emptiness expresses itself in gluttony. His hunger for food is a metaphor for his feeling that he is a hollow man.

Since he craves to win the approval of others, Daniel1 is just as likely to be manipulated or rather to let himself be manipulated by others. He places his celebrity at the service of a cult for no apparent reason other than

5   *La Possibilité d'une île*, p. 19.

there seems to be no good reason not to. His lack of strong convictions means that he has no moral compass to guide him through events. As a result, he acquiesces in the deception of the cult followers when their leader is killed and, more seriously, in the defenestration of the prophet's killer, even though he does not want it. He is not sufficiently strong in himself to resist what others want him to do.

Pierce claims that memory and language operate together to create the personality. However, they merely produce an *effet de personnalité*. There is more to what makes the individual what he or she is than Pierce's laws would have us believe. Memory is not all there is. Although the clones have all the memories of their progenitors, they are manifestly not the same people. We do not mistake Daniel24 for Daniel1. The clone is much more insipid. He is a pallid version of his progenitor.

The opening of the chapter headed Daniel1, 2 (which returns to the narrative of Daniel1) is disconcerting if we take Pierce's maxims to be the simple truth:

> Il m'est à peu près impossible aujourd'hui de me souvenir *pourquoi* j'ai épousé ma première femme; si je la croisais dans la rue, je ne pense même pas que je parviendrais à la reconnaître. On oublie certaines choses, on les oublie réellement; c'est bien à tort qu'on suppose que toutes choses se conservent dans le sanctuaire de la mémoire; certains événements, et même la plupart, sont bel et bien *effacés*, il n'en demeure aucune trace, et c'est comme s'ils n'avaient jamais été.[6]

If what Pierce says is true then, forgetting is to lose part of one's personality. However, forgetfulness constitutes part of Daniel1's personality and helps define the way he relates to the world in which he lives. It is more than a failure of memory. Forgetting is the paring away of memories. The human personality is shaped both by what it retains and what it discards. Furthermore, the discarded is never completely erased. It still is the case that, despite his claim that he has forgotten them, these events have in some way shaped him and made him who he. The events may not be in his memory but they are nonetheless a part of who he is. Forgetting them

6   *La Possibilité d'une île*, p. 29.

does not make the experiences cease either to have an effect or to exist – the 'comme si' of the final sentence does not undo experiences. It is only an *effet de disparition*. By Daniel1's own admission, we forget so much that if memory were indeed the foundation of the personality, then precious little of our individuality would be left.

What makes us who we are is more complicated than Pierce's laws would have us believe. Memories do help shape us but they seem also to imprison us. The clones pore over the records left by their original in what is a kind of self-imposed prison – in that they deliberately choose not to open the door and leave. Their role is not to wander in the world, having a life. Instead they are bound to the memories of their ancestors. Consequently, forgetting becomes not just a mechanism that entails loss but also a mechanism that frees. Daniel1 is no longer encumbered with his first wife. He is free.

Yet such freedom is not completely positive. It is Daniel1's disconnection from the woman he married that allows him to forget her so easily. He does not value her as a person. Indeed the reader may well wonder what Daniel1 does value. His approach to his sketch-writing is similar in that he is as little committed to his subjects as he is to his wife. He concentrates on winning the approval or admiration of his audience but does not really care about what he is doing. Thus he can gleefully produce sketches entitled: 'ON PRÉFÈRE LES PARTOUZEUSES PALESTINIENNES', describing it as the summit of his career without giving any thought to the underlying tragedy of the conflicts in the Middle East nor to the offense he might be causing. He trivialises the serious for its shock value and revels in the reaction that it will create. It will further his status. His stance is manipulative rather than principled.

Not that Daniel1 fails to acknowledge that principles are important – but they are to be used tactically, something that he does very successfully in handling controversy. He distracts people from the immediate issue of his outrageousness towards something that they will feel compelled to defend, freedom of speech. He is in fact inducing a form of forgetfulness – the issue of offensiveness is erased as though it did not exist. With his new girlfriend, Isabelle, at his side to offer advice, he strategically manages the furore that he is causing. He is astute enough to know that the key to winning (which is nothing more than having the bulk of the public take his side) is not by convincing them to support the original point at issue but rather to fight on a principle round which everyone can rally. The strategy is a successful version of the strategy the Raëlian paedophiles in *Lanzarote* when they attempt to make the central issue one of good parenting rather than abuse. Isabelle and Daniel1 treat freedom of speech the same way scientists treat a cell when they set about cloning a sheep. Freedom of speech is a concept waiting to have their particular interpretation inserted into it. All that matters is that the new organism is capable of sustaining itself. In reality Daniel1 cares as much for the principle of freedom of speech as he does about the position of women in Palestinian society or about the alleged hypocrisy of paternalistic sexual mores.

The earlier attempts at cloning were based on the belief that the worn-out body can be replaced and the personality transferred into its new home – just as a programme can be downloaded to a new computer. In short the idea is that just as all our files can be moved to a new computer when the old one is ready for the scrap heap, so our personality, that which is really us, can be moved to a new body so allowing us to achieve immortality. Pierce's breakthrough is to link memory and language by pointing out that language functions as a carrier of memory. Daniel24 speaks of three types of memory – 'cognitive, procédurale ou affective'. Pierce's analogy only works for one of the three, the cognitive. The others are left out. Thus what can be transferred from one body to another is limited in scope. Yet it is this very limitation that adds to the sense of verisimilitude. Real breakthroughs rarely provide all the answers. They are advances but often contain within themselves the limitations that will be their own undoing. In this case, the limited transfer accounts for the rather pallid character of the future clones. Compared to their progenitors, they are colourless. The other two forms of memory (motor memory and affective memory) have not been transferred. Daniel24 and Daniel25 are missing an essential part of the human experience.

Motor memory relates to the body and affective memory to feelings. We might perhaps recall the image of Michel in *Extension du domaine de la lutte* in his hospital bed, losing his sense of self as his limbs seem not to be subject to his will. That the body is crucial to how we experience ourselves in the world is demonstrated by the fact that the effect of mind-altering or mood-altering drugs takes place at the level of the body. Thus there is clearly an inadequacy in Pierce's model and the technology deriving from it – no matter how attractive it might appear.

Within the logic of the narrative, this also has the virtue of verisimilitude in that, as already pointed out above, scientific breakthroughs rarely provide complete answers but rather move us on to a new set of problems. If the cultists see that the neo-humans will solve the problems that come with being mortal beings, then the neo-humans themselves see that they will be succeeded by the 'Futurs'. They regard themselves as only the provisional stage, the intermediaries. All scientific progress moves from intermediary state to intermediary state, never finding definitive answers. Solutions and problems are indivisible.

The problem, however, lies not just in the limitation arising from the fact that only the cognitive memory can be transferred. The personality is not an essence that determines our acts but something that we create as we live out our lives – even if we forget the events. Daniel₁ is shaped by his marriage and separation. We continue to shape ourselves until we die. Life is first and foremost a process. Human beings are works in progress. They are not fixed. What is transferred to the clones, on the other hand, appears to have been fixed at the point of transfer. What is preserved is the memory of a life, not the living personality which should, if it is to be truly a living personality, continue to have experiences that can be remembered.

Houellebecq's characters wrestle with scientific problems and come up with plausible solutions that we feel would work given scientific knowledge. Characters working on a problem do not have a single revelation that solves all problems. Rather, progress results from gradual advances. More than one person contributes to the solution – and that solution is not necessarily perfect. Indeed, in arriving at the solution, there may be false starts and blind alleys. Characters may be unable to realize the full potential of their breakthroughs. In *Les Particules élémentaires* it is those who come after Michel and who carry on his work that create the neo-humans.

Miskiewicz, whom Daniel₁ nicknames 'Savant' and who is known to the clones as Slotan₁, devises a process that can only be partially realized and needs to be supplemented. (The triple naming of the same person is both an indication of the complexity that Miskiewicz will, ironically, seek to simplify and an indication that Miskiewicz is, like Danieli, a set of façades or *effets de personnalité*, each symbolised by a name, which contains no core or essence.)

Pierce's insight was to see language as another means of preserving memories and that this could be harnessed to enhance the cloning process. Memories can be moved from one body to another via language. The unspoken or unwritten assumption is that language is the 'support adéquat' of the memory:

> Les trois lois de Pierce allaient mettre fin aux tentatives hasardeuses de downloading mémoriel par l'intermédiaire d'un support informatique au profit d'une part du transfert moléculaire direct, d'autre part de ce que nous connaissons aujourd'hui sous le nom de *récit de vie*, initialement conçu comme un simple complément, une solution d'attente, mais qui allait à la suite des travaux de Pierce, prendre une importance considérable. Ainsi, cette avancée logique majeure allait curieusement conduire à la remise à l'honneur d'une forme ancienne, au fond assez proche de ce qu'on appelait jadis l'*autobiographie*.[7]

Thus the view that we are really minds that can be disembodied and downloaded like computer files is, he recognises, too distant from what science and technology allow us to do for it to be the basis of a practical application. Instead, the mechanism turns out to be a technology that is much older. However, the solution is not perfect. The phrase 'solution d'attente' is treated almost nonchalantly – in an intermediary position in the sentence – but this only serves to reinforce its status as the intermediary technology that permits a way forward to be found. It is also the adaptation of an existing 'technology' – the book. By writing an autobiography the writer allows his or her own personality to be preserved. The thoughts that preserve the personality are transmitted by language when they are read.

The '*récit de vie*' is not enough on its own to provide the mechanism by means of which the personality is transferred into a new body. If it were,

---

7   *La Possibilité d'une île*, p. 27.

what would prevent that personality being transferred into multiple bodies or into a body that is not related to the original? The little phrase 'transfert moléculaire direct' explains that the personality is dependent on both the autobiography and the transfer of genetic material. This ties the *'récit de vie'* to the body from which it derives. We are lead to suppose that the new person is a product of both biological and intellectual processes. It is only later that more precision is given when Daniel24's successor, Daniel25, informs us that what happens is 'l'injection dans le nouvel organisme des protéines extraites de l'hippocampe de l'organisme ancien'.[8] The hippocampus is believed to be associated with the retention of memory. This is enough to strengthen the plausibility of the narrative.

So, the *'récit de vie'* is a central part of the technology used to perpetuate the line of neo-humans. Yet that was not its primary purpose. The first *'récit de vie'*, the prototype that set the pattern from which the others derived, started out as something quite different. It was one of the unintended consequences of the murder of the prophet and his replacement by Vincent. This is a reminder that in a world, despite the characters' intentions, things have a way of taking an unexpected turn – a detour. This is evident as Daniel1 describes how the *'récit de vie'* came about and what its original purpose was. The setting is the strange and unearthly landscape of Lanzarote:

> Au moment où nous longions de nouveau cette plage étrange, au sable noir parsemé de petits cailloux blancs, je tentai de lui expliquer ce besoin que j'éprouvais d'une confession écrite. Il m'écouta avec attention et après que nous nous fûmes garé [*sic*] sur le parking, juste devant le hall des départs, il me dit qu'il comprenait, et me donna l'autorisation d'écrire ce que j'avais vu. Il fallait simplement que le récit ne soit publié qu'après ma mort, ou du moins que j'attende pour le publier, ou d'ailleurs pour le faire lire à qui que ce soit, une autorisation formelle du conseil directeur de l'Église – à savoir le triumvirat qu'il formait avec Savant et Flic. Au-delà de ces conditions que j'acceptai facilement – et je savais qu'il me faisait confiance – je le sentais pensif, comme si ma demande venait de l'entraîner dans des réflexions floues, qu'il avait encore du mal à démêler.[9]

8   *La Possibilité d'une île*, p. 245.
9   *La Possibilité d'une île*, p. 308.

The purpose of Danielı's story is not to pass on his personality but to purge the guilt he feels for his part in the cover-up that follows the death of the cult's prophet. The purpose of confession is to seek absolution, forgiveness for the sin committed. The impulse is of a piece with what we know of his character. He is not a man capable of taking responsibility. He drifts through life rather than living it with passion and commitment. He travels but travels light. He is drawn towards women who ultimately fail to have deep and meaningful relationships with him. In seeking to write the story of the events on Lanzarote, he is disburdening himself of his role in an important episode.

The reaction of Vincent is no less interesting in that it shows his motivation for allowing this. Houellebecq's cult does not quite fit the stereotype. Vincent readily agrees to Danielı's request. One would have imagined that the last thing they would have wanted was for the truth to come out. More importantly, however, is the concluding sentence which shows that Vincent, the imaginative artist, is beginning to think about possibilities that might be created by Danielı's intention:

> En effet, Vincentı nous apprend que c'est à la suite de cette conversation avec Danielı sur le parking de l'aéroport d'Arrecife qu'il eut pour la première fois l'idée du *récit de vie*, d'abord introduit comme une annexe, un simple palliatif en attendant que progressent les travaux de Slotanı sur le câblage des réseaux mémoriels, mais qui devait prendre une si grande importance à la suite des conceptualisations logiques de Pierce.[10]

Thus the mechanism for the transmission of personality derives, like some other scientific discoveries, from chance, from an imaginative grasp of the significance of opportunistic events – it is a detour, a 'détournement' of the '*récit de vie*' from its original purpose. However, even Vincent does not see the full importance of what he is doing. He discovers what works before he understands fully how it works.

The autobiography, together with the transfer of molecular material, is one of the ways in which the personality can be passed on. However,

10   *La Possibilité d'une île*, p. 310.

this step forward also contains its own limitation. The autobiography is not a work in progress but a completed artefact:

> Il était recommandé aux humains d'aboutir, dans toute la mesure du possible, à un récit de vie *achevé*, ceci conformément à la croyance, fréquente à l'époque, que les derniers instants de vie pouvaient s'accompagner d'une sorte de révélation. L'exemple le plus souvent cité par les instructeurs était celui de Marcel Proust, qui, sentant la mort venir, avait eu pour premier réflexe de se précipiter sur le manuscrit de la *Recherche du temps perdu* afin d'y noter ses impressions au fur et à mesure de la progression de son trépas.
>
> Bien peu, en pratique, eurent ce courage.[11]

There is some humour in the image of the great and not so great writers getting up from their death beds to write about the experience to dying. The laconic comment at the end casts a humorous shadow over the preceding paragraph. Houellebecq is however, raising the issue about how complete a complete account of one's life can be – an issue already raised in the eighteenth century by Laurence Sterne. How can an account keep pace with an ongoing experience? The experience will always give rise to an excess of material. It is an issue that also arises in *Plateforme* where the narrator envisages his own disappearance. Michel incorporates his own death into life but as a future event. Life recounted and life lived are thus reunited in a fixed, unchanging document.

The clones do not have any new experiences. They are cut off from experience – literally and metaphorically – in their isolated living units. The clones avoid having any new experiences. They are dedicated to preservation not to advance. With them progress stops dead. Thus rather than being beacons in a post-apocalyptic world, they seek to isolate themselves from what is left of humanity. It is significant that when characters do indeed leave their unit, they are not allowed to return and their line is terminated. Thus the neo-humans become a remnant cowering in a protected bunker afraid to face the challenges that lie outside.

11   *La Possibilité d'une île*, p. 93.

Death is the event which prevents you from ever changing your mind again. The author can have no further 'révélation', no sudden messages into his or her brain which will change what is already there. A personality based on memory cannot entertain new experiences because that would change (i.e. annihilate) the memory as currently constituted. What this means for the process of cloning is that what is passed on cannot be altered, nor can it be added to. In a sense the autobiography imprisons the recipient. It is not so much that Daniel24 and Daniel25 absorb the story so that it becomes a part of them. Rather, they are absorbed by it. That is why they are set to writing commentaries. They have no life of their own, no experiences outside the ones bequeathed by their ancestors.

This is another respect in which the clones are like the tourists in *Plateforme*, as Granger Remy points out above. Tourists follow the script prepared for them by the *Guide du routard* or its equivalent, observing rather than doing. The clones are even more constrained. Nothing happens to them. Unlike their predecessors, they do no have much interaction with others except through the attenuated medium of the computer screen. Living in isolated units, they have nothing to do other than contemplate the lives of their predecessors. With its electrified fence, the living unit is not unlike a prison. Imprisonment is the condition of their existence. They cannot live as free beings, forging their own destiny but must review the life of their original. What they write is not a '*récit de vie*' but a commentary. They have no lives.

The neo-humans are not superior human beings but attenuated ones. Indeed, their physical bodies have been altered in ways that may be presented as advances:

> Il est ironique de penser que la RGS, conçue au départ pour de simples raisons de convenance esthétique, est ce qui allait permettre aux néo-humains de survivre sans grande difficulté aux catastrophes climatiques qui allaient s'ensuivre, et que nul ne pouvait prévoir à l'époque, alors que les humains de l'ancienne race seraient presque entièrement décimés.[12]

---

12 *La Possibilité d'une île*, p. 375.

Clearly the changes to the human form brought about by RGS ('Rectification Génétique Standard' – Standard Genetic Rectification) have allowed the neo-humans to survive the changes in climate. The very term, with its use of initials, reeks of the sort of scientific bureaucracy that was found in *Les Particules élémentaires*. There is also a strong suggestion that the unusual and idiosyncratic are to be expunged. Nothing will be permitted that does not fit in with the norm – a norm that has been predetermined.

As with the '*récit de vie*', what happens is not what was intended. Something that was meant to be cosmetic turns out to be suited to future unforeseen conditions. Indeed, it is this very accident of history that does most to undermine any notion of the inherent superiority of the neo-humans. The changes were not chosen to make them more robust but to make them aesthetically more pleasing. Thus the changes were not like those of evolution which strengthen the species and make it a better fit with its environment. Secondly, the disasters were unforeseen and so no-one could have planned for them anyway. The survival of the neo-humans is the result of luck and luck is not a basis for superiority since the lucky do not control events – they are victims. Even when they benefit from what happens, that only serves to underline their lack of control.

There is thus more that an element of chance in the final form of our successors – and a strong element of humour in the fact that it originates in quasi-pornographic images. Vincent, in an attempt to enhance the attraction of the cult for existing and new members, has launched a campaign stressing the importance of fostering sexual relations as a means of attaining a fulfilled life:

> C'est alors qu'on prit conscience d'un détail qui dans les premiers moments d'enthousiasme, avait échappé à tous: dans son désir de stylisation, Vincent s'était largement éloigné d'une représentation réaliste du corps humain. Si le phallus était assez ressemblant (encore que plus rectiligne, imberbe, et dépourvu d'irrigation veineuse apparente), la vulve se réduisait dans ses dessins à une fente longue et fine, dépourvu de poils, située au milieu du corps, dans le prolongement de la raie des fesses, et qui pouvait certes s'ouvrir largement pour accueillir des bites, mais n'en était pas moins impropre à toute fonction d'excrétion. Tous les organes

excréteurs, plus généralement, avaient disparu, et les êtres ainsi imaginés, s'ils pouvaient faire l'amour, étaient à l'évidence incapables de se nourrir.[13]

What Vincent sketches is only a suggestion of humanity, one that is intended to direct attention to a particular aspect of our existence. The designs stress the sexual but seek to eliminate those aspects of existence that are linked to eating and excretion. This design does reflect some important prejudices and it is the starting point of the Standard Genetic Modification, as devised by Miskiewicz. It is a meeting of science and art, in a manner reminiscent of Tisvalde as described in *Les Particules élémentaires*. It is also an example of an idea being developed in ways that the proposer had not envisaged. Nevertheless, both Vincent and Miskiewicz have conscious or subconscious prejudices against the digestive system. The former sees it as unaesthetic and the latter as inefficient, preferring a system of nutrition based on photosynthesis. Both men find unacceptable in different ways the decomposition of food in the alimentary canal – perhaps because, in their search a means of circumventing death, they do not want to deal with a natural process that is based on decay.

The Standard Genetic Modification is the product of current and attitudes and practices within the cult. The sect seems to pay little heed to what it eats. Meals are Spartan and seem not to be eaten with much pleasure. It is an unavoidable necessity, to assuage hunger. However, hunger, in *La Possibilité d'une île* as elsewhere in Houellebecq, goes beyond the physical need to fill an empty stomach. It is an awareness of lack that can be unbearable. This is an intensely painful experience, a metaphysical one, as is exemplified by Daniel1's account of his reaction to his son's suicide:

> Le jour du suicide de mon fils, je me suis fait des œufs à la tomate. Un chien vivant vaut mieux qu'un lion mort, estime justement l'Ecclésiaste. Je n'avais jamais aimé cet enfant: il était aussi bête que sa mère, et aussi méchant que son père. Sa disparition était loin d'être une catastrophe; des êtres humains de ce genre, on peut s'en passer.[14]

---

13   *La Possibilité d'une île*, pp. 370–371.
14   *La Possibilité d'une île*, pp. 29–30.

This is a complex passage, revealing a complicated person. There is something dysfunctional about this personality. Yet as Danielı proclaims his indifference, his account suggests otherwise. What he does remember is eating eggs. On a symbolic level, the eggs evoke fertility and birth. The tomato used to have an alternative name – love apple or 'pomme d'amour'. The physical hunger that has to be satisfied is indicative that at some level he is aware of emptiness, a hole at the centre of his existence. He needs love.

This emptiness manifests itself in further ways. Danielı, as we have seen, is a man without values. He has no moral centre, no authentic personality to which he can be true. This emptiness means that Danielı does not feel sufficient in himself. His personality is empty shell – like those he discards when he cooked and ate the eggs. The way in which he satisfies his physical hunger points to another, more serious emptiness within him.

This spiritual hunger also shows up in his addictions, which are attempts to satisfy feelings of inadequacy. Danielı is addicted to sex and to the need to feel a connection with people, but he also craves to be admired, to be rich and famous. The themes of hunger and fame are linked at the outset of the novel in the incident of the German and the sausage, which furnishes the material for young Daniel's first stage success. Nevertheless, it is in his relationship with Estherı that Danielı's emptiness manifests itself most clearly. His neediness drives him towards her and, such is its power, it drives her away from him. The relationship between Danielı and Estherı is intense and dysfunctional. The dependency is such that it triumphs over all other considerations. The personality of Danielı develops in unhealthy ways and he ends up stalking the girl.

Neo-humans' absence of hunger is ambiguous. Is the drawing an indication that by eliminating hunger and the need to satisfy it, the neo-humans will also have succeeded in tackling the metaphysical hunger that we feel? Or is it an indication that by tackling physical hunger, one has treated only a symptom of human malaise (our lack of ease with ourselves, our 'disease') rather than the profounder issues. The question is: has the problem been properly dealt with or merely repressed? And might that repressed one day return? Indeed, by not giving neo-humans the means of feeding themselves, might one not also be indicating that they do not have the means of assuaging that spiritual hunger, should it recur?

However, that is not the only issue raised by the genetic modification of the human body. As Daniel1 points out the human beings depicted in the drawing are incapable not just of feeding themselves but also of excreting. This is not deemed necessary because if these humans do not feed themselves, then they will not find it necessary to eliminate the toxic wastes that our living bodies produce. The absence of excretory organs brings to the fore issues of cleanliness and filth.

The neo-humans live in a physically antiseptic environment. They are protected from the mess and debris outside their cocoons and do not physically interact. All communication is through the computer and they sustain themselves by means of sun, water and mineral salts. Once in the outside world, Daniel25 has to confront a quite different world, one that is messy and disordered. The technical objects that fascinated Daniel1 and possession of which were an indication of his worth in the eyes of others are here little more than the flotsam and jetsam of a destroyed civilisation. They are the droppings of a vanished way of life.

What remains of humanity, the dregs, are scavengers. They are in awe of their successors. Seeking to placate Daniel25, one of the women appears to offer him sexual favours. The clone sees 'son trou, qui était énormément velu'.[15] The bodily hair emphasizes the difference between the carnality of the human and the clean lines of the neo-humans, the realisation of Vincent's drawings. The hairs indicate messiness and a lack of definition that contrasts with the latter's clarity. The word 'trou' is deliberately vague, at this point. Are we dealing with the vagina or the anus? Is Daniel25 being offered the excremental organ? If so, is it a sign of respect or is it an insult. Whatever, the answer, the word 'trou' also signals an absence. The emptiness at the heart of human experience has not been filled.

Daniel25 at first accepts the invitation to fill this empty hole:

> En m'approchant, je fus saisi par l'odeur pestilentielle qui émanait de son entre-cuisse. Depuis mon départ j'avais perdu mes habitudes d'hygiène néo-humaines, mon odeur corporelle était légèrement plus prononcée, mais cela n'avait rien à voir avec la puanteur qui émanait du sexe de la sauvage, mélange de relents de

---

15   *La Possibilité d'une île*, p. 460.

merde et de poisson pourri. Je reculai involontairement; elle se redressa aussitôt, toute son inquiétude réveillée, et rampa vers moi; arrivée à la hauteur de mon organe, elle approcha sa bouche. La puanteur était moins insoutenable mais quand même très forte, ses dents étaient petits, avariées, noires.[16]

Smell is not one of the elements that figure largely in Houellebecq's prose. He tends to go for the visual, as do his characters. Daniel1 writes sketches and later film scenarios. We remember the landscape of Lanzarote, Bruno's walk down the Boulevard Saint-Michel and the Rue de la Harpe or the remains of Michel's grandmother in a plastic bag. The incorporation of pornographic elements in the fiction further strengthens this bias and if Michel in *Plateforme* discusses Agatha Christie's *The Hollow* as an outstanding accomplishment, it is perhaps because the enigma is articulated round a murder scene which constitutes the most striking tableau in Christie's work. The image created in the mind is just as important – as Tisserand finds – and the reason for encouraging the chosen humans to rise from their death-beds to write is that they might have a 'révélation'. Smell does not feature much, if at all.

In this instance, the impact of smell is enormous because it is so rare. Even here, the use of the verb 'émaner', which tends to apply to light, liquids and particles, brings the olfactory close to the visual. Indeed, Houellebecq uses the verb twice instead of an alternative such as 'provenir' which would have been more general. Unlike the visual, however, smell is repulsive. This is the first time that a character in one of Houellebecq's novels is actually repulsed by the prospect of sex. That repulsion is conveyed through smells associated with decay and dirt because waste products and decaying fish are reminders that we too will decay and die.

Even the mouth, source of nourishment, smells of decay, though less strongly. Interestingly, the description of the teeth as 'petites, avariées, noires' returns us to the visual but now the visual is contaminated and the sight of the teeth is disgusting rather than attractive. Her teeth have been damaged by eating and this causes the bad smell that comes from her mouth. Both ends of the digestive system repulse – realising what was

16   *La Possibilité d'une île*, pp. 460–461.

only implicit in the drawings of Vincent: eating and excreting are bodily functions with which the neo-humans, like their creators have problems. They seek to repress those problems rather than deal with them or accept them. The search for immortality is not so much an attempt to prolong life as to eliminate death. The scene between Daniel25 and the human woman is a return of the repressed. The malodorous body evokes the smell of the decomposing corpse.

There is an interesting conundrum here which may be the result of an authorial lapse or it may be something else. The question is: if the neo-humans do not eat and do not excrete, how does Daniel25 manage to find a way to describe the smells emanating from the woman? Both excrement and rotting fish are outside his area of experience. However, they are not outside the area of Daniel1's experience. It is important to keep in mind that the clones preserve their link with the original in two ways. The one that has been most prominent in this study is the 'récit de vie'. However, the other should not be neglected – the transfer of material from the hippocampus of the original. Since the hippocampus is associated with the memory function of the brain, it is not implausible to assume that some element of memory is transmitted in this way. The two methods are meant to be fit together. Daniel25 himself speaks of the two processes as being a 'méthode hybride entre le biochimique et le propositionnel'.[17] Interestingly, the hippocampus is located next to that part of the brain associated with the olfactory function. It is possible therefore to conclude that the transfer of the experiences also takes place at a direct level. Daniel25 has access to areas of experience that cannot be preserved in a book. He has Daniel1's human experience of smells and these are called upon here. As was pointed out earlier, one cannot be someone's clone just because one has read their autobiography. Something more is required and the genetic transfer provides that extra element.

Thus Daniel25 is able to identify dirt. Humanity cannot avoid dirt and cannot preserve itself from contamination. The cult's obsession with removing the excretory processes reflects a desire not only to avoid contamination

17   *La Possibilité d'une île*, p. 246.

but also not to contaminate. This is unrealistic and the clones can only live up to this if they are isolated in the living units. Once outside, things are different. Fox, the dog who has accompanied Daniel25, is found one morning in obvious pain:

> En lissant son poil je découvris rapidement une petite surface bombée, grise, large de quelques millimètres: c'était une tique, je reconnus l'aspect pour avoir lu la description dans des ouvrages de biologie animale. L'extraction de ce parasite était, je le savais, délicate; je retournai à mon sac à dos, pris des pinces et une compresse imbibée d'alcool. Fox gémit faiblement, mais resta immobile au moment où j'opérais: lentement, millimètre par millimètre, je parvins à extraire l'animal de sa chair; c'était un cylindre gris charnu, d'aspect répugnant, qui avait grossi en se gorgeant de son sang; ainsi était constitué le monde naturel.[18]

This time, Daniel25 gives us the source of his knowledge of ticks. Emphasis is on the visual, describing the appearance of the skin and then the parasite itself. The tentative rhythm reflects the slow, careful operation. Daniel25 cares for the dog and does not want him to suffer. By the same token, the quiet and stillness of Fox reflects a closeness and trust in Daniel25, an echo of the unconditional love that the original Fox gave to Isabelle and Daniel1.

Beyond this, however, the extract dwells on the repugnant. The tick causes pain and that is reflected in the changed appearance of the dog's skin. Furthermore, when extracted, it looks disgusting. It is swollen because of the blood it has consumed. Houellebecq uses the verb 'se gorger' to suggest that the parasite is feeding not to keep itself alive but excessively and at the expense of another living being. It is selfish. The verb 'boire' would have conveyed something less threatening. However, this is part of the 'monde naturel'. It is indeed painful for the dog but it is Daniel25 who judges that the parasite is repugnant.

What disturbs Daniel25 is the act of feeding. If Daniel1 was able to find comfort in a dish of eggs, his successor has an attitude resembling that of Vincent and Miskiewicz. A tick is nothing but an alimentary canal. It feeds, therefore it is. It is a hunger that knows no end. Vincent and Miskiewicz are uncomfortable with this part of the human experience. They

---

18   *La Possibilité d'une île*, p. 442.

are not uncomfortable with displays of sexuality but with the manifestation of hunger. It is a sign of our weakness, our dependence on a process
of decomposition that exists within the human body. It leaves the body
vulnerable to what it ingurgitates. But it also parallels the way personality
functions. As empty shells, our personalities are empty spaces that need to
be filled. We are susceptible to the thoughts of others which we process in
our minds and in turn others are susceptible to our thoughts. The Standard
Genetic Rectification is a closing off of the alimentary canal. However, it
is also a metaphor for sealing within the clones the emptiness at the heart
of the human personality and indicates that the neo-humans have no way
of finding the spiritual nourishment they need.

Furthermore, the 'récit de vie' is a closing off of the mind. The clones
are influenced by only one person – the progenitor. They comment on only
one life, the progenitor's. Their spirit is in a closed circuit, a mental system
that feeds on itself, a recirculation of the same ideas rather as photosynthesis, the system on which the clones' new alimentary process is based, is
a circulating system. The clones are isolated as far as possible.

However, complete isolation is impossible. Light and air are needed
as are mineral salts. The clones are able to communicate with each other
though not in the immediate ways of their ancestors. There is still something
of the human about them. Daniel25 is in theory capable of having sex with
the woman. Most importantly, the need to feed is still there. The clones
need to take in nourishment from the environment, just as humans do.

The disgust at the appearance of the tick may therefore indicate a more
profound malaise. Just as Vincent and Mickiewicz were uncomfortable with
what is the basic human process, the need to feed, so Daniel25 finds in the
parasite an unacknowledged reminder of a side of his nature that has been
repressed. The clones are like the ticks in so many ways. What is noticeable
about the clone chapters is the absence of activity. What do they do? They
observe, they comment and enter into sporadic contact with each other.
They do not produce anything. They are consumers, nothing more. They
live off what is already there but do not actually produce anything. When
they die and are replaced by an identical model – all ticks look the same.
This perhaps is the point. The clones feed off the planet and contribute

nothing in return. Despite the Standard Genetic Rectification, the neo-humans are hungry mouths that are insatiable.

Ironically, the hunger that was part of Daniel1's tragedy is extrapolated and now constitutes what the clones are. The very thing that Vincent and Miskiewicz sought to suppress turns out to be the essence of the clones. They have a want that will never be satisfied. The neediness, the lack of values is what has been passed on. This is the nature of humanity and the neo-humans are trapped in it. Just as Daniel1 lacks the values that would give him an authentic life, so the clones lack any purpose. They are copies of an original and as copies lack any possibility of authenticity since it is a pre-requisite of authenticity that one is true to oneself. However, the clones do not have a self to be true to – any more than their ancestors did. They cannot be delivered of the emptiness within.

On one level, the link between the cult and the science needed to carry out cloning is simple. It is financial. The cult has money and Miskiewicz will do what it takes in order to get the financial backing he needs. As often, within organisations, people with differing motivations can work together. Miskiewicz can collaborate with the prophet because they both believe in the importance of cloning for the future of humanity. His research is parasitically attaching itself to the cult – a different kind of knowledge system – in order to feed. This in fact mirrors what the other characters do. The prophet himself uses the cult to feed his delusions. He needs to be worshipped. Indeed his needs are similar to those of Daniel1 who tags along because he is fêted as a VIP. Both men are little more than images that need to be maintained by the attention of others.

Image and reality are fused. The death of the prophet and his replacement by Vincent is staged as a resurrection in the full glare of the media. The destruction of the physical body of the prophet in the volcanic crater and his staged 'resurrection' shows to what extent the image is the person. What matters is what is presented. The absence of authentic substance (the fact that this is not the prophet but a substitute) is of no importance. The cult then is not, as might be expected of a religion or other spiritual practice, a means of finding one's inner truth. It is mechanism that allows

the emptiness that is at the heart of humanity to be covered by an image.
It is a distraction.

The cult is a fabrication that does not deal with our fundamental
problem – while keeping up the pretence that it does. Perpetuating life is
only a distraction from the fact that the characters do no really have lives
worth living. It is this despair that drives Isabelle towards suicide and, at
the end, Danielı himself. What is perpetuated is emptiness not a full life.
The clones are pointless. Life is meaningless not because we die but because
we are empty inside ourselves. Our fear of aging is only a symptom of this.
It stems from our location of value not within ourselves but in externals, in
how other people rate us rather than in how we accept ourselves for who
we are. If we locate our worth in the judgement others make on our bodies,
then the decay of the body is an attack on our sense of value. Death is the
ultimate loss because it completely destroys the body.

The narrator is a also cultivator of his image. That is where he places
his sense of worth. He is lured into the cult because it looks upon him as
he looks upon himself. He is a VIP. This is something he revels in:

> Nous [Danielı and Vincent] n'allions pas jusqu'à fumer en présence du prophète;
> mais de temps en temps au cours des conférences on sortait ensemble s'en griller
> une, ce fut assez vite tacitement admis. Ah, VIPitude.[19]

This is humorous at Danielı's expense, a wry, ironic humour. The gap
between his self-importance and the reality of the privilege it accords is
obvious. What is debatable is the extent to which Danielı is aware of this.
His concluding remark is certainly ironic as far as the reader is concerned.
However, is Danielı aware of how petty his advantage is or is he does he
really believe that he has such a high status? The answer lies somewhere
between the two. There is an ambiguity in Danielı's attitude that reproduces
the attitude of the prophet and his followers towards Danielı's smoking.
He is allowed to do it but the permission is given 'tacitement'. It is a knowing deception that does not even acknowledge that it is a deception. It is

19   *La Possibilité d'une île*, p. 119.

an act. Similarly, Danielı's concluding words are a little flourish that leaves us in doubt as to whether or not he is in on the joke.

What is not in doubt is that, as far as Danielı and the cult are concerned, the façade should not be questioned. Daniel wants his status as a VIP. This is because there is nothing else. The cult wants that status because it will give them additional kudos. The fact that these people need him is a further indication that the cult is just as hollow. It needs to convince people by carefully cultivating its image. If it were confident of its own inherent value it would not need him. There is mutual parasitism.

This is not to say that the cult is a deliberate fraud, a conscious effort to deceive – even though some of the adherents may have questionable motives and there is good reason to suspect that Miskiewicz is more interested in funding for his experiments than in the theology. What is more troubling is that the cult not only fails to address feelings of worthlessness, it reinforces them. Indeed, it must do so in order to survive. It depends for its existence on maintaining the very problem it should be dealing with. It does not look on our feelings of worthlessness as a challenge. Existentialist philosophers accept that we are not sustained by a god-given set of values but take this as an invitation to forge values. The cult does the opposite. Its story is the story of a humanity that is basically powerless to find its own salvation. Human beings are not responsible for their own existence.

The cult believes that human beings are the creation of beings from outer space, the Élohim, who will one day return to share their power and knowledge with us. Implicit in this belief, even if not openly stated, is the view that if our origins are elsewhere, then so is our home. We are alienated from the planet on which we live. We do not belong. Additionally, our relationship to the Élohim is that of children to their parents. They are more advanced than we are. The story infantilises us and makes us dependent on the Élohim. We achieve our sense of worth through our belief that we were created by these advanced beings and that one day, not through our own merits but by their gift, we will achieve worth. The very promise denies what it would grant.

If the cult cannot depend on truth, then it is compelled to manage effects. This is what underpins its substitution of Vincent for the dead prophet. It is quite prepared to jettison that which it no longer needs in order to maximise its effectiveness. Like Danielı, the cult plays many parts in order to create a following. This is the only consistent pattern. There is a major re-orientation under the next generation of leaders and the myth of the Élohim is quietly abandoned. It is no surprise to discover that the neo-humans have a quite different mythology:

> Au commencement fut engendrée la Sœur suprême, qui est première. Furent ensuite engendrés les Sept Fondateurs, qui créèrent la Cité centrale. Si l'enseignement de la Sœur suprême est la base de nos conceptions philosophiques, l'organisation politique des communautés néo-humaines doit à peu près tout aux Sept Fondateurs [...][20]

The language is formal and hieratic, as though a quotation from sacred writ. The foundation myth is quite different from that recounted by the Élohimites and yet it has the same purpose – to convince its followers that they are powerless and depend on a higher authority. Thus the Supreme Sister and the Seven Founders are the source of wisdom and the curious formulation 'Sœur suprême' is nicely ambiguous in a way reminiscent of the cult's attitude to Danielı's nipping out for a quick smoke. The 'Sœur' indicates that she is on the same level as the rest of us while 'suprême' undermines that, suggesting a more powerful being. Ambiguity is part of a belief system which seems to rest on a sense of the impossible. The use of 'Sœur' indicates that there might have been a father – but the passive, 'fut engendrée', suggests the opposite. It does not make sense but that is the point. The myth of the 'Sœur suprême' is a mystery that is meant to block scrutiny rather than invite us in. Like the cult's myth of the Élohim, it fosters the belief that the neo-humans owe everything to something outside themselves and this encourages a feeling of powerlessness. The myth goes on to state that the neo-humans are only transitional beings. They will be superseded when the 'Futurs' come, bringing with them the possibility of a more fulfilled life. This means that the clones are not the goal of evolution, even one assisted by the cult. Such a status would confer worth.

20   *La Possibilité d'une île*, p. 424.

Daniel24 describes his existence as 'une vie calme et sans joie'.[21] He complains that unlike the dog, Fox, he cannot experience happiness because he cannot experience unconditional love: 'Que l'amour inconditionnel soit la condition de possibilité, cela les humains le savaient déjà, du moins les plus avancés d'entre eux'.[22] Daniel24 knows what is missing: the unconditional love that does not depend on anything outside itself to sustain it. Yet he is incapable of experiencing it. He is in the position of knowing what is wrong but feeling powerless to do anything.

Daniel24 does not deny the existence of values – he just does not see how he can access them:

> La bonté, la compassion, la fidélité, l'altruisme demeurent donc près de nous comme des mystères impénétrables, cependant contenus dans l'espace limité de l'enveloppe corporelle d'un chien. De la solution de ce problème dépend l'avènement, ou non, des Futurs.
>
> Je crois en l'avènement des Futurs.[23]

The phrase, 'contenus dans l'espace limité de l'enveloppe corporelle d'un chien', recalls the eggs that provided the food Daniel1 ate the day his son died. The virtues are like the yoke and white of the egg. They feed our hunger for values and fill up the space in our souls – just as the eggs fill our empty stomachs. Daniel24 locates the virtues in the dog and in so doing denies them to himself. These immense, limitless abstractions are contained in a physical space that lies beside him, a message of value in an envelope that he cannot open. Yet he realizes that this is a problem that must be solved. The last line is an expression of qualified hope but one that seems to depend more on a miracle than on any definite notion of what to do.

Daniel24 understands the problem but does not have it within himself to do anything. So, he ends up fading out to be replaced by Daniel25. However, the latter changes the pattern of existence once he has finished

21 *La Possibilité d'une île*, p. 77.
22 *La Possibilité d'une île*, p. 78.
23 *La Possibilité d'une île*, p. 79.

his commentary on the story of Daniel1. His role has come to an end. There is nothing more for him to comment on. Faced with this emptiness, he does what his predecessors fail to do. He leaves the unit in which he lives, impelled to search for something to assuage the metaphysical hunger no neo-human can escape. By leaving, Daniel25 ceases to comment and instead starts to encounter the world outside the limited set of experiences that he has been given. He starts to lead his own life rather than going back to the beginning of Daniel1's story – a cycle of repetition, a closed circuit that prevents life moving forward. The text may label this section of the book 'epilogue' but this understates the importance of the fact that Daniel25 is able to go beyond his ancestor's words. He is not imprisoned by the story any longer. Daniel1 no longer determines Daniel25's role.

There is something unexpected about the departure. That, however, is one of the themes of the book. Running alongside the theme of planning, of determining in advance what will happen, there is also the theme of the unexpected. As a scenario writer, Daniel1 predetermines what will happen in his sketches and his films. Nothing happens unless he has written it. However, life is different. The cult plans for the return of the Élohim. It seeks to build an embassy that will greet them on their arrival – a sort of magic not unlike that of the cargo cults. However, things go awry and the result is the neo-humans – not part of the plan. There is thus a tension between control and the inability to control. Ultimately, life happens while we are making other plans. The irruption of the unexpected, causing a change of course, is not unlike the opening of *Lanzarote*.

Plans seek to circumscribe actions and eliminate the unexpected. Disruption shows us that there is a possibility of something else. The title of the novel is a tribute to the ambiguous, disruptive forces that can change things for good or ill. Uncertainty of outcome lies at the heart of the ambiguous notion of 'possibilité'. Optimistic planning in order to achieve a desired outcome can and does result in frustration. The anxiety that accompanies a visionary like Michel in *Les Particules élémentaires* stems from his impulse to control events and his inability to do so. He can only cope by taking Xanax, a palliative that lessens the pain and allows him to cope but which does not solve the problem.

Giving up control and surrendering to possibility allows the unexpected to arise. However, before accepting this, it is well to remember that this sort of philosophy comes close to the New Age thinking that gets short shrift in *Les Particules élémentaires*. Houellebecq's vision does not favour abdication of the will or of our capacity to plan. It starts from the realisation that there is no point in making a decision to surrender to the unexpected because ironically in deciding to surrender to it and invite it into our lives, we are somehow domesticating it. Surrendering to the unexpected makes it part of the rules by which we live. The activities at the camp seek to harness the forces of change and integrate them. The participants plan for the unexpected whereas in fact the unexpected occurs whether we will or not. It disrupts. 'Changement' is inevitable and irresistible. The unexpected occurs causing us to lose control – as Bruno loses control of the car on is way to the centre. It was not a decision to lose control. It was something that showed that total control is impossible.

At the same time, Houellebecq also demonstrates the complexity of the issue. Control is not something to be denigrated, to be cast out as a stultifying force that inhibits us. Driving without control of a vehicle is not a life-enhancing experience. We need to plan if things are to be done. Without foresight and attempts to control events, nothing would be accomplished. However, we also need to know is that control can be undone by the unexpected. This is a much more realistic vision of the reality of life than that espoused by the New Agers as Bruno encounters them.

This tension or balance between control and surrender to the unexpected is most tellingly articulated in *La Possibilité d'une île* in the figure of Vincent. On the one hand he is the person who allows control to be reasserted after the death of the prophet. Indeed by enhancing the role of Jerôme, whom Daniel1 calls 'Flic', he increases the amount of control that operates in the cult. However, when we first meet him, he is an artist and as an artist he is aware of, or working towards an awareness of, the deep forces that underpin existence. What he achieves culminates in the installation viewed, or more accurately experienced, by Daniel1. The irony is that Vincent, the person who facilitates the creation of the neo-humans, is also the one who allows an alternative experience of what our experience might be about. This is certainly unexpected.

Danielı is receptive to the experience:

Les vers sublimes me revinrent immédiatement en mémoire, comme si ils avaient
toujours été présents dans un recoin de mon esprit, comme si ma vie entière
n'avait été que leur commentaire plus ou moins explicite [...]²⁴

A poem by Baudelaire returns like a memory. What happens to Danielı is
similar to the experience of the narrator at the start of *Lanzarote*, though
now the thought that irrupts into the mind is richer. The word 'commentaire' reverses the relationship between life and commentary. A commentary should follow the life and illuminate it. The clones provide glosses
and explanations that fill out the story of a live already lived. By claiming
that his life is a commentary on the poem, Danielı is making the poem
a prophetic vision. The present can be foretold or foreordained by a past
text. Time is made to run backwards in defiance of normal laws and cause
and effect are reversed.

What is happening here also foreshadows the process of cloning and
use of text to pass on a previous life. The quotation above suggests that
Danielı could be considered a clone of Baudelaire. Eight lines of the poet's
La Mort des pauvres follow. In them death is seen ambiguously not just as
a rest from life but one of the drivers of our lives. It shows the body being
given comfort and nourishment, rather than being starved into nothingness, a mere bag of bones. One of the things that we know about Danielı
is that he is actually quite wealthy and seems to think it important that
he possess high-status material things. He enjoys staying in fine hotels.
He constantly reminds us just how much money he has in the bank – he
certainly knows his own price. Yet the poem is about the '*pauvres*'. Danielı
is indeed poor and hungry but in another sense: he lacks self-worth. His
poverty is spiritual.

Danielı describes the lines as being 'sublimes' and the sublime is always
unsettling, taking us beyond the boundaries of normal experience. It has
the power to inspire dread as well as ecstasy. What causes us to look up in
wonder may cause us to look down at the horror of the grave. Danielı's

24   *La Possibilité d'une île*, p. 409.

experience of Vincent's installation is a journey to the heart of mysteries normally kept hidden. It explores not the world beyond life but the world beyond the material:

> J'avais l'impression de me mouvoir à l'intérieur d'un espace laiteux, isotrope, qui se condensait parfois, subitement, en micro-formations grenues – en m'approchant je distinguais des montagnes, des vallées, des paysages entiers qui se complexifiaient rapidement puis disparaissaient presque aussitôt, et le décor replongeait dans une homogénéité floue, traversée de potentialités oscillantes.[25]

Daniel1 is exploring not a literal landscape but the world of his imagination. It is an 'espace laiteux', a space where nourishment will be provided and hunger satisfied. It is a descent into the underworld in order to be reborn. However, in this womb, Daniel1 is still able to perceive geographical features that would normally be part of the world outside. Inner and outer are being confused and the effect is of total disorientation or reorientation. There is a sense of flow but the direction is uncertain. All that Daniel1 can know is that he is experiencing a rich complexity that is full of ever-changing possibilities.

In this unsettling experience, very notion of self begins to mutate and Daniel1 becomes, as the adverb indicates, a stranger to himself:

> Étrangement, je ne voyais plus mes mains, ni aucune autre partie de mon corps. Je perdis très vite toute notion de direction, et j'eus alors l'impression d'entendre des pas qui faisaient écho aux miens: lorsque je m'arrêtais ces pas s'arrêtaient eux aussi, mais avec un léger temps de retard. Tournant mon regard vers la droite j'aperçus une silhouette qui répétait chacun de mes mouvements, qui ne se distinguait de la blancheur éblouissante de l'atmosphère que par un blanc légèrement plus mat. J'en ressentis une légère inquiétude: la silhouette disparut aussitôt. Mon inquiétude se dissipa: la silhouette se matérialisa à nouveau, comme surgie du néant.[26]

---

25 *La Possibilité d'une île*, p. 410.
26 *La Possibilité d'une île*, p. 410.

It may be remarked that this surreal scene where Danielı is describing his loss of his sense of direction is written in strict accordance with the rules governing the past tenses in French. The Past Historic is the main tense and gives a sense of flow and direction. What Danielı is experiencing is a plenitude that denies nothing. It does not throw out law and order just because it recognises the worth of the unexpected, of wandering from the predetermined. Nothing can be excluded.

Comparing this sense of losing control over one's body with earlier examples is most instructive. Michel in his hospital bed in *Extension du domaine de la lutte* also experiences a sense of separation from his limbs but in that instance the sense was one of loss of power rather than of the tapping into ever-changing potential. In *Les Particules élémentaires*, the integrity of the body is linked to a sense of self. Cancers attack the body structure and the sight of the remains of Michel's grandmother being gathered into a plastic bag is a statement of hopelessness.

In *La Possibilité d'une île*, the loss of the sense of self is accompanied by an uncanny rediscovery of the self – the self is experienced as other, as a ghost that returns to haunt Danielı. But this ghost is reversed. It is a black silhouette in a white environment. This is Danielı's shadow side, the part of himself that he has repressed. Its return arouses feelings of anxiety. This anxiety causes the silhouette to disappear – it is again repressed if only momentarily. However, Danielı simply allows the feeling to be one more passing experience. He does not hold on to it or seek to suppress it. So, it simply passes and when it does, the silhouette returns. Feelings are neither good nor bad, experiences to be resisted or prolonged. They simply are.

Experiencing feelings does not, however, mean that the intellect has been abandoned. Danielı realizes that this installation is made possible by computer technology – it derives from the same technology that was used to design the putative embassy. This is rich is irony. The cult's belief may be a false one but its attempts to act out that fraud have made possible the rich, life-enhancing experience that Danielı is now having. The world of art is intimately related to the world of science and technology.

The other self disappears and Danielı feels himself merging with the experience. Now he feels absorbed into something bigger, or perhaps it is absorbed into him. The result is a feeling of expansion, of opening out rather than of being hedged in:

> Je n'entendais même plus ma propre respiration, et je compris alors que j'étais *devenu* l'espace; j'étais l'univers et j'étais l'existence phénoménale, les micro-structures étincelantes qui apparaissaient, se figeaient, puis se dissolvaient dans l'espace faisaient partie de moi-même, et je sentais miennes, se produisant à l'intérieur de mon corps, chacune de leurs apparitions comme chacune de leurs cessations. Je fus alors saisi par un intense désir de disparaître, de me fondre dans un néant lumineux, actif, vibrant de potentialités perpétuelles; la luminosité redevint aveuglante, l'espace autour de moi sembla exploser et se diffracter en parcelles de lumière, mais il ne s'agissait pas d'un espace au sens habituel du terme, il comportait des dimensions multiples et toute autre perception avait disparu – cet espace ne contenait, au sens habituel du terme, rien.[27]

The phrase 'au sens habituel du terme' occurs twice, an echo of itself just as the silhouette is an echo of Daniel1. Language itself is part of the experience. It is in and through language that Daniel1 is making sense of what is happening. He is finding his place in the universe and more importantly the place of the universe in him. If he only found the former, it would reduce him to the status of cog in a machine. He experiences himself as much more.

This imaginative grasp of the complex fit of Daniel1 and the world is couched in a language that is heavy with negatives. The images of light are counterbalanced with the image of the 'néant' and the negative constructions. These negatives are not a stripping away, an excision of the parts, but rather a merging of the self and what is not the self. It forces us to consider what meaning is. The way the word 'rien' is being used at the end of the quotation indicates that it is not absence but rather a silhouette, a presence that is also an absence.

The imagery of science, particularly that pertaining to space, is used poetically. Science is not inimical to the imagination. It is not what causes us to be alienated but indeed can serve to heal our sense of not belonging. The violence of some of the imagery, particularly 'exploser' is not a symptom of

---

27   *La Possibilité d'une île*, p. 411.

dislocation but rather of pent-up energy being released, energy that is not contained or controlled, but which just is. As the term Big Bang reminds us, explosions are both creative and destructive.

All of this experience is dynamic, full of energy. It is not some still, transcendent moment that exists outside time and space. Movement is part of the experience. It is a process. And like all processes, it must change. Experiences are to be experienced, not held. What Daniel1 goes through is not a loss of self 'au sens habituel du terme':

> Je demeurai ainsi, parmi les potentialités sans forme, au-delà même de la forme et de l'absence de forme, pendant un temps que je ne parvins pas à définir; puis quelque chose apparut en moi, au début presque imperceptible, comme le souvenir ou le rêve d'une sensation de pesanteur; je repris alors conscience de ma respiration, et des trois dimensions de l'espace, qui se fit peu à peu immobile; des objets apparurent de nouveau autour de moi, comme de discrètes émanations du blanc, et je parvins à sortir de la pièce.[28]

As though to emphasize the complexity of what is happening, the verb 'demeurer' is used to indicate that stillness is part of this process: remaining in situ is a part of losing oneself in the cosmos. Time passes but it is uncounted.

The return to the real is treated subtly. First, just as the experience began with a loss of awareness of the breath, so it starts to conclude with a return of that awareness. Solidity returns as a dream of solidity and the multiple dimensions of the imagination are reduced to three. The paragraph ends with Daniel leaving the room. The experience is not taken from him – he participates in its ending.

Vincent calls this experience love. But it goes beyond what Daniel1 and others have experienced as love up until now. It is all the feelings and emotions that Daniel24 believes are locked up in the envelope that is Fox. This is what is missing from the major characters in Houellebecq's fiction. The unconditional love that Fox offers is not something that they can share. Some characters do appear to have found love but this always has

---

28   *La Possibilité d'une île*, p. 411.

conditions attached, the most important condition being that it should last. Love is not felt to be love if it does not last. This is what destroys the Michel of *Plateforme*. He cannot accept that his love for Valérie is a process. He sees it as a state, something to be made permanent. Hence, when the bomb goes off and Valérie is killed, he is emotionally devastated and has a nervous breakdown. The bomb explosion demonstrates his inability to control. Michel is unable to accept this. His love is clinging. It is based on neediness, not a sense of plenitude. It is desire for an absent or separated other, not a feeling of communion. Daniel1 elsewhere demonstrates the same neediness. His relationship with Esther is based on his neediness, his hunger. It is not a love that is unconditional. The experience that the installation provokes is an experience that goes beyond desire. There is no absent object (no 'I miss you') to stimulate and maintain the burning, destructive passion that is desire. Instead, Daniel1 finds in himself the answers. The only obstacle is his anxiety, an obstacle that moves on when he accepts it.

Yet this scene is not a moment of salvation. It is a turning point, certainly, but also a re-turning point. Daniel1 returns to his own life, his own hunger – it is after this that he stalks Esther. We may well wonder why it has not lasting impact. The answer is given almost immediately in the text: 'Il était presque impossible, dis-je à Vincent un peu plus tard, de demeurer vivant dans un tel endroit plus de dix minutes'.[29] Daniel1 does not have the strength to withstand such an overwhelming vision. It could be a statement that applies to all of us.

Despite his vision, Daniel1 seeks to hold on to his familiar life. He returns to the comfortable, luxury hotel, the Lutetia, and resumes his life – he chooses 'demeurer vivant'. Life, as we have seen in *Les Particules élémentaires*, is a process of disintegration and proves to be so here. This time, as in *Extension du domaine de la lutte*, the disintegration is psychic. Daniel1 is resuming the downward spiral. He attempts to hold on to the people and places that he knows but this is futile. He ends up facing his own

29 *La Possibilité d'une île*, p. 412.

nothingness, what he calls *'la terreur pure de l'espace'*.[30] This is not space as plenitude that embraces and enfolds but as an absence that threatens to devour him. The hunger that is the emptiness inside him finds an echo in the world outside. His final reflections are an ironic reversal of the experience of the installation:

> Je ne sens plus de haine en moi, plus rien à quoi m'accrocher, plus de repère ni d'indice; la peur est là, vérité de toutes choses, en tout égal au monde observable. Il n'y a plus de monde réel, de monde senti, de monde humain, je suis sorti du temps, je n'ai plus de passé ni d'avenir, je n'ai plus de tristesse ni de projet, de nostalgie, d'abandon ni d'espérance; il n'y a plus que la peur.[31]

This is an emptying out. Daniel₁ has no map to guide him – if indeed he ever had one. This contrasts with Daniel25, a few pages later, able to navigate his way by memory through a changed Spanish landscape. Even if at times he is thrown off course, he still has a sense of direction and purpose. Daniel₁ not so much loses his sense of purpose as discovers that he never really had one. He was animated not by an inner set of values but by the image that he sought to create in other people's mind. He lived in fear of what they might think and so turned to various control strategies to manage that image. All that he is left with is fear, an empty dread. It is not fear of anything in particular – just a fear that is nameless and purposeless.

Daniel₁ is experiencing a contraction of his world. Space closes in on him and the emptiness of fear consumes him:

> L'espace vient, s'approche et essaie de me dévorer. Il y un petit bruit au centre de la pièce. Les fantômes sont là, ils constituent l'espace, ils m'entourent. Ils se nourrissent des yeux crevés des hommes.[32]

The irony is that at the moment of self-effacement, when the author is facing emptiness, the language itself is so full of meaning. The passage contains the final words of Daniel₁ and yet it is not the final word of the

---

30   *La Possibilité d'une île*, p. 427.
31   *La Possibilité d'une île*, p. 427.
32   *La Possibilité d'une île*, p. 428.

novel. Indeed, the image of the ghosts that terrorise Daniel1 could be his vision of the parasitic clones, wraith-like attenuations that feed on the lives of their predecessors.

Daniel24 pointed out that it was desirable to record the moment of death because it was believed that some great revelation was vouchsafed at such a moment. This is in fact what happens here. The irony is that the revelation is not a message of hope but of despair. The hunger that animated Daniel1 and which the Standard General Rectification sought to repress is here exteriorised and returns to devour humanity. The image is of monstrous entities eating the eyes of the living – a cruel image, expressing pain and horror. These ghosts are unlike the silhouette in the installation, a form that reflected the subject. Instead, they occupy the centre of the room, pressing in on Daniel1 so as to choke the life out of him. He loses all.

Yet if the clones are nourished by the words of their predecessor, it is also possible to argue that the narrator's life story needs the commentary that the clones provide. Daniel1's words always require or suggest other meanings. They are themselves hungry for commentary. Thus the '*récit de vie*' is never read in isolation but always calls forth a commentary which supplements it in some way.

In the light of this, the departure of Daniel25 can be seen as moment of renunciation. No longer content or desirous of holding to the life of his ancestor, he leaves. He escapes the clutches of his ancestor. He is no longer under the obligation to keep alive the story of Daniel1's life. This does not mean that his escape is a definitive release. It is not a moment of salvation, when he discovers meaning in his life. Rather, he goes in search of that meaning or of a life in the first place. His leaving his living unit does not diminish his hunger.

Indeed, as he approaches Lanzarote (or the place that it has become) he experiences a loss of water and runs out of mineral salts. And so, he experiences the symptoms of hunger. His spiritual hunger has a physical manifestation. Reaching the ocean, gives him access to water and salt and ensures his survival. It allows his life to continue. However, it gives him something more:

C'était donc cela que les hommes appelaient la mer, et qu'ils considéraient comme la grande consolatrice, comme la grande destructrice aussi, celle qui érode, qui met fin avec douceur. J'étais impressionné, et les derniers éléments qui manquaient à ma compréhension de l'espèce se mirent d'un seul coup en place. Je comprenais mieux, à présent, comment l'idée de l'infini avait pu germer dans le cerveau de ces primates; l'idée d'un infini accessible, par transitions lentes ayant leur origine dans le fini. Je comprenais aussi comment une première conception de l'amour avait pu se former dans le cerveau de Platon.[33]

This is another account of where we come from. The sea is the source of life but it is also the source, according to Daniel25, of our philosophies. It is the sea that intimates infinity and also suggests that the infinite can be present in the finite. What Daniel25 experiences is a moment of enlightenment akin to that of Daniel1 when he viewed the installation. Indeed, Vincent calls his installation 'Love' and Daniel25 sees love as being one of the concepts that has it origins in the contemplation of the eternal movement of the sea. In contemplating the sea, we become aware of a greatness that is near us and which is absent from us. The sea is a symbol of something that we lack but which will complete us. The reference to Plato takes up an earlier quotation from Plato's *Symposium* where love was the force that impelled a human to look for his or her other half – the part that would render them complete beings once again.

Vincent's installation is recalled. The 'espace laiteux' that Daniel1 experiences is the counterpart of the ocean itself, the sea which is bathed in sunlight and composed of water and mineral salts providing the nourishment that Daniel25 needs. There is something archetypal about these closing pages. Daniel25 has returned to the womb of existence. It is a rebirth.

There is an ambiguity about the sea. It consoles but it also destroys. Daniel25 does not shy away from the pain. There is a maturity of emotion rather than a rush of optimistic enthusiasm. It is as though the experience is a humbling one. In the installation, Daniel1 experienced a feeling of his own power and the power of the universe. Now, Daniel25 faces his own insignificance, his own weakness. If he sees the sea as consoling it is because

---

33   *La Possibilité d'une île*, p. 483.

he sees himself as needing, or being likely to need, consoling. His sense of life's fragility is clear in the verbs that follow. This is change as wearing away, wearing down – even if done gently. Things deteriorate. They cannot be preserved. When Daniel1's camera is retrieved by Daniel25 in the ruins of his house in Almería, it is no longer functional. The object survives but its purpose and value do not.

That is why the cloning experiment is an aberration. In attempting to fix the present, it is trying to swim against the tide – a futile effort. The project sought to preserve life by arresting it. This is what Daniel25 finally recognises:

> Je compris, alors, pourquoi la Sœur Suprême insistait sur l'étude du récit de vie de nos prédécesseurs humains; je compris le but qu'elle cherchait à atteindre. Je compris, aussi, pourquoi ce but ne serait jamais atteint.[34]

We may surmise that the 'Sœur Suprême' seeks use the 'récit de vie' to educate the clones so that they follow the life that they study. Even if this supposition is incorrect, it does not matter. The passage is not more or less meaningful as a result. Life cannot be prescribed or circumscribed in this way. It is in the presence of the sea that Daniel25 realizes that the life-force cannot be resisted. This leads to the important realisation: 'J'étais indélivré'. It is a realisation that Daniel25 accepts. Knowledge and enlightenment do not bring salvation. This is a bleak conclusion.

Throughout Houellebecq's fictions we meet characters who are dissatisfied with their lives. They do not like where they live. The dislike the conditions under which they live. The seek change or they seek to control. In some cases they seek to distract themselves from the hunger that tells them that they are in some way lacking. Yet despite all their efforts, they fail to satisfy their fundamental longings. *La Possibilité d'une île* ends differently:

> Je me baignais longtemps, sous le soleil comme sous la lumière des étoiles, et je ne ressentais rien d'autre qu'une légère sensation obscure et nutritive. Le bonheur n'était pas un horizon possible. Le monde avait trahi. Mon corps m'appartenait

---

34 *La Possibilité d'une île*, p. 483.

pour un bref laps de temps; je n'atteindrais jamais l'objectif assigné. Me rêves
étaient peuplés de présences émotives. J'étais, je n'étais plus. La vie était réelle.[35]

Our last encounter with Daniel25 shows him in the sea. He is experiencing
life in its mutability. The experience is 'nutritive', a quality that is ongoing
and which affirms the continuity of the hunger it feeds. Just as Daniel1 was
able to accept a feeling of anxiety while in Vincent's installation, so Daniel25
is able to accept and deal with his hunger. That is part of life. It is pointless
to strive for life to be other than it is. There is no horizon beyond which lies
happiness and to that extent the world has betrayed him. The way to make
the most of life is to be realistic, to accept that things are the way they are.
Hope must give way to realism. If Voltaire's Candide embraces realism by
cultivating his garden, then in the anti-Eden that is post-Apocalypse Lanzarote, Daniel25 takes care of his body. The penultimate sentence accepts
our paradoxical status as beings that are also imbued with nonentity. All
Daniel25 can do is accept his body for the length of time it is granted to
him – not seek uselessly to prolong existence. The final lines are an acceptance, shot through with humility, of the reality of life and of the fact that
it cannot be changed. Daniel25 no longer struggles.

35   *La Possibilité d'une île*, p. 485.

Select Bibliography

Blanton, Casey, *Travel Writing: The Self and the World* (London, Routledge, 2002).

Carlston, Jacob, 'Écriture houellebecquienne, écriture ménipéenne?', in *Michel Houellebecq sous la loupe*, edited by Murielle Lucie Clément and Sabine van Wesemael, Collection Faux Titre no. 304 (Amsterdam and New York, Éditions Rodopi, 2007), pp. 19–30.

Clément, Murielle-Lucie, *Houellebecq, Sperme et Sang*, Collection Approches Littéraires (Paris, L'Harmattan, 2003).

—— *Michel Houellebecq revisité: L'écriture houellebecquienne*, Critiques Littéraires (Paris, L'Harmattan, 2007).

Cohen, Erik, *Thai Tourism: Hill Tribes, Islands and Open-ended Prostitution, Collected Papers*, Studies in Contemporary Thailand, 4 (Bangkok, White Lotus Press, 1996).

Cramer, Kathryn, 'Hard Science Fiction', in *The Cambridge Companion to Science Fiction*, edited by Edward James and Farah Mendlesohn (Cambridge, Cambridge University Press, 2003), pp. 186–196.

Daniell, Steven, '*Plateforme*', *World Literature Review*, 76 (3–4) (Summer–Fall, 2002), p. 110.

Delorme, Julie, 'Du guide touristique au roman. *Plateforme* de Michel Houellebecq', in *Michel Houellebecq sous la loupe*, edited by Murielle Lucie Clément and Sabine van Wesemael, Collection Faux Titre no. 304 (Amsterdam and New York, Éditions Rodopi, 2007), pp. 287–300.

Dumas, Nathalie, 'Lutte à 99 F: La vie sexuelle selon Michel H et Frédéric B.', in *Michel Houellebecq sous la loupe*, edited by Murielle Lucie Clément and Sabine van Wesemael, Collection Faux Titre no. 304 (Amsterdam and New York, Éditions Rodopi, 2007), pp. 215–225.

Friese, Heidrun, 'The Limits of Hospitality', *Paragraph*, Vol. 32, No. 1 (2009), pp. 51–68.

Granger Remy, Maud, 'Le tourisme est un posthumanisme: Autour de *Plateforme*', in *Michel Houellebecq sous la loupe*, edited by Murielle Lucie

Clément and Sabine van Wesemael, Collection Faux Titre no. 304 (Amsterdam and New York, Éditions Rodopi, 2007), pp. 277–286.

Hillis Miller, Joseph, *Fiction and Repetition* (Oxford, Basil Blackwell, 1982).

Holloway, Richard, *Looking in the Distance* (Edinburgh, Canongate Books, 2004).

Houellebecq, Michel, *Extension du domaine de la lutte* (Paris, Éditions Maurice Nadeau, 1994) (Hbk), (Paris, J'ai Lu, 2003) (Pbk).

—— *Les Particules élémentaires* (Paris, Flammarion, 1998) (Hbk), (Paris, J'ai Lu, 2003) (Pbk).

——*Lanzarote* (Paris, Flammarion, 2000) (Hbk), *Lanzarote et autres textes* (Paris, Librio, 2002) (Pbk).

—— *Plateforme* (Paris, Flammarion, 2001) (Hbk), (Paris, J'ai lu, 2001) (Pbk).

—— *La Possibilité d'une île* (Paris, Fayard, 2005) (Hbk), (Paris, Livre de Poche, 2007) (Pbk).

—— 'Sortir du XXᵉ siècle', *Nouvelle Revue Française*, no. 561 (April 2002), pp. 117–121.

Loselle, Andrea, *History's Double: Cultural Tourism in Twentieth-Century French Writing* (New York, St Martin's Press, 1997).

Midgley, Mary, *Science and Poetry* (Abingdon, Routledge Classics, 2006).

Noguez, Dominic, *Houellebecq en fait* (Paris, Fayard, 2003).

Ní Loingsigh, Aedín, 'Tourist Traps: Confounding Expectations in Michel Houellebecq's *Plateforme*', French Cultural Studies, Vol. 16, No. 1 (February 2005), pp. 73–90.

Place-Verghnes, Floriane, 'Houellebecq/Schopenhauer: Souffrance et désir gigognes', in *Michel Houellebecq sous la loupe*, edited by Murielle Lucie Clément and Sabine van Wesemael, Collection Faux Titre no. 304 (Amsterdam and New York, Éditions Rodopi, 2007), pp. 123–132.

Pruche, Yvon, *Amours siamoises: la prostitution en Thaïlande* (Aire-sur-l'Adour, Atura, 2001).

Rabosseau, Sandrine, 'Houellebecq ou le renouveau du roman experimental', in *Michel Houellebecq sous la loupe*, edited by Murielle Lucie Clément and Sabine van Wesemael, Collection Faux Titre no. 304 (Amsterdam and New York, Éditions Rodopi, 2007), pp. 43–51.

Ryan, Chris and Hall, C. Michael, *Sex Tourism: Marginal People and Liminalities* (London and New York, Routledge, 2001).

Sayer, Frédéric, 'Transformations de symboles: Michel Houellebecq et Bret Easton Ellis', in *Michel Houellebecq sous la loupe*, edited by Murielle Lucie Clément and Sabine van Wesemael, Collection Faux Titre no. 304 (Amsterdam and New York, Éditions Rodopi, 2007), pp. 145–155.

Seabrook, Jeremy, *Travels in the Skin Trade: Tourism and the Sex Industry* (London and Chicago, Pluto Press, 1996).

St-Onge, Simon, 'De l'esthétique houellebecquienne', in *Michel Houellebecq sous la loupe*, edited by Murielle Lucie Clément and Sabine van Wesemael, Collection Faux Titre no. 304 (Amsterdam and New York, Éditions Rodopi, 2007), pp. 67–80.

Viard, Bruno, 'Faut-il en rire ou faut-il en pleurer? Michel Houellebecq du côté de Marcel Mauss et du côté de Balzac', in *Michel Houellebecq sous la loupe*, edited by Murielle Lucie Clément and Sabine van Wesemael, Collection Faux Titre no. 304 (Amsterdam and New York, Éditions Rodopi, 2007), pp. 31–42.

Wesemael, Sabine van, *Michel Houellebecq: Le plasir du texte*, Approches Littéraires (Paris, L'Harmattan, 2005).

Index

abuse 6, 123, 130, 134, 161, 169, 180
Adams, Tim 171–172
alcohol 12, 14, 15, 80
animal 9, 61, 82, 96, 108, 177, 193
art 56, 67, 94, 95, 188, 204
Aspect, Alain 58, 69, 71, 75
authentic 158, 159, 160, 177, 189, 195
authenticity 176, 177, 195
authorities 16, 22, 23, 139
autobiography 44, 182, 183, 184, 186, 192

Baudelaire, Charles 16, 202
Baudrillard, Jean 63–64
Belgium 117, 120, 127, 129
beliefs 65–66, 87, 126, 128, 169
boundaries 2, 41, 118, 120, 122, 202
Bourdieu, Pierre 63, 64
bureaucracy 16, 18, 187
Burma 142, 156

Camus, Albert 27, 59, 89
cancers 89
Carlston 52–53, 65
cars 17, 51, 73
chaos 13–14, 41, 99
children 6, 23, 43, 57, 62, 89, 109–110, 123,
    126–127, 129, 137, 142, 149, 155, 197
Clément, Murielle Lucie 13, 17, 52–54,
    98, 166, 168, 172
clones 9, 11, 43, 53, 99, 172–175, 177–181,
    185–186, 192–196, 198, 202, 209,
    211
cloning 56, 129, 172, 174, 180, 182, 186,
    195, 202, 211
Cohen, Erik 146, 148–151, 153

competition 30, 56, 67, 70, 78, 157
control 2, 12, 19–21, 28–29, 42, 44,
    47–48, 73, 77, 80, 82, 85, 87–88,
    91, 126, 141, 162, 164, 168, 187,
    200–201, 204, 207–208, 211
Cramer, Kathryn 64–66
creation 101, 159, 173–174, 197, 201
crime 14, 43, 126
Cuba 159
cult 7, 11, 65, 75, 106, 109–110, 114–116,
    122, 129, 134, 173, 177, 181, 184,
    187–188, 192, 195–198, 200–201,
    204
culture 1, 55, 58, 91, 123, 137, 141–142

danger 26, 28, 108–110, 113, 118, 122, 136,
    166
Debord, Guy 81–82
Deleuze, Gilles 81–82
Delorme, Julie 17, 133
derivative 5, 8, 9, 12, 157
desire 13, 17, 33, 35, 40, 43, 45, 47, 60–61,
    65, 86, 98, 105, 107, 111, 116–118,
    120, 122, 125, 134, 138, 154, 192, 207
domination 36, 47, 62
drugs 25, 80, 86, 92, 162, 181
Dumas, Nathalie 13, 15

Einstein, Albert 70
emptiness 24, 50, 96–97, 154–155, 165, 172,
    177, 189–190, 194–196, 200, 208
Epicurus 72
evolution 7, 65, 79, 87–89, 114, 137, 187,
    198
exploitation 9, 133, 134, 137, 155, 168

fiction 2, 3, 6, 8, 13, 25, 52–54, 59, 63–64,
    73, 106, 114, 121, 130, 135, 137, 139,
    145–146, 150, 191, 206
France 54–56, 58, 76, 134–135, 137
French 1, 16, 51, 52, 54–55, 57–58, 76, 103,
    113, 119, 140, 143–144, 147, 162,
    167, 169, 204
Friese, Heidrun 133–134, 142
future 1, 5, 6–9, 11, 25, 37, 74, 86, 88, 91,
    100, 110, 114, 125, 134, 173–174,
    180, 185, 187, 195

Gates, Bill 55, 57, 90
Giraldus Cambrensis 95, 99
globalization 2, 76, 103
Granger Remy, Maud 172, 173, 186

health 166, 168
Hillis Miller, Joseph 26
horror 84, 109, 124, 202, 209
hospitality 133–135, 142, 162, 169
human 1–3, 7, 9, 11, 16, 18, 22, 24, 26,
    31–32, 36, 42, 51, 54–56, 59, 61–63,
    65, 70, 72–73, 78, 79–81, 84,
    88–91, 96–98, 100, 103–104, 116,
    118, 120–122, 152–153, 169, 172–
    174, 178, 180, 186–187, 189–190,
    192–194, 197, 200, 210
humanity 7, 9, 42, 61, 65, 70, 82, 86,
    87–89, 91, 97–99, 129, 171, 173,
    177, 185, 188, 190, 195–197, 209
humans 8, 9, 62, 69, 82, 98–99, 121, 172,
    174, 181, 187, 189–192, 194, 198
hunger 107, 116, 121, 177, 188–189, 193,
    195, 199–200, 203, 207–209,
    211–212

image 21–22, 50, 61–62, 76, 78, 83, 96,
    103, 109, 118, 125, 130, 135, 154, 159,
    176, 180, 185, 191, 195, 196–197,
    205, 208, 209

intellectuals 63–64
Islam 119–121, 134–135, 140

Kells, Book of 6, 43, 46, 66, 93–98, 100
knowledge 1, 3, 6–7, 24, 29, 39, 49, 64,
    66–68, 70–71, 80, 92, 100, 109,
    116, 121, 124, 130, 138, 140–141, 143,
    152, 157, 159, 175, 181, 193, 195, 197

lack 1, 3, 8, 18, 21, 23–25, 29–31, 35–36, 40,
    56–57, 64, 73, 76, 84, 86, 102, 104,
    110, 112, 119, 124, 126, 133, 149, 151,
    155–156, 159–160, 165, 176–178,
    187–190, 195, 210
language 28, 30, 33, 36, 42, 64–65, 67,
    112–113, 135, 139–140, 143, 164,
    175–178, 180, 182, 198, 205, 208
lesbians 101, 104, 113, 122
Loselle, Andrea 140

machines 7, 82, 159, 171–172
Malraux, André 63–64
masturbation 30, 40, 116
memories 7, 39, 174, 178–179, 182
memory 7, 175, 178, 180, 181, 182, 183, 186,
    192, 202, 208
metaphor 11, 52, 64, 81, 177, 194
Midgley, Mary 72
mind 2, 8, 13, 16–17, 19, 29, 30, 33, 35,
    38–39, 85–86, 92, 100, 103–105,
    113, 120, 140, 143, 148, 181, 186,
    191–192, 194, 202, 208
monstrosity 109, 117, 119, 120
monstrous 101, 103, 111, 120, 123, 125, 209
myth 34, 173, 198

neo-humans 8, 99, 100–101, 173–174,
    181–183, 185–187, 189–190, 192,
    194–195, 198, 200–201
network 22–23, 25, 33, 44, 48, 58, 87, 97
Ní Loingsigh, Aedín 167

Noguez, Dominique 14, 135, 137, 140, 143–145, 153, 155

paedophile 103–104, 110, 117, 122, 126, 128–129, 135–137, 155, 159
paedophilia 2, 104, 108, 113, 122, 127, 129, 135, 137, 155
parasite 193–194
parents 6, 23, 85–86, 125–129, 135–136, 149–150, 155, 159, 197
patients 26–29
physics 65, 69, 71, 74, 76, 90, 93
Place-Verghnes, Floriane 53, 54
Plato 14, 210
pleasure 26, 37, 60, 81, 113, 126–127, 142, 161, 188
Podolsky, Boris 70
Proust, Marcel 55, 65, 185
Pruche, Yann 144–145
psyche 19, 104, 107
purity 61, 76, 147

Rabosseau, Sandrine 53, 58–59, 65, 69, 97
reader 1, 2, 26, 41–43, 46, 52, 54, 60–61, 73, 83, 111, 123, 125, 127, 135, 140, 143–144, 148, 153, 156, 163, 166–167, 174–175, 179, 196
reality 1, 15, 27, 32, 38, 41–42, 46, 61, 66, 84, 92, 95, 100, 106, 111, 115, 118, 120, 134, 145–146, 148, 162, 180, 195–196, 201, 212
religions 64, 82, 87, 94, 121
Rosen, Nathan 70
Ryan, Chris and Hall, C. Michael 168

Sartre, Jean-Paul 63–64
Sayer, Frédéric 98
science 28, 59, 63–68, 70, 72–74, 80, 87–88, 91, 94–95, 97, 114, 121, 124, 128–129, 137, 182, 188, 195, 204–205

Seabrook, Jeremy 145–146, 148–150, 153
sex-tourism 2–3, 133–135, 137, 141, 144–146, 149–151, 154–155, 159, 161–162, 166–168
sex-tourists 9, 133, 135, 149, 154
sex-trade 138, 146–147, 150, 154
sexuality 31, 32, 88, 102, 120, 128, 137, 194
Snoop Doggy Dogg 55, 56, 57, 90
society 15, 26, 34, 41, 44, 47, 53, 59, 63–64, 66, 84, 106–107, 116–117, 119, 126, 128–130, 137–138, 142–143, 148, 152, 154, 159, 180
St-Onge, Simon 53–54, 56
struggle 2, 8, 11, 19, 30–31, 35, 42–45, 47, 50, 63, 67, 70, 78, 90, 128
suicide 7, 45, 81–83, 172, 188, 196
Swift, Jonathan 163, 174

technology 56, 181–183, 204
Thailand 141–142, 145–146, 149, 153, 155, 164
tourism 105, 133–134, 137, 140, 142, 145, 157, 161, 166–169
tourists 9, 123, 134, 140, 141–144, 151, 159–161, 167–168, 186
travel 17, 19, 44, 94, 102–105, 107–110, 113, 115, 124, 133, 141, 158

universe 5, 17, 51, 54, 66–67, 69, 72, 78, 87–88, 92, 96–98, 100, 205, 210

Viard, Bruno 52–53
violence 27, 31, 32, 36, 37, 48, 49, 74, 122, 135, 137, 138, 164, 169, 205
Vorilhon, Claude 114, 115, 124, 129

Wagner, Walter 98
Wesemael, Sabine van 13, 17, 52–54, 65–66, 82, 91, 98, 101, 172
Worton, Michael 171, 172

Modern French Identities

Edited by Peter Collier

This series aims to publish monographs, editions or collections of papers based on recent research into modern French Literature. It welcomes contributions from academics, researchers and writers in British and Irish universities in particular.

Modern French Identities focuses on the French and Francophone writing of the twentieth century, whose formal experiments and revisions of genre have combined to create an entirely new set of literary forms, from the thematic autobiographies of Michel Leiris and Bernard Noël to the magic realism of French Caribbean writers.

The idea that identities are constructed rather than found, and that the self is an area to explore rather than a given pretext, runs through much of modern French literature, from Proust, Gide and Apollinaire to Kristeva, Barthes, Duras, Germain and Roubaud.

This series reflects a concern to explore the turn-of-the-century turmoil in ideas and values that is expressed in the works of theorists like Lacan, Irigaray and Bourdieu and to follow through the impact of current ideologies such as feminism and postmodernism on the literary and cultural interpretation and presentation of the self, whether in terms of psychoanalytic theory, gender, autobiography, cinema, fiction and poetry, or in newer forms like performance art.

The series publishes studies of individual authors and artists, comparative studies, and interdisciplinary projects, including those where art and cinema intersect with literature.

Volume 1   Victoria Best & Peter Collier (eds): Powerful Bodies.
             Performance in French Cultural Studies.
             220 pages. 1999. ISBN 3-906762-56-4 / US-ISBN 0-8204-4239-9

Volume 2   Julia Waters: Intersexual Rivalry.
             A 'Reading in Pairs' of Marguerite Duras and Alain Robbe-Grillet.
             228 pages. 2000. ISBN 3-906763-74-9 / US-ISBN 0-8204-4626-2

Volume 3   Sarah Cooper: Relating to Queer Theory.
             Rereading Sexual Self-Definition with Irigaray, Kristeva, Wittig
             and Cixous.
             231 pages. 2000. ISBN 3-906764-46-X / US-ISBN 0-8204-4636-X

Volume 4   Julia Prest & Hannah Thompson (eds): Corporeal Practices.
             (Re)figuring the Body in French Studies.
             166 pages. 2000. ISBN 3-906764-53-2 / US-ISBN 0-8204-4639-4

Volume 5   Victoria Best: Critical Subjectivities.
             Identity and Narrative in the Work
             of Colette and Marguerite Duras.
             243 pages. 2000. ISBN 3-906763-89-7 / US-ISBN 0-8204-4631-9

Volume 6   David Houston Jones: The Body Abject: Self and Text in
             Jean Genet and Samuel Beckett.
             213 pages. 2000. ISBN 3-906765-07-5 / US-ISBN 0-8204-5058-8

Volume 7   Robin MacKenzie: The Unconscious in Proust's *A la recherche
             du temps perdu.*
             270 pages. 2000. ISBN 3-906758-38-9 / US-ISBN 0-8204-5070-7

Volume 8   Rosemary Chapman: Siting the Quebec Novel.
             The Representation of Space in Francophone Writing in Quebec.
             282 pages. 2000. ISBN 3-906758-85-0 / US-ISBN 0-8204-5090-1

Volume 9   Gill Rye: Reading for Change.
             Interactions between Text Identity in Contemporary French
             Women's Writing (Baroche, Cixous, Constant).
             223 pages. 2001. ISBN 3-906765-97-0 / US-ISBN 0-8204-5315-3

Volume 10   Jonathan Paul Murphy: Proust's Art.
             Painting, Sculpture and Writing in *A la recherche du temps perdu.*
             248 pages. 2001. ISBN 3-906766-17-9 / US-ISBN 0-8204-5319-6

Volume 11   Julia Dobson: Hélène Cixous and the Theatre.
             The Scene of Writing.
             166 pages. 2002. ISBN 3-906766-20-9 / US-ISBN 0-8204-5322-6

Volume 12   Emily Butterworth & Kathryn Robson (eds): Shifting Borders.
             Theory and Identity in French Literature.
             VIII + 208 pages. 2001.
             ISBN 3-906766-86-1 / US-ISBN 0-8204-5602-0

Volume 13   Victoria Korzeniowska: The Heroine as Social Redeemer in
             the Plays of Jean Giraudoux.
             144 pages. 2001. ISBN 3-906766-92-6 / US-ISBN 0-8204-5608-X

Volume 14   Kay Chadwick: Alphonse de Châteaubriant:
             Catholic Collaborator.
             327 pages. 2002. ISBN 3-906766-94-2 / US-ISBN 0-8204-5610-1

Volume 15   Nina Bastin: Queneau's Fictional Worlds.
             291 pages. 2002. ISBN 3-906768-32-5 / US-ISBN 0-8204-5620-9

Volume 16   Sarah Fishwick: The Body in the Work of Simone de Beauvoir.
             284 pages. 2002. ISBN 3-906768-33-3 / US-ISBN 0-8204-5621-7

Volume 17   Simon Kemp & Libby Saxton (eds): Seeing Things.
             Vision, Perception and Interpretation in French Studies.
             287 pages. 2002. ISBN 3-906768-46-5 / US-ISBN 0-8204-5858-9

Volume 18   Kamal Salhi (ed.): French in and out of France.
             Language Policies, Intercultural Antagonisms and Dialogue.
             487 pages. 2002. ISBN 3-906768-47-3 / US-ISBN 0-8204-5859-7

Volume 19   Genevieve Shepherd: Simone de Beauvoir's Fiction.
             A Psychoanalytic Rereading.
             262 pages. 2003. ISBN 3-906768-55-4 / US-ISBN 0-8204-5867-8

Volume 20   Lucille Cairns (ed.): Gay and Lesbian Cultures in France.
             290 pages. 2002. ISBN 3-906769-66-6 / US-ISBN 0-8204-5903-8

Volume 21   Wendy Goolcharan-Kumeta: My Mother, My Country.
             Reconstructing the Female Self in Guadeloupean Women's Writing.
             236 pages. 2003. ISBN 3-906769-76-3 / US-ISBN 0-8204-5913-5

Volume 22   Patricia O'Flaherty: Henry de Montherlant (1895–1972).
             A Philosophy of Failure.
             256 pages. 2003. ISBN 3-03910-013-0 / US-ISBN 0-8204-6282-9

Volume 23   Katherine Ashley (ed.): Prix Goncourt, 1903–2003: essais critiques.
             205 pages. 2004. ISBN 3-03910-018-1 / US-ISBN 0-8204-6287-X

Volume 24   Julia Horn & Lynsey Russell-Watts (eds): Possessions.
             Essays in French Literature, Cinema and Theory.
             223 pages. 2003. ISBN 3-03910-005-X / US-ISBN 0-8204-5924-0

Volume 25   Steve Wharton: Screening Reality.
             French Documentary Film during the German Occupation.
             252 pages. 2006. ISBN 3-03910-066-1 / US-ISBN 0-8204-6882-7

Volume 26   Frédéric Royall (ed.): Contemporary French Cultures and Societies.
             421 pages. 2004. ISBN 3-03910-074-2 / US-ISBN 0-8204-6890-8

Volume 27   Tom Genrich: Authentic Fictions.
             Cosmopolitan Writing of the Troisième République, 1908–1940.
             288 pages. 2004. ISBN 3-03910-285-0 / US-ISBN 0-8204-7212-3

Volume 28   Maeve Conrick & Vera Regan: French in Canada.
             Language Issues.
             186 pages. 2007. ISBN 978-3-03-910142-9

Volume 29   Kathryn Banks & Joseph Harris (eds): Exposure.
             Revealing Bodies, Unveiling Representations.
             194 pages. 2004. ISBN 3-03910-163-3 / US-ISBN 0-8204-6973-4

Volume 30   Emma Gilby & Katja Haustein (eds): Space.
             New Dimensions in French Studies.
             169 pages. 2005. ISBN 3-03910-178-1 / US-ISBN 0-8204-6988-2

Volume 31   Rachel Killick (ed.): Uncertain Relations.
             Some Configurations of the 'Third Space' in Francophone Writings
             of the Americas and of Europe.
             258 pages. 2005. ISBN 3-03910-189-7 / US-ISBN 0-8204-6999-8

Volume 32   Sarah F. Donachie & Kim Harrison (eds): Love and Sexuality.
             New Approaches in French Studies.
             194 pages. 2005. ISBN 3-03910-249-4 / US-ISBN 0-8204-7178-X

Volume 33   Michaël Abecassis: The Representation of Parisian Speech in
             the Cinema of the 1930s.
             409 pages. 2005. ISBN 3-03910-260-5 / US-ISBN 0-8204-7189-5

Volume 34   Benedict O'Donohoe: Sartre's Theatre: Acts for Life.
             301 pages. 2005. ISBN 3-03910-250-X / US-ISBN 0-8204-7207-7

Volume 35   Moya Longstaffe: The Fiction of Albert Camus. A Complex Simplicity.
             300 pages. 2007. ISBN 3-03910-304-0 / US-ISBN 0-8204-7229-8

Volume 36   Forthcoming.

Volume 37   Shirley Ann Jordan: Contemporary French Women's Writing:
             Women's Visions, Women's Voices, Women's Lives.
             308 pages. 2005. ISBN 3-03910-315-6 / US-ISBN 0-8204-7240-9

Volume 38   Forthcoming.

Volume 39   Michael O'Dwyer & Michèle Raclot: Le Journal de Julien Green:
             Miroir d'une âme, miroir d'un siècle.
             289 pages. 2005. ISBN 3-03910-319-9

Volume 40   Thomas Baldwin: The Material Object in the Work of Marcel Proust.
             188 pages. 2005. ISBN 3-03910-323-7 / US-ISBN 0-8204-7247-6

Volume 41   Charles Forsdick & Andrew Stafford (eds): The Modern Essay
             in French: Genre, Sociology, Performance.
             296 pages. 2005. ISBN 3-03910-514-0 / US-ISBN 0-8204-7520-3

Volume 42   Peter Dunwoodie: Francophone Writing in Transition.
            Algeria 1900–1945.
            339 pages. 2005. ISBN 3-03910-294-X / US-ISBN 0-8204-7220-4

Volume 43   Emma Webb (ed.): Marie Cardinal: New Perspectives.
            260 pages. 2006. ISBN 3-03910-544-2 / US-ISBN 0-8204-7547-5

Volume 44   Jérôme Game (ed.): Porous Boundaries : Texts and Images in
            Twentieth-Century French Culture.
            164 pages. 2007. ISBN 978-3-03910-568-7

Volume 45   David Gascoigne: The Games of Fiction: Georges Perec and Modern
            French Ludic Narrative.
            327 pages. 2006. ISBN 3-03910-697-X / US-ISBN 0-8204-7962-4

Volume 46   Derek O'Regan: Postcolonial Echoes and Evocations:
            The Intertextual Appeal of Maryse Condé.
            329 pages. 2006. ISBN 3-03910-578-7

Volume 47   Jennifer Hatte: La langue secrète de Jean Cocteau: la *mythologie
            personnelle* du poète et l'histoire cachée des *Enfants terribles.*
            332 pages. 2007. ISBN 978-3-03910-707-0

Volume 48   Loraine Day: Writing Shame and Desire: The Work of Annie Ernaux.
            315 pages. 2007. ISBN 978-3-03910-275-4

Volume 49-50 Forthcoming.

Volume 51   Isabelle McNeill & Bradley Stephens (eds): Transmissions:
            Essays in French Literature, Thought and Cinema.
            221 pages. 2007. ISBN 978-3-03910-734-6

Volume 52   Forthcoming.

Volume 53   Patrick Crowley: Pierre Michon: The Afterlife of Names.
            242 pages. 2007. ISBN 978-3-03910-744-5

Volume 54   Nicole Thatcher & Ethel Tolansky (eds): Six Authors in Captivity.
            Literary Responses to the Occupation of France during World War II.
            205 pages. 2006. ISBN 3-03910-520-5 / US-ISBN 0-8204-7526-2

Volume 55   Catherine Dousteyssier-Khoze & Floriane Place-Verghnes (eds):
            Poétiques de la parodie et du pastiche de 1850 à nos jours.
            361 pages. 2006. ISBN 3-03910-743-7

Volume 56   Forthcoming.

Volume 57   Helen Vassallo : Jeanne Hyvrard, Wounded Witness:
            The Body Politic and the Illness Narrative.
            243 pages. 2007. ISBN 978-3-03911-017-9

Volume 58   Marie-Claire Barnet, Eric Robertson & Nigel Saint (eds):
             Robert Desnos. Surrealism in the Twenty-First Century.
             390 pages. 2006. ISBN 3-03911-019-5

Volume 59   Michael O'Dwyer (ed.): Julien Green, Diariste et Essayiste.
             259 pages. 2007. ISBN 978-3-03911-016-2

Volume 60   Kate Marsh: Fictions of 1947: Representations of Indian
             Decolonization 1919–1962.
             238 pages. 2007. ISBN 978-3-03911-033-9

Volume 61   Lucy Bolton, Gerri Kimber, Ann Lewis and Michael Seabrook (eds):
             Framed! : Essays in French Studies.
             235 pages. 2007. ISBN 978-3-03911-043-8

Volume 62-63 Forthcoming.

Volume 64   Sam Coombes: The Early Sartre and Marxism.
             330 pages. 2008. ISBN 978-3-03911-115-2

Volume 65-66 Forthcoming.

Volume 67   Alison S. Fell (ed.): French and francophone women facing war /
             Les femmes face à la guerre.
             301 pages. 2009. ISBN 978-3-03911-332-3

Volume 68   Elizabeth Lindley and Laura McMahon (eds):
             Rhythms: Essays in French Literature, Thought and Culture.
             238 pages. 2008. ISBN 978-3-03911-349-1

Volume 69   Forthcoming.

Volume 70   John McCann: Michel Houellebecq: Author of our Times.
             229 pages. 2010. ISBN 978-3-03911-373-6

Volume 71   Jenny Murray: Remembering the (Post)Colonial Self:
             Memory and Identity in the Novels of Assia Djebar.
             258 pages. 2008. ISBN 978-3-03911-367-5

Volume 72   Susan Bainbrigge: Culture and Identity in Belgian Francophone
             Writing: Dialogue, Diversity and Displacement.
             230 pages. 2009. ISBN 978-3-03911-382-8

Volume 73-74 Forthcoming.

Volume 75   Elodie Laügt: L'Orient du signe: Rêves et dérives chez Victor Segalen,
             Henri Michaux et Emile Cioran.
             242 pages. 2008. ISBN 978-3-03911-402-3

Volume 76   Suzanne Dow: Madness in Twentieth-Century French Women's
             Writing: Leduc, Duras, Beauvoir, Cardinal, Hyvrard.
             217 pages. 2009. ISBN 978-3-03911-540-2

Volume 77   Myriem El Maïzi: Marguerite Duras ou l'écriture du devenir.
             228 pages. 2009. ISBN 978-3-03911-561-7

Volume 78   Forthcoming.

Volume 79   Jenny Chamarette and Jennifer Higgins (eds): Guilt and Shame:
             Essays in French Literature, Thought and Visual Culture.
             231 pages. 2010. ISBN 978-3-03911-563-1

Volume 80   Forthcoming.

Volume 81   Margaret-Anne Hutton (ed.): Redefining the Real: The Fantastic in
             Contemporary French and Francophone Women's Writing.
             294 pages. 2009. ISBN 978-3-03911-567-9

Volume 82   Elise Hugueny-Léger: Annie Ernaux, une poétique de la
             transgression.
             269 pages. 2009. ISBN 978-3-03911-833-5

Volume 83   Peter Collier, Anna Magdalena Elsner and Olga Smith (eds):
             Anamnesia: Private and Public Memory in Modern French Culture.
             359 pages. 2009. ISBN 978-3-03911-846-5

Volume 84   Adam Watt (ed./éd.): Le Temps retrouvé Eighty Years After/80 ans
             après: Critical Essays/Essais critiques.
             349 pages. 2009. ISBN 978-3-03911-843-4

Volume 85   Louise Hardwick (ed.): New Approaches to Crime in French
             Literature, Culture and Film.
             237 pages. 2009. ISBN 978-3-03911-850-2

Volume 86-87 Forthcoming.

Volume 88   Alistair Rolls (ed.): Mostly French: French (in) Detective Fiction.
             212 pages. 2009. ISBN 978-3-03911-957-8

Volume 89   Bérénice Bonhomme: Claude Simon : une écriture en cinéma.
             359 pages. 2010. ISBN 978-3-03911-983-7